Binsey: Oxford's Holy Place
Its saint, village, and people

Edited by

Lydia Carr, Russell Dewhurst,
and Martin Henig

Archaeopress

Gordon House
276 Banbury Road
Oxford OX2 7ED

www.archaeopress.com

ISBN 978 1 905739 84 4

© Archaeopress, The Parochial Church Council of St Frideswide's Church Osney with St Margaret's Binsey, and the individual authors 2014

Cover illustrations: *At Binsey, near Oxford 1862*, watercolour and ink by George Price Boyce (Cecil Higgins Art Gallery) (front cover and background); St Margaret's, Binsey (Simon Carr) (back cover)

Printed and bound in Great Britain by Marston Book Services Ltd, Oxfordshire

All rights reserved. No part of this book may be reproduced, stored in retrieval system, or transmitted, in any form or by any means, electronic, mechanical, photocopying or otherwise, without the prior written permission of the copyright owners.

In memory of Shay Gee, former churchwarden, and his faithful companion Millie

Binsey church and village in relation to Godstow (N) and Botley (S), Port Meadow (E) and the county boundary on the Seacourt Stream (W).
Extract from the 1919 Ordnance Survey Town Map of Oxford (6 inches to 1 mile).

Contents

Forewords iii
Christopher Lewis and Clare Sykes

Introduction and Acknowledgements v

Contributors vi

A Poet's View: St Margaret's Church at Binsey ix
Nigel Speight

The Legends of Saint Frideswide 1
John Blair
Part One – Saint Frideswide Reconsidered 1
Part Two – Thornbury, Binsey: A Probable Defensive
Enclosure associated with Saint Frideswide 57
With a contribution by Maureen Mellor
Author's Addendum, 2014 74

St. Frideswide's Binsey as Sacred Space 75
Martin Henig

Pilgrimage to Binsey: Medieval and Modern 81
Lydia Carr

The Clergy of Binsey 89
Russell Dewhurst

Life in Binsey as Recorded in the Church Registers 95
Carl Boardman

Binsey: A Church in its Landscape 100
Julian Munby

Binsey and Lewis Carroll 116
Edward Wakeling

Gerard Manley Hopkins and 'Binsey Poplars' 123
Beatrice and Peter Groves

The Perch and its Predecessors 135
Mark Davies

Meeting God at Binsey: Holy Ground, then and now 143
Martin Henig

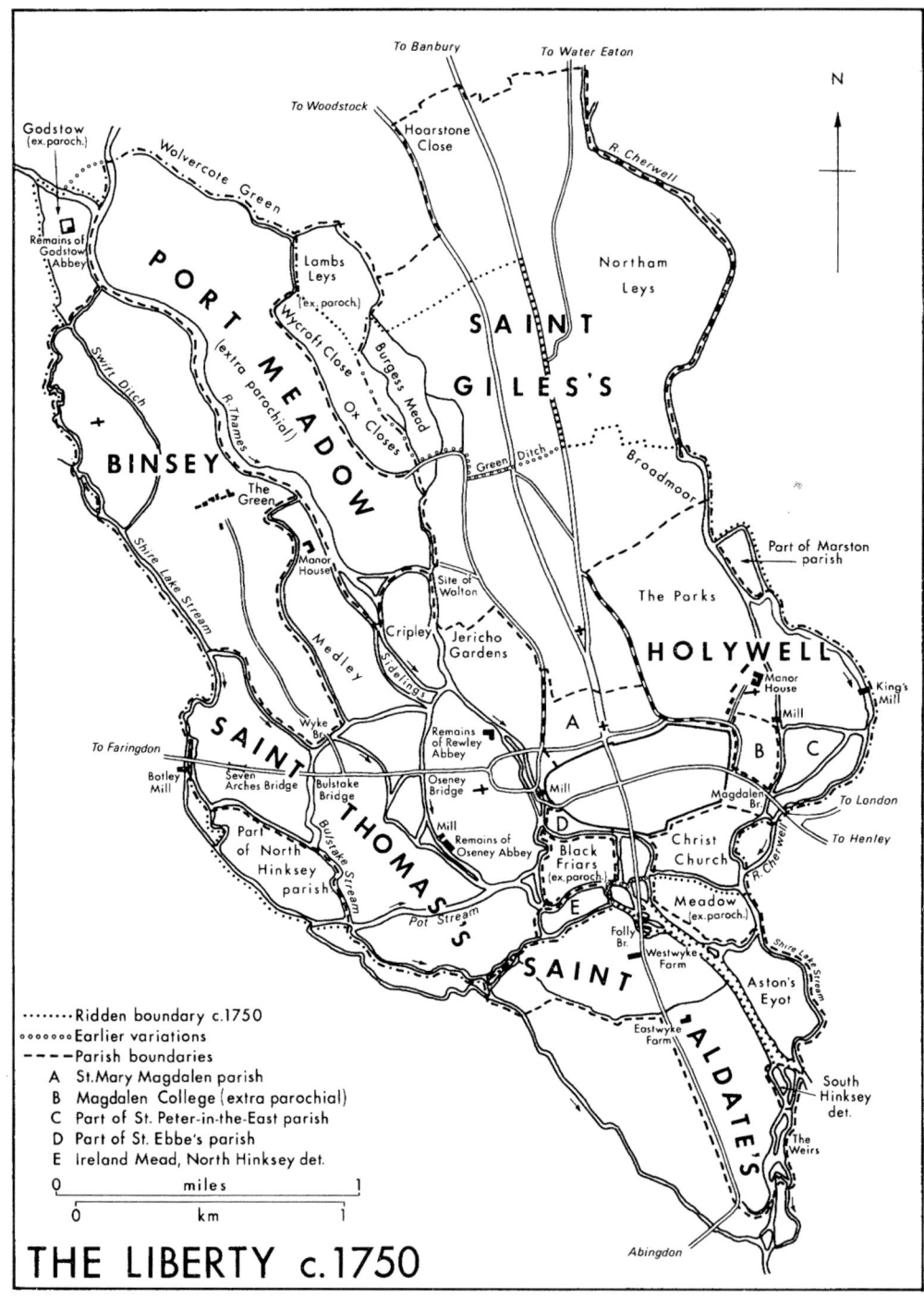

The parishes of Binsey and St Thomas in relation to the Liberty of Oxford, the parishes and extra-parochial areas.
Source: Crossley, VCH Oxon iv, 267; Courtesy of the Victoria History of Oxfordshire Trust and the University of London.

Forewords

Binsey's charm depends on its history but also on its current character. It is, of course, related to its voraciously academic and vastly more populous neighbour and yet it is 'of itself' and continues to be happily rural.

Christ Church loves its tie, for since the 12th century at least, Binsey was owned by St Frideswide's monastery and the current college/cathedral is the monastery's successor. To which add the link of Alice, whose Wonderland included both Christ Church and Binsey's holy healing/treacle well, without which no Mad Hatter's Tea Party would be complete.

Then there was the present: the brand new tradition of the fete, with its roast pig and its chicken-beauty competition, the second prize for which was won a year or two ago by a chicken who sent her apologies: too shy to come. There is the serious business of farming with pick-your-own alongside Longhorn and Aberdeen Angus cattle. There are houses to renovate, streams to clear and houses to renovate.

Best of all, the saying 'Church then Perch': two glorious focal points of Binsey, summing up the essentials of life, namely relatedness to God and to community, both of which Binsey does with aplomb.

This is a splendid book which Binsey deserves.

The Very Reverend Christopher Lewis, Dean of Christ Church

For many hundreds of years the Church of St. Margaret of Antioch, within the hamlet of Binsey, has been a place of pilgrimage and sanctuary. Set within sight of the dreaming spires and with the sound of the ring-road close at hand, Binsey is a rural idyll that calms the nerves and soothes the souls of those who visit. As we journey through life, we need places where earth and heaven meet, where we can find ourselves again and commune with God and seek healing through his divine grace. Binsey has been that place for both ancient and modern pilgrims and I pray it will continue to provide that unique gift to the people and visitors of Oxford.

Clare Sykes, Rector of Osney Benefice
March 2013

Extract showing Binsey church from field map of Binsey by Richard Davis of Lewknor, 1792
Courtesy of the Archivist and Governing Body of Christ Church (MS maps Binsey 2)

Introduction and Acknowledgements

Binsey is a village to the west of Oxford, on the south bank of the main channel of the River Thames, opposite Port Meadow, which has been an open space belonging to the burgesses of Oxford since late Saxon times. Although now within the ring-road, the village is essentially rural and unspoilt. The hub of Binsey is a row of cottages and the Perch Inn on one side of the village green. At one time when the river was wider there was a ferry here taking travelers across to Oxford. The church, its present building no earlier than the 12th century though on an older site, lies a third of a mile distant. Its association with Oxford's patron saint St Frideswide alone makes this an evocative place for anyone with an interest in the origins of this great University city. Its holy well, dedicated to St Margaret like the church itself, was a place of resort for those with eye problems or desirous of a child: Katharine of Aragon's lack of success in conceiving a male heir after resort to the well in a sense precipitated the English Reformation! Later associations, which include Charles Dodgson and Alice Liddell as well as Gerard Manley Hopkins and C. S. Lewis, render Binsey a place for the literary as well as the religious pilgrim.[1]

This book is a collection of essays on aspects of Binsey and its environs. It is not a guidebook so much as an evocation of the place, dwelling on specific aspects from the busy river to the tranquil and silent churchyard; from the poplars, great-grandparents of the present trees along the river and Hopkins' great poem on them, to the personalities who served the village community; from the Binsey of St Frideswide's time to the community of the present day.

Apart from the authors of the various contributions we would like to thank Christ Church and its Dean the Very Revd Christopher Lewis, the PCC of St Frideswide's with Binsey, which will receive the royalties of the volume, Father Anthony Rustell, the former Rector of Osney Benefice, and his successor the Revd Clare Sykes, the present Rector. Julian Munby, currently churchwarden has been helpful in many ways, especially in helping to check the Latin texts of the early life of St Frideswide. We would also like to thank those who provided photographs, especially Karl Wallendszus, Edward Wakeling, John Lee, Julian Munby, Sue Dewhurst and Katie Seal; and the painter Simon Carr, of New York City, who generously provided a beautiful sketch of the church. The editors and the Parochial Church Council of the parish of St Frideswide with St Margaret's are most grateful to Dr David Davison and to Archaeopress for taking on the publication of this book.

Our grateful thanks go out to you all!

---

[1] Many visitors make a pilgrimage to the church, drawn by a haunting episode in the tragic autobiographical love story by Lewis's pupil and friend Sheldon Vanauken, A Severe Mercy (London 1977), 122 and 224.

Contributors

John Blair has been a Fellow in History at The Queen's College, Oxford, since 1981. His academic interests centre on the history, archaeology, architecture and landscape of medieval England. Oxfordshire has been the focus of much of his research, and he is a former editor of *Oxoniensia*.
john.blair@queens.ox.ac.uk

Carl Boardman was Hulme exhibitioner in Modern History at Brasenose College Oxford, and did postgraduate work in Archive Studies at University College London. After working at the Harrowby MSS Trust and setting up the King Edward VI Foundation Archive in Birmingham, he returned to Oxford where he became County Archivist in 1988. With the bringing together of Oxfordshire Record Office and Oxfordshire Studies in 2008 he became overall History Services Manager, and ran the joint Oxfordshire History Centre in Cowley. His books include *Oxfordshire Sinners & Villains* and *Foul Deeds & Suspicious Deaths*, though he secretly prefers moonlighting as a crime novelist.
c.boardman@bnc.oxon.org

Lydia Carr came to Binsey as a teenager and returned years later as an Oxford graduate student reading history and archaeology. Her first solo book, the eponymous biography *Tessa Verney Wheeler*, was published by the Oxford University Press early in 2012. She is a writer and editor based in New York City.
carr.lydia@gmail.com

Mark Davies is an Oxford local historian, pubic speaker, and guide with a particular interest in the history and literature of the city's waterways. He has lived on a narrowboat on the Oxford Canal since 1992, and is the author of: *Our Canal in Oxford* (1999), *A Towpath Walk in Oxford* (2001/2012), *The Abingdon Waterturnpike Murder* (2003/2008), *Stories of Oxford Castle* (2005/2006), *Alice in Waterland* (2010/2012) and *Alice's Oxford on Foot* (2014). The second and latter two of these publications contain sections on Binsey. His historical and literary tours generally explore less-visited parts of Oxford, away from the crowded city centre and University colleges. www.oxfordwaterwalks.co.uk.
mark.oxford1@btinternet.com

Russell Dewhurst first visited the treacle well as an undergraduate in 1996. He was Priest-in-Charge of St Frideswide's, Oxford and St Margaret's, Binsey between 2005 and 2009, and is now Vicar of Ewell in the Diocese of Guildford.
rdewhurst@mac.com

Peter Groves is parish priest of St Mary Magdalen, Oxford, and Lecturer in Theology at Worcester College, Oxford. Having served his curacy in Essex, he returned to Oxford in 1999 and worked at Pusey House and then Keble College before serving as Chaplain and Fellow of Brasenose College. He is a member of Theology Faculty in the University of Oxford, where he teaches doctrine. He has published articles on systematic and doctrinal theology, as well as on the Oxford Movement and the poet Gerard Manley Hopkins, in a number of books and journals.
peter.groves@theology.ox.ac.uk

Beatrice Groves is a lecturer in Renaissance literature at Trinity College, Oxford. She is the author of *Texts and Traditions: Religion in Shakespeare, 1592–1604* (OUP, 2007) and numerous articles on early modern literature.
beatrice.groves@ell.ox.ac.uk

Martin Henig has lived in west Oxford for many years, teaching archaeology in Oxford University and writing widely on Roman religion and art, and is currently engaged in research on Roman sculpture from London. The second edition of his book *The Heirs of King Verica* (2002) appeared in 2010, in the same year in which he was ordained. He now serves as Assistant Priest in the Osney Benefice. The parish includes St Margaret's, Binsey, which has been a special place for him ever since he came to Oxford over forty years ago. He writes: 'Believing as I do that all parts of our lives are interconnected, I feel privileged to be allowed to bring together my love of historic monuments and beautiful landscape with the strong feelings for sacred space and spiritual exploration which are so central to my Christian faith'.
martin.henig@arch.ox.ac.uk

Julian Munby is head of Buildings Archaeology at Oxford Archaeology and is a churchwarden at St Margaret's.
jtmunby@gmail.com

Nigel Speight has lived in Oxford teaching and writing since coming up to St Johns to read English in 1967. His student pilgimages to Binsey were more to The Perch than the church, but some bits of the poem included here fell into place soon after his first visit to St Margaret's. His first love in poetry was Hopkins, so the sense of how Binsey inspired him has always amplified the joy of a walk across Port Meadow to revisit the experience. Try it very early, amidst the birdsong, on a translucent summer morning.
nigespeight@gmail.com

Edward Wakeling is a long-standing member of the Lewis Carroll Society. He has written widely on Carroll over the last three decades, and among his publications is the first unabridged edition of *Lewis Carroll's Diaries* in ten volumes. He has written on Carroll's photography, letters, mathematics, puzzles and games, and logic. As a recognised Carrollian scholar and collector, he is frequently called upon to contribute to conferences, exhibitions, and television programmes around the world.
edward@wakeling.demon.co.uk

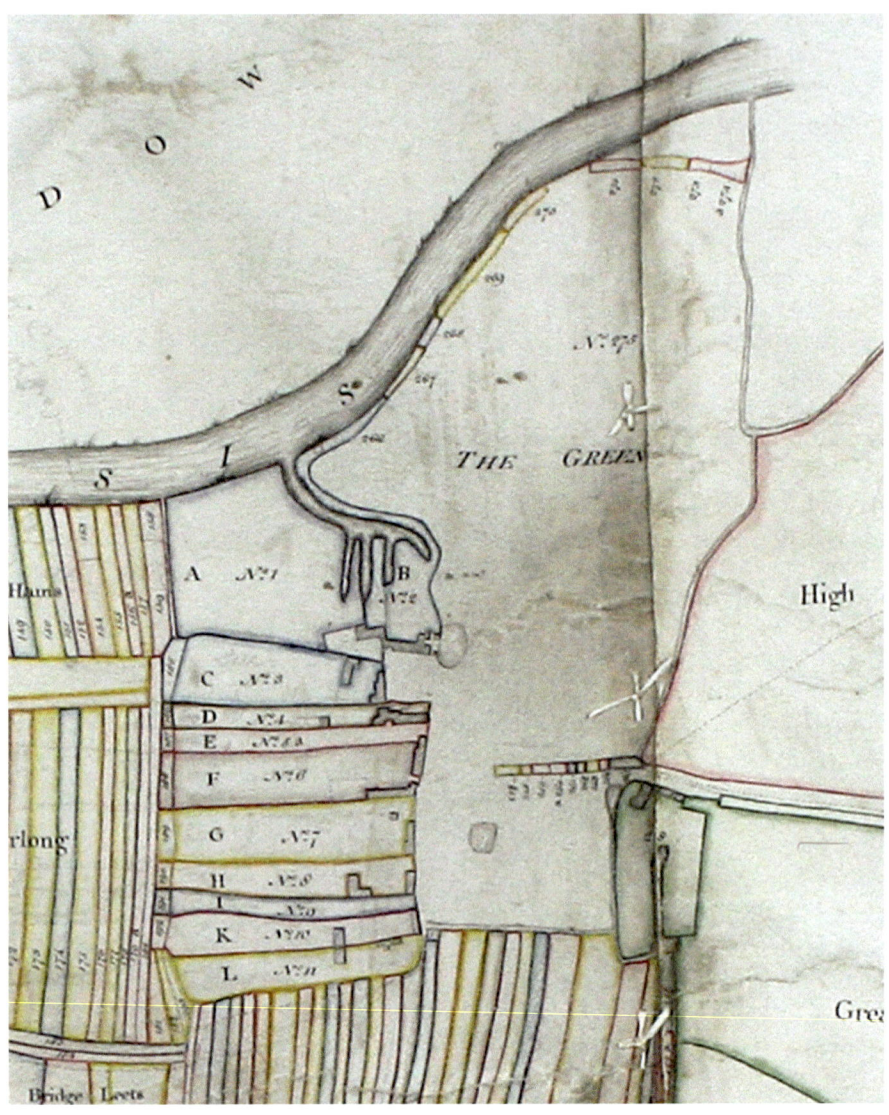

Extract showing Binsey village and green from field map of Binsey by Richard Davis of Lewknor, 1792
Courtesy of the Archivist and Governing Body of Christ Church (MS maps Binsey 2)

A Poet's View: St Margaret's Church at Binsey

NIGEL SPEIGHT

Cathedrals insist that God is
Where They are, not everywhere. Up-
Right, and highly strung, they point,

Dogmatically, at nothing, bringing
Down to earth a Deity for whom great
Heights can be no Revelation.

Great Abbeys are worse – imperialist
War museums, all cluttered and stuck up with
Statesmen & soldiers, prelates & poets,
Kings, flags, Britannias and latinate lies.

A plaque in the Abbey?
You know what to do…
Just kill foreign jonnies
Until they kill you.

****

But push here and the door is always open.
For this is a wholly simple church, teaching
Humility with humility. It leaves you
Alone with your reasons for stepping

Inside. Near cattle, sheep and goats, it's like
A stable. But once it has you face to face
Or looking through its eyes, it's a living
Skull that cups a silence strewn with prayer,

The life-time offerings too, from regular souls,
Standing to sing amidst their families,
With ancestors at peace beneath their feet.
Now pilgrims come, not for Magnificence,

But since a miracle, it's said, has happened here.
There's many kinds of sight can be restored.
Some leave believing they are rinsed within,
With holy water from the wishing well

Closing over the head of all their sin.
They feel the phoenix in these ashen greys.
No moral doubts assault the victories
Still celebrated in this ancient place.

For they've been won in private wars by ones
Surprised to feel here irretrievably
Found – caught by this elemental Christian hold
That intimates the infinite space around.

THE LEGENDS OF SAINT FRIDESWIDE

JOHN BLAIR

Part One – Saint Frideswide Reconsidered

Reprinted with permission from *Oxoniensia* 52 (1987), pp 71–127.

SUMMARY

Introduction: *William of Malmesbury's brief account of St. Frideswide, long considered the only worthwhile source for the Frideswide legends, is re-interpreted as a mere summary of older material which also formed the basis of a full-scale early 12th-century* Vita *('Life A'). During c.1140–70 Life A was re-written, almost certainly by the scholar and Prior of St. Frideswide's Master Robert of Cricklade, in a more elegant and elaborate version ('Life B'). In Life A the princess, pursued by the lecherous King Algar, flees by boat from Oxford to Bampton where she hides in 'a wood called Binsey'. This blunder, which shows that the compiler of 'Life A' was ignorant of local topography, nonetheless suggests that the Frideswide legend in its pre-12th-century form included separate episodes associated with Bampton and Binsey. Life B resolves the confusion by adding a chapter in which Frideswide returns towards Oxford but stops for a while at Binsey, where she builds a nunnery in a secluded place called 'Thornbury' and obtains by her prayers the still-extant holy well. The Lives may include elements of genuine tradition. Frideswide, as a king's daughter and the first head of a minster founded by her father c.700, is highly plausible in the general contemporary context. Other evidence hints at a mid-Saxon province centred on Eynsham and probably including Oxford and Bampton, both of which had royal minsters by at least the 10th century; thus the association of Frideswide's cult with these two centres, spaced out along the Thames on either side of Eynsham, rings true. Life A may preserve a hint that the early minster at Oxford had three churches, dedicated to the Holy Trinity, St. Mary and All Saints. Life A says that Frideswide was buried on the south side of St. Mary's church on 19 October 727; Life B adds that King Æthelred enlarged the church after 1002 in such a way that the grave was thereafter central. 'Thornbury' at Binsey is tentatively interpreted as a monastic retreat-house, its boundaries perhaps reflected in a surviving earthwork.*

   Appendix A: *Edition of Life A. (pp.23–31)*
   Appendix B: *Edition of Life B. (pp.31–45)*
   Appendix C: *Narratives describing the re-discovery (1111×1180) and first translation (12 February 1180) of Frideswide's relics. After the re-foundation of the minster as an Augustinian priory, the canons became afraid that monks of Abingdon had stolen the bones. They opened the grave secretly at night and found an empty stone coffin; digging deeper, they found a skeleton which was identified as Frideswide's by a miraculous sign. At a ceremony in 1180 the Archbishop of Canterbury translated the bones from this grave into a raised feretory. (pp.46-8)*
   Appendix D: *At Bomy in northern France is a cult of St. Frideswide ('Ste. Frévisse') associated with a chapel, hermitage and holy spring. The known hagiographical 'traditions' are post-medieval importations from Oxford, but a charter of 1187 mentions St. Frideswide's well and appears to associate it with the old parish church and cemetery, then being down-graded to the status of a chapel. The cult may possibly have reached Bomy from Oxford in the late 10th or 11th century through links between the English and Flemish Churches. (pp. 48–56)*

ACKNOWLEDGEMENTS

My main thanks are to Richard Sharpe and Michael Lapidge for their painstaking criticism of the texts, and to Edward Impey for his splendid fieldwork at Bomy. I am also very grateful to Theresa Webber for advice on the palaeography of the Nero EI and Laud

Misc. 114 MSS; to the British Library, the Bodleian Library, and the Libraries of Gonville and Caius College, Cambridge, and Balliol College, Oxford, for access to the MSS; to Mme. Martine le Maner for supplying Xeroxes from Saint-Omer; to Peter Foote and Paul Bibire for advice on Robert of Cricklade's works; and to Steven Bassett, Martin Biddle, Ralph Davis, Antonia Gransden, Tom Hassall, Patrick McGurk, Henry Mayr-Harting, Alan Thacker, Rodney Thomson and David Wilson for all their suggestions. Pat Lloyd's quick and accurate typing has been a very great help. It is also appropriate to mention two names from the past: Miss L.I. Guiney, whose collection of transcripts (now Bodl. MS Lat. Misc. c.72) has proved extremely useful; and the Revd. G.E.C. Rodwell, vicar of Bampton, whose correct identification of *Bentonia* ('The Flight of St. Frideswide', *Jnl. Brit. Archaeol. Assocn.* n.s. xxii (1916), 85–9) has passed almost unregarded.

INTRODUCTION

It was fitting that the first volume of *Oxoniensia,* published in 1936, should contain an article on Oxford's patron saint by the leading Anglo-Saxonist of the day.[1] The rough handling which St. Frideswide's *Vita* received there from Sir Frank Stenton is all the more unfortunate, for it has barred it from serious attention for half a century.[2] Stenton wrote of Frideswide:[3]

> No materials for her life were available to the first generation of Anglo-Norman hagiographers, and the earliest writer to sketch the outline of her legend is the historian William of Malmesbury, writing shortly before the year 1125. According to him, Frideswide was a king's daughter, sought in marriage by a king from whom she escaped, at first into a nameless woodland refuge, and then into the town of Oxford. Her pursuer was struck with blindness as he approached the gates of the town, but was soon restored to sight by her intercession, and she, freed from his importunities, proceeded to found a monastery in the town, where she spent the rest of her life. It is a meagre story, and the men of later generations were not satisfied with it. Before the end of the thirteenth century, Frideswide had been provided with a father named Didanus and a mother named Safrida; the king who pursued her was called Algar, and the place of her final retirement was changed from Oxford to a neighbouring wood called Thornbury, afterwards known as Binsey. There is no reason to think that these details represent any real tradition; the personal names in the story show that it cannot have been written down before the late twelfth century, and carry no suggestion that it comes from any older source. It clearly stands for an attempt to give some appearance of substance to one of the most nebulous of English monastic legends.

This verdict rests on two assumptions: that the detailed *Vita* is a mere embroidery of Malmesbury's simple narrative; and that this embroidery occurred in the 13th century when all things pre-Conquest had grown dim. The second assumption is simply wrong: the full story, unlikely names and all, survives in a manuscript which can scarcely be later than *c.*1140 and which is not the original exemplar of its text. This in turn calls the first assumption into question: the Life cannot have been composed much, if at all, later than Malmesbury's narrative, and the possibility is open that Malmesbury was merely summarising a longer story which already existed in written form.

The two 12th-century versions of the Life have never been edited or compared, and to do so is the main purpose of this paper.[4] It will also try to assess their value as evidence

---

[1] F.M. Stenton, 'St. Frideswide and her Times', *Oxoniensia,* i (1936), 103–12.
[2] E.F. Jacob, *St. Frideswide. the Patron Saint of Oxford* (1957) identifies the two 12th-century versions of the Life, but his discussion of the manuscripts is so riddled with confusions that he cannot have carried out any systematic collation. In fact the most thorough discussion to date remains that of James Parker, *The Early History of Oxford* (O.H.S. iii, 1885), 86–106, though this too is vitiated by misunderstandings of the relationships between the sources.
[3] Stenton op.cit. note I, 104–5.
[4] A full translation of *Life A* has been published as J. Blair, *Saint Frideswide, Patron of Oxford* (Perpetua Press, 1988).

for Anglo-Saxon Oxford and its environs, and to suggest a context for Frideswide's minster church in the light of historical, archaeological and topographical work since Stenton's time. Evidence is also presented for the rediscovery and translation of Frideswide's bones, and for her cult at Bomy in France.

MALMESBURY, 'LIFE A' AND 'LIFE B': THE THREE 12TH-CENTURY SOURCES AND THEIR INTER-RELATIONSHIP

William of Malmesbury's account of St. Frideswide occupies a brief passage in his *Gesta Pontificum,* written, like the rest of that work, in or shortly before 1125.[5] He goes on to note that Roger bishop of Salisbury established regular canons under Prior Wimund in Frideswide's former nunnery, a change which evidently occurred during 1111–22.[6] The story is compressed and summary, one of many such which William recounts in the course of his survey of ecclesiastical England.

The Life itself, in the two versions designated here 'Life A' and 'Life B', is a different matter: a full-scale *Vita* of the normal kind designed for monastic readings, replete with miracles and other edifying material. Life A is quite short, and is written in bald, rather clumsy Latin. It borrows many phrases from the Vulgate, and Frideswide herself, who is said to know the Psalms by heart, quotes them copiously. The only complete manuscript (British Library, MS Cotton Nero EI (ii) ff.156–7^v) is an addition, in a Worcester hand of *c.*1110–40 which may be John of Worcester's, to a late Anglo-Saxon legendary; textual evidence (below, pp.25–6) suggests a possibility that some passages were not present in the archetype. The currency of Life A may have been mainly in the West Midlands, for there was evidently another copy at Hereford (below, p.25). Two abridgements of a slightly different and possibly earlier text are extant, but a text similar or identical to the Nero manuscript was used for the compilation of Life B.

Life B survives in three manuscripts, the earliest a Pershore collection written *c.*1150–80 (below, pp.31–2). The author claims in his prologue that by assembling information from 'chronicles', 'volumes of authentic histories' and 'catalogues of English saints', he has proved that 'that man, whoever he was', who previously wrote her life was further from error than critics of his simple style have claimed. Clearly this refers to Life A, of which Life B is essentially a more stylish and literary re-working. The text is padded out to twice its original length, though many phrases (especially from Frideswide's direct speech) are repeated verbatim. Life B was thereafter the favoured source, and nearly all the late medieval abridgements in Latin and English derive from it.[7]

At this point it will be convenient to present English versions of the three sources. Malmesbury's brief narrative may be translated in full:

> In old times there was in the city of Oxford a monastery of nuns, where rests the most holy virgin Frideswide. A king's daughter, she spurned a king's bed, avowing her chastity to the Lord Christ. But the king had set his heart upon marrying the virgin, and when prayers and flatteries had been spent in vain he prepared to take her by force. Frideswide learnt of this, and fled into a wood. No refuge could be secret from the lover, no coldness

---

[5] William of Malmesbury, *De Gestis Pontificum Anglorum,* ed. N.E.S.A. Hamilton (Rolls Ser. lii, 1870), 315; see discussion of date in A. Gransden, *Historical Writing in England c.550–c.1307* (1974), 168.
[6] J.C. Dickinson, *The Origins of the Austin Canons and their Introduction into England* (1950), 113–15.
[7] These include: the incomplete version printed J. Mabillon, *Acta Sanctorum Ordinis S. Benedicti,* iii.1 (2nd ed.), 524–6 (*BHL* 3163); the Life in Tynmouth's *Sanctilogium* (Brit. Lib. Cotton Tiberius E I ff.85^v–7), whence Capgrave's *Nova Legenda Anglie* (*BHL* 3165); the late 15th–century Sarum breviary lessons *(Breviarium ad Usum Insignis Ecclesie Sarum,* eds. F. Proctor and C. Wordsworth, iii (1886), 938–42); the Latin metrical version *(BHL* 3168; and the middle English verse life in the *South English Legendary* (Carleton Brown, *A Register of Middle English Religious and Didactic Verse,* ii (1920), No. 1815). Some of these are discussed more fully (though with confusions in the relationships between them) in Jacob op.cit. note 2.

of heart could deter him: he followed the fugitive. So once again, when the young man's frenzy became plain, with God's help she entered Oxford at dead of night by means of hidden ways. By morning the persistent lover had hastened there too, and the girl, now despairing of flight and too weary to go any further, prayed to God for protection for herself and punishment for her persecutor. As he passed through the town gates with his thegns, a heaven-sent blow struck him blind. Understanding the wrongfulness of his persistence, he placated Frideswide by means of messengers and recovered his sight as quickly as he had lost it. Thus it came about that kings of England are afraid to enter or lodge in that town: it is said to bring ruin, and they all shrink from the danger of putting it to the test. So the woman, secure in her maidenly victory, established a monastery there where she ended her days, submitting to her bridegroom's call.

The Latin texts of Lives A and B are edited below (pp.23–45). The following parallel summaries aim to give the essential ingredients of the story, while condensing Life B's discursive style. The section numbers in bold type correspond with those in the editions below:

A	B
	1 (Prologue). Concerning the life and virtues of the most blessed virgin Frideswide, beloved brethren, I have gathered into one volume all that I could learn in chronicles, in volumes of authentic histories or in catalogues of English saints. It is obvious from this that that man, whoever he was, who wrote the most holy virgin's Life was in many ways far from error, despite the scorn of those who, affecting to despise his simple style, show that they value ornament more than substance.
2 St. Augustine converted the English, and priests, churches and believers multiplied greatly. At length there was a king of Oxford named Didan. He married a godly woman named Sefrida, who produced a daughter. The king ordered her to be baptised, and they called her Frideswide.	**2** In about the year 727, when the word of God was bearing fruit among the savage race of the English who had invaded Britain, a sub-king, named Didan, a catholic and upright man, adorned the city called in the Saxon tongue Oxford and in Latin *Boum Vadum*. He took a worthy wife named Safrida, who gave him an heir (to his qualities rather than to his estates), an only daughter. She was baptised, and he ordered her to be called Frideswide.
3 She was carefully brought up, and from the age of five she was entrusted to a matron called Ælgifu to learn her letters. Already chosen as a vessel of the Holy Spirit, she studied earnestly, learnt the Psalter within six months, and based her whole life on the precepts of Holy Scripture, always longing to dwell in the house of the Lord.	**3** After five years of careful upbringing, she was entrusted to a religious matron called Algiva to her letters. How happily she showed everyone that she was fore-chosen as a vessel of the Holy Spirit! Who could not marvel at this five-year-old maiden learning the 150 psalms in about five months? None of her peers could envy her; she was so humble and gentle that she seemed more like a slave-girl than a princess, respectful and compassionate to all. She not merely heard but practised the divine word, storing it in her heart; she spent her time in tears, sighs and groans, always longing to dwell in the house of the Lord.

4 Sefrida died. Didan built a church in Oxford, and had it dedicated in honour of the Holy Trinity, the Virgin Mary and All Saints. Frideswide asked him to give her the church, which he did. She studied to serve God by day and night in vigils and prayers. Despising the world, she gave all that she had to the poor; she always wore a hair shirt, and her food was barley-bread with a few vegetables and water. All the English marvelled at such virtue in one so young, and the king rejoiced to see his only daughter a vessel of the Holy Spirit.

5 Frideswide asked her father's permission to take the nun's habit. Rejoicing, Didan summoned Orgar, bishop of Lincoln, whom he caused to consecrate his daughter together with twelve other noble virgins. Didan then had a refectory, dormitory and cloister built for the nuns, assigned religious men to serve them, and gave the estates and villages of St. Mary and a third part of the city of Oxford to provide the nuns' food.

6 So Frideswide studied to mortify her body and nourish her soul. Didan fell sick, gave his treasure to the poor, and died after receiving the Eucharist. Bereft of both parents, Frideswide trusted all the more in the Holy Spirit; she resolved to kneel a hundred times by day, and to mortify her flesh a hundred times by night.

7 One night, while her companions slept, she was thus occupied alone in the oratory which she had built for herself. A devil appeared, bedecked with gold, silver and gems and surrounded by demons. Pretending to be Christ, he offered her the crown of eternal life and invited her to adore him. But she rejected him scornfully, made the sign of the cross, and he vanished howling, leaving her to pursue her devotions unperturbed.

4 Before she reached marriageable age her mother died, leaving her to her father's protection. She exhorted him to look to the welfare of his soul; he, grieving for his wife and urged on by his daughter, built a church within the city boundary and had it dedicated in honour of the Holy Trinity, the Virgin Mary and All Saints. He gave it to his daughter as she asked him; there she applied herself to devotion and to mortification of the flesh. She slept on the bare earth; this princess, brought up to banquets, ate only simple vegetables with barley-bread, and drank only water. O unhappy men of today who make gods of their bellies, who pretend to religion in their dress but deny it in their way of life! England was agog; all marvelled to see the frail sex at so young an age surpassing masculine strength, and her father rejoiced.

5 Rejecting all hope of mortal posterity, Frideswide obtained her father's permission to take the nun's habit, doubtless foreseeing that after his death someone might try to force her into marriage. Knowing that Christ's blood had redeemed her, she sickened of fine clothes; wedded with the ring of faith, she despised gold and gems. Rejoicing, Didan summoned the bishop of the next diocese and ordered him to give her the nun's habit. About twelve noble girls, following her example, left all to serve the Lord, and although they could not equal her merits, they strove to share with her the heavenly kingdom. Buildings appropriate for religious uses were constructed beside the church through the king's generosity. So the sweet singing of psalms and hymns could be heard there by day and night.

6 The king fell sick and, strengthened by the Eucharist, slept with his fathers, ending his days in a good old age. Bereft of both parents, Frideswide sought her father in heaven the more earnestly: she fasted and prayed, kneeling a hundred times by day, a hundred times by night.

7 But who can be good, yet avoid the envy of him who is supremely bad? The Devil, unable to seduce Frideswide's soul, tried to deceive her by pretending to be Christ. Simulating heavenly light but surrounded by demons, he invited her to adore him, offering her eternal life without the pains of death. Guided by the Holy Spirit she rejected him scornfully, and he vanished howling, leaving her to pursue her devotions unperturbed.

8 Algar king of Leicester, a villainous man hateful to God, succeeded to the kingdom after Didan's death. He sent envoys to her with this message: 'King Algar wants to take you in marriage, but if you object he will have you dragged to a brothel.' Frideswide answered: 'I am betrothed to the King of all kings, whom it would be shameful to leave to obey a slave. As for your threat, the soul cannot be polluted except by consent of the will [quotes Psalm cxviii.6]'.

9 The envoys threatened to take her by force. Frideswide invoked God's help [quotes Psalms x.20.1 and xxxv.2–3], and they were struck blind. The citizens of Oxford fell terrified at her feet, begging her to pray for them.

10 Wishing to return good for ill, she invoked God [quotes Psalm lxxxvi.15], begging him to restore the envoys' sight so that the people might know his mercy. As all replied 'Amen' their eyes were opened, and they fell at her feet, praising God.

11 The envoys reported back to Algar. Enraged, he cried that her magic arts would not save her from him. As Frideswide prayed that night, an angel appeared to her, promising Christ's protection [quotes Psalm xvii.8]: she should go with chosen companions to the river, where a boat and boatman provided by God would take them to safety.

12 Frideswide took two of her sisters to the Thames. There they found a boat, with a young man of angelic appearance who invited them to embark. Guided by the Lord, they arrived within an hour at the town called Bampton. They left the boat, and the young man vanished. Fearing

8 The Devil, thus foiled, tried again: he inflamed the wicked King Algar with love for Frideswide, prompting him to seek to despoil her of the nun's habit. Algar, thus maddened, sent messengers to take Frideswide willy-nilly. Swiftly travelling a great distance, they came to her and said: 'King Algar desires you as partner for his bed and kingdom: he will not be denied.' She answered humbly, 'If I could marry anyone, I would have no objection to King Algar. But since I am betrothed to the eternal King, it would be shameful to seek a mortal husband and children.' The envoys replied, 'If you refuse the king's honourable offer, you will be dragged to a brothel and suffer great dishonour.' 'God will protect me', she answered, 'and in any case the body cannot be polluted except by consent of the will.'

9 The envoys, persisting in their folly, prepared to take her by force. Frideswide invoked God's help [quotes Psalms x.20.1 and xxxv.2–3]. How great is God's wisdom! See these wicked men, already blind in their souls, now restrained by physical blindness. The miracle stupefied the city; all fell at her feet, begging her to pity the envoys.

10 Unable to harden her heart, she invoked God [quotes Psalm lxxxvi.15], begging him to restore their sight so that the people might know his mercy. As all replied 'Amen' their eyes were opened, and they fell at her feet asking pardon. 'Do not attribute it to me', she answered, 'but to the Saviour's mercy and the faith of these people. Remember this, and leave nuns alone in future.'

11 The envoys reported back to Algar. Enraged, he cried that her magic arts would not save her from him: before she should insult him thus, he would hand her over to the pleasure of pimps. He rode off in a fury towards Oxford. But God protects those who trust in him: as Frideswide prayed that night, an angel appeared and warned her of the coming danger. Frideswide was aghast; but the angel told her that Christ would protect her, and punish Algar with perpetual blindness. She should go with chosen companions to the Thames, where they would find a boat and boatman provided by God to guide them.

12 Thanking God, Frideswide took two of her sisters to the Thames. There they found a boat, with a young man of beautiful appearance who invited them to embark. Within an hour they travelled ten miles, and were deposited below the town called Bampton, whereupon the boat and

the wicked king's snares, the nuns went into a wood called Binsey, not far from that town; they followed a path to an abandoned swineherds' hut which was completely overgrown with ivy. Frideswide made the sign of the cross, and entered with her companions.

13 The wicked king reached Oxford with his henchmen, intent on defiling the vessel hallowed for God; but as he entered the city he was struck blind. It is thought to have come about in this way that kings never enter Oxford. He remained blind for the rest of his life, always plotting injuries to Frideswide. She, continuing ceaselessly in prayer and meditation, stayed in the wood for some three years.

14 A girl of Bampton, who had been blinded by a devil nearly seven years earlier, was told in a dream to go to the nuns' dwelling and wash her eyes with the water in which Frideswide had washed her hands. In the morning she told her father; he led her to Frideswide's dwelling, waited until she washed her hands, and wiped the water on the girl's eyes, which were immediately cured. They returned home, praising the Saviour's power displayed in Frideswide.

boatman vanished. They found a path near that town, which led into the heart of a wood not far away. There they found a hut built to protect pigs in bad weather, long abandoned and so completely overgrown with ivy that no entrance was visible. Frideswide made the sign of the cross, and entered with her companions to await God's will.

13 Meanwhile the wicked king reached Oxford, and tried by threats and promises to learn from the inhabitants where Frideswide had gone. Nobody could tell him, and the enraged king swore to sack the city. But as he approached the North Gate he was struck blind, and learnt the fate of those who defy God. He returned home obdurate, and remained blind for the rest of his life. Because of his just punishment, no king of England has dared to enter Oxford since. But Frideswide, as though transported into a desert, continued ceaselessly to serve and venerate God. She remained in the wood for some three years, but not unknown to the locals: for the light of God cannot be hidden for long.

14 In Bampton was a girl of good family whom the Devil had struck blind. She was told in a dream to go to the nuns' dwelling and wash her eyes with the water in which Frideswide had washed her hands. In the morning she told her parents, who congratulated her, went to the hut, knocked loudly, and asked to be present while Frideswide washed her hands. The girl seized the water, wiped it on her eyes, and at once she could see. How pure a virgin, that what might have been thought dirty could thus cleanse! Silence, all who question the Redeemer's promise, 'Not a hair of your head shall perish': he who can restore sight through the dirty water in which his handmaid has washed, can restore our bodies at the Resurrection. Stupendous miracle! Returning home joyfully, they proclaimed it throughout the region.

15 But the wise virgin feared to pour out her oil, lest none remained for her lamp when the Bridegroom came. Embarrassed by the admiring crowds, she decided to hide. So calling together her companions, she said, 'It is time to return to our monastery: our sisters, grieving for us, may have gone astray.' So they travelled swiftly by boat to the estate called Binsey near the city. Here they disembarked, and Frideswide decided to stay for a while in solitude: their sisters in Oxford could

16 A youth named Alward in the village called Seacourt was chopping wood with an axe on a Sunday, forgetful of the Lord's Resurrection, when his hands stuck to the haft and felt as though on fire. He was led in great pain to Frideswide, and fell at her feet. Moved by pity, she invoked God and asked him to cure the sufferer. As the by-standers answered 'Amen' she made the sign of the cross, and the youth was cured; he returned home praising God. So Frideswide's name became famous through the region.

17 Some fishermen were asleep one night in a boat, when one of them was seized by a demon. He laughed madly, strangled one of his companions, and tried to tear him with his teeth. The others bound him and led him to Frideswide's oratory. She invoked God to free his creation laid low by the enemy of mankind, made the sign of the cross, and commanded Satan to depart. The man fell senseless; she ordered him to be unbound, and commanded him in Christ's name to arise. He got up in his right mind and glorified God. His name was Leowin.

18 God worked many other miracles through Frideswide. One day she said to her companions, 'Let us return to our monastery.' So they went by boat to Oxford, where they were honourably received by the citizens and clergy. When Frideswide had just entered the town, a leprous youth ran up and said 'I charge you, virgin Frideswide, to give me a kiss in

come there easily, and it would be protected from the crowds of townsfolk. On that estate was a secluded spot, called *Thornbiri* because it was overgrown with many kinds of thorns, lonely and suitable for devotion. Here she built an oratory and other appropriate buildings. The nuns could not conveniently draw water from the stream, so she obtained by her prayers a well which still remains, and performs healing works for many who drink from it [*or* for many praying there]. Here she hoped to shun the company of men.

16 Why are you trying to hide, virgin beloved of God? The Lord said that a city placed on a mountain cannot be hidden, and that the humble will be exalted. Although you are crucified to the world, the wretched still seek you out. Behold the unhappy youth of the village called Seacourt, who was chopping wood with an axe on a Sunday, forgetful of the Lord's Resurrection, when his hand stuck to the haft and felt as though on fire. As the wretch cried out and his parents wept, they remembered the miracle of the blind girl and determined to visit Frideswide. Indeed I applaud your faith: drag her out and make her show her merits! Crossing the river, they brought him to Frideswide's dwelling and said, 'Cure this youth, suffering through his own fault; for we know that if you want to, you can.' Will you send them home unrequited? No: moved by pity, she invoked God and asked him to cure the sufferer. As she made the sign of the cross, his hand was freed from the haft and he regained full health.

17 Shortly afterwards, some fishermen were asleep in their boat at dead of night, when one of them was seized by a demon. He grabbed one of his companions, and tried to tear him with his teeth and strangle him. The others overpowered him, tied his hands behind him, and led him to Frideswide's dwelling. She prayed, made the sign of the cross, and commanded Satan to depart. The author of death thus ejected, the man fell as though dead. She commanded him to rise in Christ's name; he got up in his right mind, and proclaimed the miracle wherever he went.

18 God worked so many miracles through Frideswide that it is hard to believe her mortal. One was of such outstanding virtue that it cannot be omitted. When the day of her death approached, sad for men but joyful for angels, she returned on horseback to her own monastery, to surrender her soul to God where she had first

Christ's name.' She made the sign of the cross, kissed him, and his leprosy was cured. Seeing her works, the people and clergy rejoiced at her coming.

served him in the nun's habit. The whole city rushed to meet her; and behold, in the joyful crowd of clergy and people, a leprous youth so disfigured with ulcers and tumours that he seemed more like a monster than a man. He approached her and said, in a raucous voice, 'I charge you, virgin Frideswide, to give me a kiss in Christ's name.' A hard request! Do you, from whose horrible form and smell hardened men recoil, ask this royal maiden to kiss you? An outrageous request, unless prompted by stupendous faith! If you were not a leper, but simply male, you could not ask a kiss from her who has never touched a man. But you answer, 'The heats of my disease, not of my sex, prompt my request. At the touch of her pure mouth the impurity of my body will vanish.' To everyone's wonder, she made the sign of the cross and then kissed the leper. Amazing miracle! What bathing in the Jordan did for Naaman, one kiss from the holy maiden did for this young man: as their mouths touched his whole body was cleansed, and his scaly skin became like that of an infant. Who could refrain from praising Christ? At the coming of such a patron, the whole city rejoiced. But as she grew in good works, so the more humbly she tamed her soul and body.

19 She continued to serve God, mortifying her body to nourish her spirit. A long time passed, and the day of reward drew near. On 12 October an angel appeared and told her, '19 October will be a Sunday, and then you will receive the crown of eternal life. Because you scorned your father's earthly palace, a heavenly hall is prepared for you'. Then a fever seized her, and her limbs began to fail. One day all the citizens came to her, and she edified them with good advice.

20 On Saturday she asked for a grave to be opened for her in St. Mary's church, saying 'Tomorrow is Sunday, and I do not wish anyone to work on my account. After the third cock-crow I shall go to my Lord, strengthened by Christ's body and blood [quotes II Tim.iv.6]. As the sickness grew she received the Eucharist, and began to bless God.

21 When very weak, she looked up and said, 'Welcome, holy virgins.' The others asked with whom she was speaking, but she said, 'Do you not see the blessed virgins of God, Catherine and Cecily?' She spoke to them further, and then said 'Now I come, my Lord.' After the third cock-

19 As the day of her death approached, the Lord's angel appeared while she prayed and said, 'On 19 October, during the night which ends with Sunday's dawn, you will end your pains and receive eternal rewards. Because you scorned your father's earthly palace, you will enter the heavenly King's chamber.' Then a fever seized her, and her limbs began to fail. The citizens came to her as to a nurse and mother, and even during her illness she edified them with good advice.

20 On Saturday evening she said to those around her, 'Dig me a grave today in the basilica of the holy Mary mother of Christ, under whose protection I shall be the safer before her son's tribunal. And since his Resurrection is celebrated tomorrow, and I shall leave this world tonight after the third cock-crow, I do not wish anyone to work on my account on such a day.' Receiving the Eucharist, she blessed the Lord.

21 Looking heavenwards, she saw approaching the virgins whom she most venerated, and addressed them, 'Welcome, blessed virgins.' How great are your mercies, O Lord! Your handmaid now coming to you need not fear Satan, who although vanquished is wont to assail victors

crow, she bade everyone farewell and passed to the Lord. In that hour such a light blazed through Oxford, and such a sweet scent filled it for three hours, that all marvelled and glorified God.

coming home, when you send these fore-runners to guard her path. The others asked with whom she was speaking, but she said, 'Do you not see the holy virgins, Catherine and Cecily?' She spoke to them further, and said, 'Now I come, my Lord.' Bidding everyone farewell, she passed to the Lord at the hour foretold. In that hour a heavenly light shone from the house in which her body lay, and the sweetest of scents filled the town.

22 A very rich man who was paralysed ordered his servants to bear him to her grave, where he instantly regained full health: he who had been dumb and lame for two years walked home praising God.

22 To leave no doubt that she lived beyond death, behold a very rich man, paralysed and dumb, borne by his servants to the feretory on which her body rested. On touching it he was cured so completely that he leapt up in praise of God and St. Frideswide.

23 A nobleman named Athelwold, who was crippled from the navel downwards, dragged himself on crutches to the church door during the funeral. The crowd prevented him from entering, but he shouted at the door, 'Chosen bride of Christ, free me from my infirmities: I know that if you want to help me, you can.' At once he was completely cured; he leapt into the church, holding up his crutches and praising God.

23 As her most chaste corpse was carried to the grave amid a great crowd, a man crippled from the navel downwards dragged himself to the funeral on crutches. The crowd prevented him from approaching the feretory, but he shouted in a loud voice, 'Bride of the Fount of mercy, how long have I wished to come to you! I could not while you lived, nor can I now that you are dead. But heal me now: for I know that you can most easily.' As all turned to look at him, his infirmity vanished; holding up his crutches, he rushed to the grave and threw them down praising God and his servant Frideswide. All congratulated him, seeing how God worked miracles through his servant even after her life.

24 The blessed virgin Frideswide passed to the Lord on 19 October 727. She was buried in St. Mary's church, on the south side, where Christ has worked many miracles through her merits.

24 She was buried in the basilica of the spotless virgin Mary, on the south side, next to the River Thames. The site of the basilica remained thus until the time of King Æthelred, who, after the burning of the Danes who had fled there, enlarged the perimeter of the basilica as he had previously vowed. It certainly happened like this, because the grave, which had previously been on one side, came thenceforth to be the middle. There Christ has worked countless miracles through her merits.

The least of our problems is the status of Life B. Clearly its author was using a text of Life A identical with, or very close to, the Nero manuscript. There are a few omissions of fact: the name and see of the bishop who consecrated Frideswide, the description of Didan's gifts to the church, the facts that Algar was king of Leicester and succeeded Didan in his kingdom, and the names of the beneficiaries of the miracles. For textual reasons it is unlikely that this material was absent from the version of Life A used by the later author (below, p.26), so probably he discarded it as dubious or irrelevant. In three cases Life B adds substantive information not in Life A, all reflecting a knowledge of Oxford topography: Algar's attempted entry through the North Gate; the Binsey episode; and the location of

Frideswide's grave after Æthelred's rebuilding of the church. As shown below (pp.14–16), the insertion of the Binsey passage rationalises Life A's gross confusion over the locations of Bampton, Binsey and Seacourt. Evidently the author of Life B either knew Oxford and its environs or had access to reliable information, whereas the author of Life A did not.

Life B must have been written before the translation of Frideswide's relics in 1180, which would otherwise have been mentioned, and in any case the Pershore manuscript is probably rather earlier than this. On the other hand, the version of Life A available to the author of Life B and to us contains spellings which can scarcely pre-date *c*.1100 (below, p.13). The prologue of Life B implies that Life A was of unknown authorship and held in doubtful repute, suggesting at least a generation or so between the two Lives. Thus the likely date-ranges are *c*.1100–30 for Life A and *c*.1140–70 for Life B.

The obvious candidate for the author of Life B is the scholar Robert of Cricklade, prior of St. Frideswide's between 1139×41 and 1174×80.[8] His literary interests certainly included hagiography, for he wrote a life of St. Thomas of Canterbury (now only known from an Icelandic version); he has also tentatively been identified as the 'Master Robert' who composed a Latin life, also now lost, of St. Magnus of Orkney.[9] A quick comparison of Life B with one of Robert's known works, *De Connubio Iacob*,[10] reveals close similarities both in style and in sentiment. At least five of Life B's scriptural quotations are also used in *Iacob*, two of them twice and one three times;[11] the author deals with similar moral themes (notably gluttony, attacked in section 4 of Life B and several times in *Iacob*); and there are some striking correspondences in style and vocabulary.[12] Given the inherent likelihood that Robert would have been interested in the patron-saint of the house of which he was prior, the attribution of Life B to him must be considered extremely strong if not conclusive.

---

[8] For Robert's dates see D. Knowles, C.N.L. Brooke and V.C.M. London, *The Heads of Religious Houses, England and Wales, 940–1216* (1972), 180. He had been succeeded as prior by Philip before the translation of Frideswide's relics on 12 February 1180 (below, pp.46–8). (There is no evidence for the precise death-date of 1180 given in some works, still less for that of 1188 given by J.B. Schneyer, *Repertorium der Lateinischen Sermones. . .*; *Beiträge zur Geschichte der Philosophie und Theologie des Mittelalters*, xliii.5 (Münster, 1974), 171–6.)

[9] Robert's works are discussed in M. Burrows (ed.), *Collectanea II* (O.H.S. xvi, 1890). 160–5; A.B. Emden, *A Biographical Register of the University of Oxford* (1957), i, 513–14; *Lexikon für Theologie und Kirche*, viii (Freiburg, 1963), 1338; R.W. Hunt, 'English Learning in the Late Twelfth Century', *Trans. Roy. Hist. Soc.* 4th ser.xix (1936), 31–3, 37–8. For the Thomas text see also P.G. Foote, 'On the Fragmentary Text Concerning St. Thomas Becket in Stock. Perg. fol. nr. 2', *Saga-Book of the Viking Society*, xv.4 (1961), 403–50; idem, introduction to *Early Icelandic Manuscripts in Facsimile*, iv (1962), 7–18; M. Orme, 'A Reconstruction of Robert of Cricklade's Vita et Miracula S. Thomae Cantuariensis', *Analecta Bollandiana*, lxxxiv (1966), 379–98. Finnbogi Guðmundsson, *Orkneyinga Saga*, Íslenzk Fornrit xxxiv (Reykjavik, 1965), xlvi–xlvii, discusses the possible identity of 'Master Robert' with Robert of Cricklade; he is known to have visited Scotland at least once in the 1160s *(Regesta Reg.Scott.* i, Nos. 223–5, 228, 260), and might have become interested in St. Magnus there.

[10] Bodl. MS Laud Misc. 725.

[11] (a) Eccli.ii.12: *Life B* sec.9, *Iacob* ff.173, 181. (b) Matt. v.14: *Life B* sec. 16, *Iacob* f.108. (c) Matt. vii.11: *Life B* sec.4, *Iacob* ff.128,169ᵛ. (d) Rom.xi.33: *Life B* sec.9, *Iacob* f.153ᵛ. (e) Philipp.iii.19: *Life B* sec. 4, *Iacob* ff.94,127ᵛ, 136ᵛ (and cf. attack on gluttony in *Iacob* ff. 147–50ᵛ).

[12] For example: (a) Novimus enim, et valde novimus, quoniam si volueris . . . *(Life B* sec. 16)/ Novi enim, et valde novi, Deus meus, quia tu es . . . *(Iacob* f.92ᵛ). (b) . . . absque corporis incommodo ... *(Life B* sec.7)/ . . corpori esse incommoda . . . ; Quis enim omnia corporis incommoda enumerare possit? *(Iacob* f.101). (c) Propterea diebus assidue et noctibus piis lacrimarum rivulis, suspiriis quoque et gemitibus, cordis mactabat hostiam in holocaustum acceptabile Domino . . . Mundi etiam fertur sic postposuisse gloriam, sic ad supernam hanelare patriam. . . *(Life B* secs.3 and 4)/ Adde etiam quia eum videre contingit in congregatione sancta, hos ieiuniis afflictos, macieque confectos, illos assidue orando, dulcibus interdum decurrentibus lacrimis ad supernam patriam hanelo desiderio suspirantes *(Iacob* f.I24). (d) . . . qua se Altissimo fore similem promittebat . . . [of the Devil] *(Life B* sec. 7)/ Immo et in hoc magis Diabolum imitatur, qui ait, 'Ero similis Altissimo' *(Iacob* f.140). (e) . . . de forma hominis nichil fere inesse videretur preter exteriora liniamenta, velut in trunco ad formam humani corporis desecto . . . *(Life B* sec.18)/ . . . nichil fere de Deo extra humani liniamenta corporis . . . ac si non forma humani corporis corporeum . . . *(Iacob* ff.157ᵛ, 158). (f) Si quando ieiunant, terra marique queritur, unde ieiunii dampnum restituatur. Sed non est hoc ieiunium quod elegi dicit Dominus *(Life B* sec.4)/ Verbi gratia ieiunas. sed ut ab hominibus abstinens videaris; non est hoc ieiunium quod elegi dicit Dominus *(Iacob* f.160).

More difficult is the relationship between Life A and Malmesbury: did he use Life A as we have it, Life A in some earlier form, or an independent source? Malmesbury often summarised, and in this case his staccato narrative has decidedly the appearance of a summary: we cannot argue from its brevity that his source was also short or simple. His account of Frideswide's flight from her suitor differs significantly from Life A, while at the same time containing some strong echoes of it:

Malmesbury	*Life A*
The king proposes marriage to Frideswide.	King Algar sends messengers to propose marriage to Frideswide, with threats if she refuses.
She rejects him, 'avowing her chastity to the Lord Christ'.	She rejects them because she is 'betrothed to Christ. King of all kings'.
He prepares to take her by force.	The messengers prepare to take her by force.
	She prays for protection for herself and punishment for them.
	The messengers are struck blind, and repent; she prays for them, and their sight is restored.
Warned of this, she hides in a wood; he follows her, and 'with God's help she enters Oxford at dead of night by means of hidden ways'.	Warned by an angel, and with miraculous help, she travels by boat to Bampton and hides in a wood 'called Binsey'.
He follows her to Oxford.	Algar sets out for Oxford, intent to violate her.
She prays for protection for herself and punishment for him.	
He tries to enter the town with his men, and is struck blind. Therefore kings are unwilling to enter Oxford.	He tries to enter the town with his men, and is struck blind. Therefore kings are unwilling to enter Oxford.
He repents and sends messengers to placate her, and his sight is restored.	He remains blind and unrepentant. She returns to Oxford some three years later.

Where the main lines of the story are concerned, it seems *prima facie* likely that Malmesbury's is the earlier version. The transformation of his over-persistent young man into Life A's wicked tyrant has didactic and dramatic advantages, whereas the reverse process does not. Likewise, the blinding of Algar at the town gates makes sense if Frideswide is trapped inside, but not if she is safely at Bampton. Her appeal for divine aid against the messengers, and their blinding, repentance and cure, in Life A, is clearly the same sequence of events which in Malmesbury's version involves the king himself.

On the other hand, Malmesbury's condensed phrases sometimes suggest an underlying longer narrative, similar in places to Life A but differently ordered. The messengers who convey the king's repentance in Malmesbury may equate with those who convey his initial demands in Life A; Frideswide's rejection of him because she is 'vowed to chastity in the Lord Christ' echoes her longer explanation to the messengers; her return to Oxford 'with God's help by means of hidden ways' recalls her voyage to Bampton with the angelic boatman. There may also be a direct echo of Life A's 'inde creditur inolevisse reges Oxinefordiam non intrare' in Malmesbury's 'hinc timor regibus inolevit Anglie illius urbis ingressum ... cavere'.

To propose that Malmesbury first formulated these passages, and that the canons of Oxford used his *Gesta Pontificum* immediately afterwards as a basis for their own saint's *Vita,* is hardly plausible. The alternative explanation is that both Malmesbury's narrative and Life A reflect some lost text, which was condensed for the former and expanded for the latter. We have Malmesbury's explicit statement that he consulted the archives of St. Frideswide's Priory, and it is more than likely that he was shown hagiographical material on this occasion.[13] This would make Life A a source of independent value, preserving elements from the earlier text: Malmesbury is useful as evidence for the main lines of the unadapted story, and Life B for a few extra details which may or may not be genuine traditions.

THE AUTHORSHIP OF LIFE A

The references to places and people show that Life A in its penultimate form (in other words the archetype of the Nero manuscript and Life B, below pp.25–6) cannot have been earlier than the late 11th century. The places mentioned are Oxford *(Oxinefordia)*, (the folk of) Lincoln *(Lincolienses)*, (the folk of) Leicester *(Leiecestrenses)*, Bampton *(Bentonia)*, Binsey *(Benesia)*, and Seacourt *(Seuecordia)*. All except Binsey correspond closely to the Domesday (1086) forms, whereas *Oxnaforda, Bemtune* and *Seofecanwyrthe* would be more likely in a 10th-century source.[14] Binsey is normally *Beneseye, Buneseia* in the 12th century, and no earlier forms are known.[15] Modernisation of place names is only to be expected, so the forms are in no sense evidence that the places were not mentioned in the hypothetical earlier source.

Apart from Frideswide herself *(Frithesuuitha)*, the people mentioned by name are her parents (King *Didanus* and Queen *Sefrida*), her nurse *(Ælfgiva)*, her suitor (King *Algarus*), the bishop of Lincoln *(Orgarus)*, and the beneficiaries of three miracles *(Alwardus, Leowinus, Athelwoldus)*. The last three are the Anglo-Norman Latin forms of standard late Old English names *(Ælfweard, Leofwine, Æthelwold)*, and may well be picked at random; perhaps the same applies to the suitor *(Ælfgar)*. 'Orgar bishop of Lincoln' looks like a crude anachronism which would be impossible before the 1090s, since the see of Dorchester was only transferred to Lincoln in 1072. But it is just possible that this reference has substance after all: between the 690s and the 720s the bishop of the old Mercian see of Lindsey was one Eadgar, who may conceivably have exercised diocesan functions in the Oxford area.[16]

As Stenton pointed out, *Sefrida* 'seems to be due to a confusion between the Old English Sæfrith and Sæthryth, which are respectively masculine and feminine names':[17] it may be a garbling of *Sæthryth*, or it may be invented. *Didanus*, on the other hand, could be a rather corrupt Latinisation of *Dæda, Dida* or *Dydda*, all evidenced by placenames. This name would occur less readily to an Anglo-Norman writer than would the others, and may be more likely to represent genuine tradition. Finally, *Frithesuuitha* and *Ælfgiva* would both be acceptable in a pre-Conquest Latin text. The fact that the name of Frideswide's nurse appears in an Anglo-Saxon form *(Ælfgiva)*, but the lecherous king's in an Anglo-Norman one *(Algarus)*, may be a sign that the more homely and inconsequential detail is the more authentic.

Textual evidence (below, pp.25–6) suggests some possibility, but no more than this, that the archetype of Life A lacked certain passages which appear in the Nero manuscript: Frideswide's invocations of God to heal Algar's messengers, the young man of Seacourt

---

[13] William of Malmesbury, *De Gestis Regum Anglorum*, ed. W. Stubbs. i (Rolls Ser. xca, 1887), 213. Dr. Alan Thacker (pers. comm.) notes that in the comparable case of St. Werburgh Malmesbury gives a miracle story, radically different from the version in Werburgh's *Vita*, which is most likely to be simply a garbled summary.
[14] *P.N. Oxon.* 19, 304: *P.N. Berks.* 465.
[15] *P.N. Oxon.* 26.
[16] Mr. S.R. Bassett (pers. comm.) suggests 'the possibility of a bishop of Lincoln deputising, during the probable vacancy of Leicester in 705–37, for the bishop of Lichfield in church matters in the southernmost part of "greater Mercia"'. Cf. *Anglo-Saxon England* 18 (1989) 1–32, 'Lincoln and the Anglo-Saxon See of Lindsey', which notes 'a number of references to a bishop of Lincoln (as opposed to Lindsey) in being before 1066, not all of which are easily dismissed as anachronisms'. Note Life B, sec. 5, has Frideswide consecrated by the bishop of the *next* diocese'.
[17] Stenton op.cit. note 1, 105n.

and the demoniac fisherman; the two posthumous miracles; the dating of Frideswide's death to 727; and the location of her grave. With these possible exceptions, the text is the work of one man: it is characterised throughout both by stylistic ineptitude and by a marked tendency to repeat catch-phrases.[18] This man can scarcely have been a professional hagiographer, and his topographical errors show that he was not local; he may well have been one of Wimund's new canons, brought from some distant Augustinian house.[19] If he was active in the Priory at some date close to William of Malmesbury's visit, he could well have re-worked, into a more unified or edifying form, a body of older material which Malmesbury also used. This material could have been of various kinds: not necessarily a single *Vita,* but brief lessons or stories, miracles collected in one or many places, and even oral traditions. In this context must be considered the central crux: the confused and inconsistent accounts of Frideswide's flight from Oxford.

THE BAMPTON–BINSEY PROBLEM

The Frideswide of popular legend hid at Binsey, where a well sprang up in response to her prayers. So well-known and well-loved is this story that her connection with Bampton is usually forgotten. But in fact it is far from clear that the Binsey episode is the more important. William of Malmesbury merely says that she 'hid in a wood'. Life A's account of her flight and exile is as follows:

> The blessed virgin arose and called two nuns, virgins dedicated with her to God. When they reached the River Thames as the angel had directed they found a boat, and sitting in it a young man with a gleaming, angelic face who thus addressed the virgins, 'Step into the boat, hallowed virgins.' They got into the boat and, guided by the Lord, arrived within an hour's space at the town called Bampton. They left the boat and at once the young man vanished from their sight. Then blessed Frideswide, fearing the wicked king's snares, went with her virgins into a certain wood called Binsey, not far from that town. There they found a path leading to a small house, built in former times by herdsmen guarding herds of swine, which was completely covered with ivy. The most holy virgin entered it with her virgins, fortifying herself with the sign of the holy cross. . . . . [Blinding of Algar.] The revered virgin stayed in that wood for about three years . . . [Miracle of the blind girl of Bampton; miracle of the young man of Seacourt; miracle of the demoniac fisherman.] One day she said to her companions, 'Let us return to our monastery.' So a boat was made ready, the blessed virgins embarked, and coming to the city of Oxford they were received with honour by the citizens and all the clergy.

Any inhabitant of Oxford must have known that Binsey is not a wood in Bampton, thirteen miles to the west, but lies less than two miles from the city (Fig. 2). The possibility of a straightforward mistake – that there was a wood in Bampton which had a name resembling Binsey and came to be confused with it – is ruled out by the miracles associated with this episode. The first, the healing of a blind girl, is explicitly located at Bampton. But the second beneficiary is a young man of Seacourt, which lay only 600 yards from Binsey church (Fig. 3);[20] obviously his miracle must relate to the genuine Binsey. It must be concluded that there were separate legends of Frideswide at Bampton and at Binsey, both involving miracles, and that Life A has conflated and confused them.

In the 12th century Binsey belonged to St. Frideswide's Priory. The townsfolk challenged the canons' ownership in 1139, and it has been suggested that the weaving of the Binsey

---

[18] I am grateful to Dr. Michael Lapidge for the following comment: 'In my view, the style of the whole is that of one rather simpleminded narrator, a man of no stylistic pretensions whatever, given to repetition of words, phrases and constructions.'
[19] Suggestion by Dr. Rodney Thomson (pers.comm.).
[20] See M. Biddle, 'The Deserted Medieval Village of Seacourt, Berkshire', *Oxoniensia,* xxvi/xxvii (1961/2). 70–84.

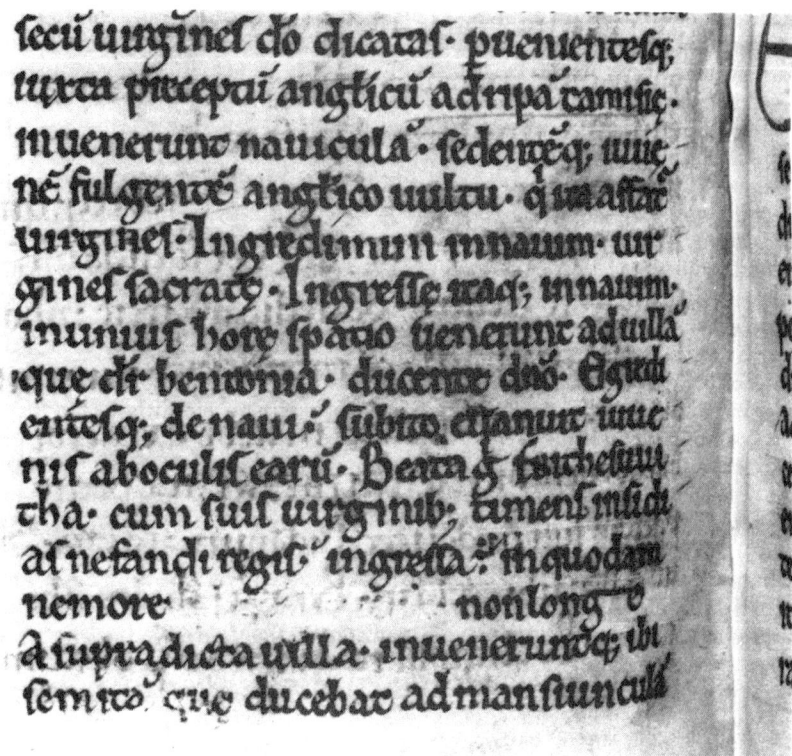

Fig. 1 The Bampton episode in Life A, from B.L. MS Cotton Nero EI (ii) f.156ᵛ. The erased words can be read as *quod dicitur Benesia* under ultra-violet light. Actual size. *Reproduced by permission of the Trustees of the British Library.*

story into Frideswide's legend was a response to this challenge.[21] But elements in the story must be older than this. The author of Life A was aware of a Binsey episode, but not of its practical utility. A story designed to bolster the legal claim would have emphasised the nuns' ownership of Binsey; it would certainly not have mis-located it so grossly. It may well be that the incompetent author of Life A framed his narrative as a vehicle for miracle stories already assigned to Bampton and Binsey respectively. In any case, the geographical confusion is itself good evidence that the body of older tradition included both a Bampton episode and a Binsey episode.

Not surprisingly, this failed to satisfy the mid 12th-century canons. The mistake must have been a prime reason for the disparagement of Life A mentioned in Life B's prologue; awareness of it is demonstrated by the erasure of the words 'called Binsey' in the Nero manuscript of Life A (Fig. 1). The author of Life B solved the problem by inserting, between the first and second Bampton miracles, a new chapter which transports Frideswide from Bampton to Binsey in time to cure the young man of Seacourt. The central passage reads:

> . . . when a boat had been made ready, and she and her companions had embarked, it went swiftly and surely by the boatmen's strength to the estate called Binsey near the city. Disembarking and surveying the scene, she decided that it would be useful to stay for a short while outside the city and devote themselves

---

[21] H. Mayr-Harting, 'The Miracles of St. Frideswide', in H. Mayr-Harting and R.I. Moore (eds.), *Studies in Medieval History Presented to R.H.C. Davis* (1985), 194.

to sweet tranquillity. The virgins whom she had left in the monastery would not find it troublesome to come there, and it would be less exposed to the townsfolk, always looking for some fresh novelty. On that estate was a place entangled with various kinds of trees, called *Thornbiri* in the Saxon tongue because of the many different species of thorns there, lonely and most suitable for devotion. Here she straightway built an oratory, and many buildings well-suited to the needs of holy people. And since the branch of the river was some way away, and she felt it inconvenient for the sisters to go there to draw water, she obtained by her prayers a well which remains to this day, and performs healing works for many who drink from it [*or* who pray there]. [22]

Thus St. Margaret's well makes it first appearance. Given that there existed a Binsey story of some kind, it may be that the author of Life B had access to independent sources or traditions. But the proprietary motive is now obvious, and is emphasised by the use of the word *predium* (estate). The same word, and the same emphasis, appear in the rubric to the Binsey section of the late medieval St. Frideswide's Cartulary: 'predium nuncupatum Bunseye . . . fuit de tempore quo S. Frideswyda corpore vixit predicto monasterio donatum'.[23] In the last analysis, it must be accepted that whereas the 12th-century canons had no vested interest in Frideswide's association with Bampton, they had a clear one in her association with Binsey. But neither episode can be dismissed, for there are independent signs that both Bampton and Binsey were places of significance, and perhaps of religious significance, in the mid-Saxon period.

THE LIVES IN THEIR HISTORICAL CONTEXT

This section assumes the premise that the 12th-century Lives contain elements of an older tradition, potentially informative about Oxford and its region in the 7th and 8th centuries. The test of these elements must be their consistency or otherwise, adduced on general grounds, with the conditions of the age to which they ostensibly refer. We must therefore examine the Frideswide legend in the broader context of royal and ecclesiastical organisation in the area, some of the evidence for which is mapped in Fig. 2.

The first Germanic colonisers of the Upper Thames were the West Saxons, whose descendants had a tradition that British strongholds at Benson and Eynsham were captured in '571'.[24] Archaeology confirms that both places lay in areas of intensive activity during the pagan Anglo-Saxon period; and when, in 634, the West Saxons became Christian, their bishopric was established at Dorchester-on-Thames near the royal headquarters at Benson.[25] But meanwhile, the rapid growth of Mercia under its great kings Penda (?626–55) and Wulfhere (658–75) was involving a relentless thrust down the Thames Valley towards London. If Frideswide was born in the neighbourhood of Oxford in the mid to late 7th century, her father and the territory which he ruled must have been subject to Mercian overlordship.

The known history of Oxfordshire in these years is essentially the history of its saints. Birinus, the Italian missionary who converted the West Saxon court, was buried at Dorchester in *c.*650; the foundation of Winchester Cathedral, and the removal there of Birinus's relics in *c.*690,[26] reflect the retreat of Wessex's north-eastern frontier in the face of Mercian expansion. Meanwhile, the Mercian nobility were being converted by a mission

---

[22] Unfortunately the readings *potantibus* and *petentibus* have equal textual weight: below, p.40 note 316.
[23] *Cartulary of the Monastery of St. Frideswide,* ed. S.R. Wigram (i–ii, O.H.S. xxviii, xxxi, 1895–6). ii, 18.
[24] *Anglo-Saxon Chronicle,* s.a. 571. (The attribution of this annal to 571 is probably arbitrary, and the date seems likely to be much too late.)
[25] G. Briggs, J. Cook and T. Rowley (eds.), *The Archaeology of the Oxford Region* (1986), map 11; *Baedae Opera Historica,* ed. C. Plummer (1896), i, 139.
[26] *Baedae Opera Historica,* ed. C. Plummer (1896), i, 140–1, ii, 143–5.

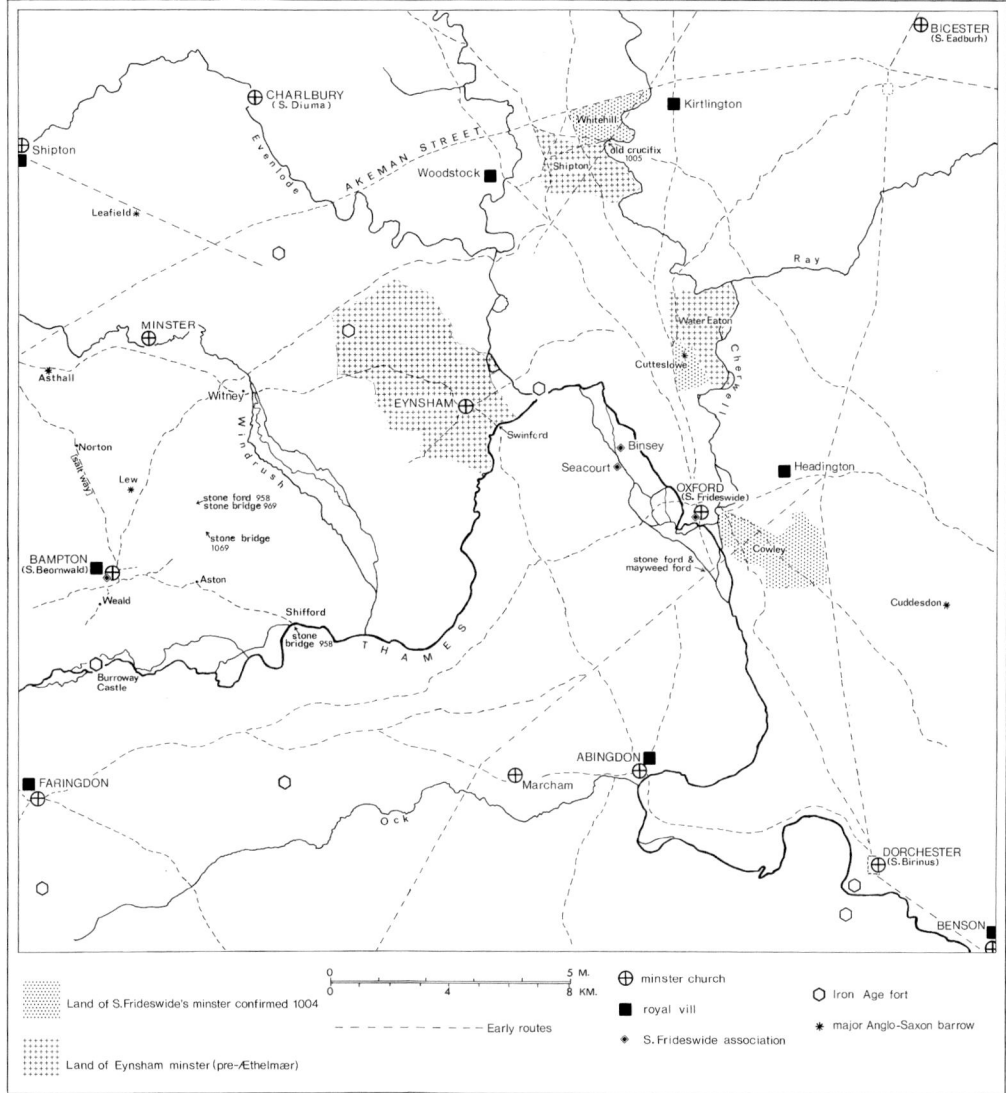

Fig. 2. The Upper Thames in the Anglo-Saxon period, showing places associated with St. Frideswide in relation to minsters, monastic estates, royal vills and select landscape features.

from Northumbria led by St.Diuma, who died in Middle Anglia in 658 in a district which Bede calls *Infeppingum*.[27] Except that this is probably identical with the *Fæpinga* of the Tribal Hidage its location is unknown, but by the 10th century Diuma's relics were enshrined at Charlbury in Oxfordshire.[28] Since the bones of important saints were rarely translated to obscure churches, this suggests that Charlbury was significant in the 7th century and perhaps that Diuma died there.

Between 660 and 700 both Wessex and Mercia saw an unparalleled number of monastic and quasi-monastic foundations, the centres of the new 'minster'-based parochial

[27] Ibid. i, 170–1.
[28] D.W. Rollason, 'Lists of Saints' Resting-Places in Anglo-Saxon England', *Anglo-Saxon England* vii (1978), 64, 90.

organisation.[29] Many were double houses, ruled by the generation of princess-saints whom James Campbell has aptly termed the 'holy cousinhood'.[30] Thus the Oxfordshire minster of Bicester housed the relics of a lady named Eadburh, reputedly a sister of King Wulfhere, whose niece St. Osyth had her own community at Aylesbury a few miles eastwards along Akeman Street.[31] So it is eminently credible that a Mercian sub-king, if this is what 'Didan' was, should have founded a monastery at Oxford and made his daughter 'Frideswide' (*Frithuswith*, 'Peace-Strong') the first abbess. Given the mid-Saxon habit of repeating name-elements within families, some relationship is possible with a pair of late 7th-century Mercian nobles whose names also began *Frith*-: Wulfhere's sub-king Frithuwold, benefactor of Chertsey minster in the early 670s and reputedly the father of St. Osyth by a sister of Wulfhere; and his kinsman Frithuric *princeps*, who founded the Leicestershire minster of Breedon-on-the-Hill.[32] The West Saxon king Æthelheard was married by the 730s to a lady named Frithugyth,[33] a close contemporary of Frideswide and conceivably even her sister. To propose an extensive *Frith*- family is conjecture; but certainly Frideswide's name and supposed parentage are wholly appropriate to the age and context in which the Anglo-Norman writers placed her.

If her father was a Mercian sub-king, how large was his kingdom? It is unlikely to have stretched south of the Thames, where West Saxon princes (such as the Cissa who founded Abingdon minster)[34] were ruling in the late 7th century. The region around Oxford was bounded east by the Tribal Hidage territory of the *Cilternsæte* and west by the Hwicce; to the north, a large tract of Oxfordshire, presumably including the *Færpinga* if they were indeed centred on Charlbury, had links with Northamptonshire and evidently belonged to Middle Anglia.[35] This leaves an area, lying roughly between the Thames to the south, Otmoor and the Chilterns to the east and south-east, and the Cotswolds to the west and north-west, for which no early tribal or territorial identity is known. It includes three places of evident importance in the Anglo-Saxon period, all of which had minster churches: Eynsham, Oxford and Bampton. Princedoms in the age of overlordship could be both artificial and transient:[36] 'Didan's' kingdom may have been much larger than this, an amalgam of territories which were later re-combined into other patterns. But it is worth suggesting that the legends which associate Frideswide with a monastery at Oxford, and with a refuge at Bampton, preserve distant memories of a Thames Valley heartland. This heartland may well be perpetuated as the 300-hide estate 'at Eynsham' which belonged to the see of Canterbury before the 820s,[37] for Eynsham stands out clearly as the dominant place: despite its later obscurity, the strong implication both of the pagan Saxon finds and of the '571' annal is that it was originally more important than Oxford.

Oxford, like Eynsham, occupies a site almost pre-determined for a major settlement: on a tongue of gravel between the Thames and the Cherwell, and at an important Thames crossing. Excavations in St. Aldate's have produced evidence for human activity along the

---

[29] See for instance J. Campbell, 'The First Century of Christianity in England', in J. Campbell, *Essays in Anglo-Saxon History* (1986), 49–67; J. Blair, 'Minster Churches in the Landscape', in D. Hooke (ed.), *Anglo-Saxon Settlements* (1988) 35–58.
[30] J. Campbell, 'Some Twelfth-Century Views of the Anglo-Saxon Past', in Campbell op.cit. note 29, 218–19.
[31] See C. Hohler, 'St. Osyth and Aylesbury', *Records of Buckinghamshire*, xviii (1966–70), 61–72.
[32] J. Blair, 'Frithuwold's Kingdom and the Origins of Surrey', in S.R. Bassett (ed.), *The Origins of Anglo-Saxon Kingdoms* (Leicester U.P., (1989), 97–107.
[33] *Anglo-Saxon Chronicle* s.a. 737.
[34] F.M. Stenton, *The Early History of Abingdon Abbey* (1913).
[35] Bassett op.cit. note 32, *passim;* G. Foard, 'The Administrative Organisation of Northamptonshire in the Saxon Period', in S.C. Hawkes,.J. Campbell and D. Brown (eds.), *Anglo-Saxon Studies in Archaeology and History,* iv (1985), 196–9.
[36] Cf. papers by D. Dumville and J. Blair in Bassett op.cit. note 32.
[37] King Coenwulf of Mercia acquired this estate from Archbishop Wulfrid in 821: see N. Brooks, *The Early History of the Church of Canterbury* (1984), 104, 138, 131–2.

line of this crossing from the 8th century onwards.[38] Frideswide's monastery, assuming that it stood where the Cathedral now stands, was at the north (or Mercian) end of the ford, on the south edge of the gravel terrace. In 1985, excavations in the Cathedral cloister revealed a cemetery which began in or around the 8th century.[39] This provides strong if indirect support for the historical existence of Frideswide and her monastery, for it shows that the late 9th-century fortified town was laid out around some existing religious site.[40]

Many 7th- and 8th-century minsters may have been mixed communities of nuns, monks and priests, the last being needed for parochial duties.[41] The presence of a female head strongly suggests that the Oxford house was of this type, as does Life A's statement that Didan provided 'religious men' to serve the nuns. The reference to a 'refectory, dormitory and cloister' speaks more of the 12th century than of the 8th. On the other hand, Life A may possibly preserve a hint that the community had more than one church. Didan is said to have had his church dedicated 'in honour of the Holy Trinity, the spotless Virgin Mary and All Saints'. The church could certainly have had a multiple dedication, but if so it is strange that Frideswide asks 'for a grave to be opened for her in the church of the blessed Mary mother of God', and is buried 'in St. Mary's church on the south side'. This problem could be resolved by supposing that the author conflated a memory of three churches, dedicated respectively to the Trinity (perhaps originally the Saviour or the Divine Wisdom),[42] the Virgin, and All Hallows,[43] in the second of which Frideswide was buried. Since the canons later believed that their church was enlarged around her grave (below, p.45), the direct predecessor of the present Cathedral must have been St. Mary's; on the other hand, one writ of Henry I is addressed to 'the church of the Holy Trinity of Oxford'.[44] Although the dedication could derive from the Augustinian priory of Holy Trinity Aldgate, which colonised St. Frideswide's,[45] it would be wrong to exclude the alternative possibility that it preserves some memory of the former main church, abandoned in favour of the lesser church containing the holy grave. Both literary and archaeological evidence shows that important mid- Saxon minsters commonly had multiple churches, sometimes on axial alignments.[46] The possibility that Alfredian Oxford was laid out around a line of churches on the edge of the gravel terrace, not around one church only, deserves further thought.[47]

---

[38] B.G. Durham, 'Archaeological Investigations in St. Aldates, Oxford', *Oxoniensia*, xlii (1977), 33–203.

[39] C.J. Scull, *Oxoniensia* 53 (1988), 21–73. Other burials from the same cemetery were published by T.G. Hassall in *Oxoniensia*, xxxviii (1973), 270–4.

[40] There are close analogies for this, notably Wareham and Cricklade: cf. J. Haslam (ed.), *Anglo-Saxon Towns in Southern England* (1984), 213–14, 106–7.

[41] Cf. Campbell and Blair, opp.cit. note 29.

[42] In two cases, at York and at Christchurch (Hants.), Domesday Book equates dedications to the Trinity with dedications to the person of Christ: see R.K. Morris, 'Alcuin, York, and the *Alma Sophia',* in L.A.S. Butler and R.K. Morris (eds.), *The Anglo-Saxon Church: Papers . . . in Honour of Dr. H.M. Taylor* (C.B.A. Research Rep. Ix, 1986), 82–3. In view of the connection between Eynsham and Oxford minsters suggested below, it is worth noting that in 1005 Eynsham was described as a monastery 'in honore Sancti Salvatoris omniumque sanctorum suorum iure dedicato': *The Eynsham Cartulary,* ed. H.E. Salter, i (O.H.S. xlix, 1907), 20. A bede-roll of 1122 includes the entries 'T[este] sanctae Trinitatis et sanctae Mariae Egneshamniae' and 'T[este] sanctae Trinitatis et sanctae Frideswidae Oxineffordensis' (A. Clapham, 'Three Bede-Rolls', in *Memorial Volume to Sir Alfred Clapham: Arch. Jnl.* cvi suppl. (1952), 49).

[43] Dr. Michael Lapidge points out (pers.comm.) that a dedication to All Saints is unlikely to pre-date the general adoption of that feast during the 9th century: see A. Wilmart, 'Un Témoin Anglo-Saxon du Calendrier Métrique d'York', *Revue Bénédictine,* xlvi (1934), 51–6.

[44] *Cart.St.Frid.* op.cit. note 23, ii, 323: 'Precipio quod ecclesia Sancti Trinitatis Oxon' et prior et canonici teneant . . .'. Cf. note 42 for 'the Holy Trinity and St. Frideswide of Oxford' at about the same date.

[45] I owe this suggestion to Dr. Richard Halsey. Cf. Dickinson op.cit. note 6, 113–15.

[46] For the most recent discussions of this phenomenon see W. Rodwell, 'Churches in the Landscape', in M.L. Faull (ed.), *Studies in Late Anglo-Saxon Settlement* (O.U.D.E.S., 1984), 15–21; S.R. Bassett, 'A Probable Mercian Royal Mausoleum at Winchcombe, Gloucestershire', *Antiq. nl.,* lxv (1985), 82–100.

[47] This idea will be developed in a later paper. The late Anglo-Saxon church seems to have been immediately north of the present Cathedral. It is noteworthy that a church in this position would be exactly on the axis of St. Aldate's church, over

Life A says that Didan endowed the monastery with rural property, described obscurely as 'the estates and villages of St. Mary', and with one-third of Oxford. By the latter, the author presumably meant the cluster of Priory tenements in the south-east quarter of the 10th-century *burh,* around the monastic precinct, some of which were known by the 1130s as 'land of St. Fridewide's altar'.[48] The first reliable source for the minster's rural holdings is Æthelred II's confirmation in 1004, which lists three manors in Oxfordshire (3 hides at Cowley, 3 at Cutteslowe and 3 at Whitehill) and one manor in Buckinghamshire (10 hides at Upper Winchendon).[49] The earliest claims of parochial jurisdiction post-date the Augustinian reform and are of a rather dubious character, though they may embody genuine information. If they do, the *parochia* extended east of the Cherwell to include the royal manor of Headington with its dependencies at Marston, Elsfield and Forest Hill.[50] The confirmation to the canons in 1122 of most of the city churches, some of which had parishes extending well outside the city boundary, is another sign that St. Frideswide's enjoyed residual minster rights over Oxford and its neighbourhood.[51] It seems clear enough that the *parochia* of Oxford must once have been contiguous with that of Eynsham, though more work is needed on its precise extent.

The rural manors provide a tantalising hint that the early history of St. Fridewide's church was in some way bound up with the minster at Eynsham. The only early source for Eynsham minster is a charter of 864, which implies that it had recently been deprived of a 5-hide estate at Water Eaton.[52] In 1005 it was re-founded as a Benedictine abbey by Ealdorman Æthelmær, who endowed it with several properties of his own acquiring.[53] But the charter specifies no source for 5 hides at Shipton-on-Cherwell, the first manor in the list after Eynsham itself: the implication must be that this belonged to the minster already. Thus the known pre-Æthelmær manors of Eynsham minster, apart from Eynsham, were Water Eaton and Shipton-on-Cherwell. It is a most striking fact that these were contiguous with the St. Frideswide's land at Cutteslowe and Whitehill respectively, both pairs of manors lying on the west bank of the Cherwell (Fig. 2).[54] It looks almost as though two 8-hide manors were divided between Eynsham and Oxford minsters, in a proportion of 5 to 3, at some date before the 864 charter. If so, the fact suggests some common element in the endowment, and perhaps in the foundation, of the two communities.

Turning to the supposed events of Frideswide's career, the central theme is perhaps the most likely to have been invented: the holy virgin persecuted by a lecherous prince, but then miraculously saved, is a standard *topos* of medieval hagiography. On the other hand,

---

which the canons of St. Frideswide's claimed rights in the 12th century: could St. Aldate's have been one of the monastic churches? [See p.56 below for further evidence.]

[48] *Cart.St.Frid.* op.cit. note 23, i, 18 ('terras que de ara Sancti Frideswidi dicuntur' in 1139), and *passim* for later references.

[49] P.H. Sawyer, *Anglo-Saxon Charters: an Annotated List and Bibliography* (1968), No.909; *Cart.St.Frid.* i, 2–6.

[50] The reference to the tithes of Headington in Æthelred's charter *(Cart.St.Frid.* i, 4–5) is a forged addition, and the authenticity of some of the 12th-century texts in Ibid. i, *passim,* is questionable. In *c.*1200 it was asserted that Headington, Marston and Elsfield chapels, and the extra-mural chapels of St. Mary Magdalen, St. Giles and St. Clement, had been built by leave of the canons of St. Frideswide's; and that the chapel of Forest Hill, and the city churches and chapels of Holy Trinity, St. Michael N., St. Peter-le-Bailey, All Saints, St. Michael S., St. Mildred and St. Aldate (half-share) had belonged to St. Frideswide's from of old: *Oseney Cartulary,* ed. H.E. Salter, ii (O.H.S. xc, 1929), 234–5.

[51] Ibid., and *Cart.St.Frid.* i, 10–11. J. Haslam, 'Parishes, Churches, Wards and Gates in Eastern London', in J. Blair (ed.), *Minsters and Parish Churches: the Local Church in Transition 950–1200* (1988), 39, comments on Oxford: 'the creation of one or possibly several sub-minsters at an early stage in the development of the *burh* would explain the large size of the parishes of churches near its gates in the later medieval period compared to that of the early minster of St. Frideswide's.' See map in *V.C.H.Oxon.* iv, 30.

[52] Sawyer op.cit. note 49, No. 210; W. de Gray Birch, *Cartularium Saxonicum,* ii (1887), No. 509.

[53] *Eynsham Cart.* op.cit. note 42, i, 19–28.

[54] For the boundaries of all four manors see J. Cooper, 'Four Oxfordshire Anglo-Saxon Charter Boundaries', *Oxoniensia,* l (1985), 15–23.

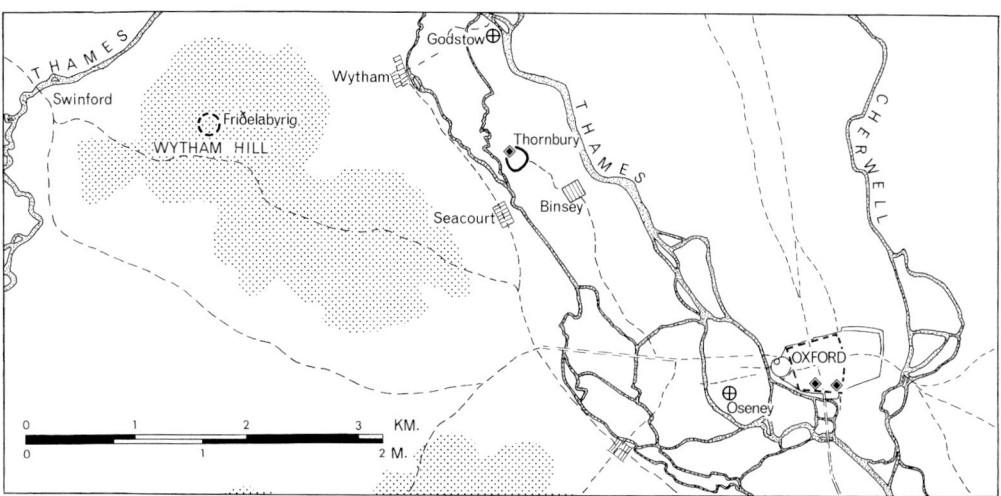

Fig. 3. The environs of Oxford and Binsey (land above 100m. stippled). The lozenge-shaped symbols denote possible mid-Saxon religious sites.

in the context of Mercian overlordship a sub-king of Leicester would be no less credible a figure than is St. Frideswide's father. The abduction of noble ladies for dynastic ends was common enough early medieval practice, and King Æthelbald of Mercia, who began his reign eleven years before Frideswide's reputed death, was accused of seducing nuns. It is not inherently unlikely that something of the sort may have happened to Frideswide.

Bampton, where she was supposed to have spent three years, could well have been important in the 8th century. In Domesday Book it appears as the most valuable royal manor in Oxfordshire after Benson.[55] From the 11th century onwards Bampton church can be recognised as a powerful minster, retaining a large parish with several subordinate chapels; in the 950s it housed a religious community venerating the relics of an obscure saint named Beornwald.[56] For present purposes, one Bampton tradition is especially interesting. Blindness and vision are prominent themes of Frideswide's legend; in the one miracle explicitly located at Bampton, a blind girl is cured when her eyes are anointed with water in which the saint has washed her hands. It is therefore rather odd that the Binsey well was not especially noted for cures of this kind: in its one appearance in the late 12th-century miracle collection it heals not blindness but deafness.[57] But there exists near Bampton church a well called 'Lady Well' traditionally believed to cure ailments, especially of the eye: the bathing of infected eyes in its water was still practised within living memory.[58] Whether or not this reflects a forgotten local tradition of Frideswide's activities, there is every reason to see Bampton as a place of sufficient temporal and spiritual status to be frequented by the royal abbess.

With Binsey the case is different: it is much too near Oxford to have had an independent minster (Fig. 3), and there is no suggestion in post-Conquest sources that its church was

---

[55] *V.C.H. Oxon.* i, 400.
[56] J. Blair, 'St. Beornwald of Bampton', *Oxoniensia,* xlix (1984), 47–55; J. Blair, 'Parish versus Village: the Bampton-Standlake Tithe Conflict of 1317–19', *Oxfordshire Local History,* ii.2 (1985), 34–47.
[57] *Acta Sanctorum: Octobris: VIII* (Brussels, 1853), p.579, No. 48.
[58] J.L. Hughes-Owens, *The Bampton we have Lost* (Bampton, n.d.), 13–14; cf. J.A. Giles, *History of the Parish and Town of Bampton* (1848), 66–8.

more than a humble chapel. But Life A shows that the legend of Frideswide at Binsey predates the 12th century, while Life B's statement that she established her chapel and well there in a secluded place called *Thornbiri* (i.e. 'thorn fortress' or 'thorn enclosure') suggests that the church lay within some earthwork or other substantial boundary. An independent source, the Godstow cartulary, says that in *c.*1100–30 the lady Ediva spent a period of prayer and solitude at Binsey, culminating in the vision which prompted her to found Godstow Nunnery.[59] So in the early 12th century Binsey was known as a place of ancient sanctity, appropriate for religious seclusion. The church lies apart from the village, on the north side of a large sub-oval enclosure defined by field-boundaries and eroded banks (Fig. 3). Excavation on the perimeter of this enclosure in 1987 revealed a sequence of boundary ditches, apparently with a massive wall; the only diagnostic finds were two sherds of 6th- to 8th-century grass-tempered pottery, one sealed by the primary silt of the first ditch.[60] It is tempting to identify this enclosure with *Thornbiri;* like the stray find of an early 8th-century *sceat* somewhere nearby,[61] it hints that an archaeological context for the Binsey legend may yet be recoverable.

Both Life B and the Godstow narrative emphasise the seclusion of Binsey: it is within easy range of the city, yet remote enough to afford undisturbed calm. If *Thornbiri* was indeed a monastic settlement, it seems best interpreted as a retreat-house used from time to time by the main community. Such establishments were familiar to Bede, who says that Bishop John of Hexham (687–706) had 'a more private house, surrounded by open woodland and a ditch, not far from Hexham church, that is almost a mile and a half . . . , in which the man of God used to retire with a few companions to pray and read quietly whenever he had the chance, and especially during Lent'.[62] Oddly enough, it is possible that Binsey was not the only such retreat-house west of Oxford (Fig. 3). The Abingdon Chronicle preserves a legend that in *c.*700 the nuns of St. Helen's Abingdon moved to Wytham, where they stayed until Wytham Hill was fortified in Offa's time (presumably with the fortress called *Frithelabyrig* in a charter-boundary of *c.*957).[63] James Parker's comment of 1885 is still valid: 'If . . . upon the death of the foundress of Abingdon, which probably happened about AD 700, the nuns moved thence to Wytham . . . , St. Frideswide, when she went to Binsey, must have found companions there.'[64] The Wytham and Binsey legends are both late and unreliable, but they also make some sense in relation to our few facts about the setting of 8th-century monasticism.

To draw together these inferences and conjectures: In the late 7th century a territory in west Oxfordshire was ruled, under Mercian overlordship, by a sub-king who may have been named something like Dida and who may have been based at Eynsham. He probably endowed minster churches, for the fashion of the time was to do so; one, perhaps the earliest and most important, was at Eynsham, and there were others at Oxford 6 miles eastwards and Bampton 8 miles westwards. His daughter Frithuswith was first abbess of the Oxford community, a 'double house' which may have had three churches. An episode in her life

---

[59] *The English Register of Godstow Nunnery,* ed. A. Clark, i (E.E.T.S. cxxix, 1905), 26.
[60] Below, pp.57–73.
[61] A 'Porcupine' *sceat* of 'series E', now in the Ashmolean Museum; a label noting the find-spot as Binsey is the only evidence for its source. Dr. Metcalf (pers. comm.) suggests a date of *c.*710–30. See D. Hill and D.M. Metcalf (eds.), *Sceattas in England and on the Continent* (B.A.R. British Ser. 128, 1984), 61, 247.
[62] *Baedae Opera* op.cit. note 26, i, 283; cf. Ibid. i, 207 for another case (Chad's *mansio remotior* near his church of Lichfield). See also E. Cambridge, 'The Early Church in County Durham: a Reassessment', *Jnl. Brit. Archaeol.Assocn.* cxxxvii (1984), 76–7.
[63] *Chronicon Manasterii de Abingdon,* ed. J. Stevenson, i (Rolls Ser. iia, 1858), 8; M. Gelling, *The Place-Names of Berkshire,* iii (E.P.N.S. li, 1976), 729–31. Unfortunately the possibility cannot be excluded that the Abingdon Chronicle refers to Wittenham Clumps, though the spelling *Witham* is more normal for Wytham.
[64] Parker, op.cit. note 2, 90–1.

was associated with Bampton, which may already have had both a royal residence and a minster church. She also spent some time at Binsey, at a retreat-house of her community within a ditched enclosure which became known as Thornbury. Always prominent in her life was the Thames, that vital thoroughfare which flowed past Bampton, Eynsham, Thornbury and Oxford:[65] it is not idly that the river is made so prominent a motif in the 12th-century Lives. She died, perhaps on the traditional date of 19 October 727, and was buried in her monastery, the nucleus of the nascent town of Oxford. Of course, this is a mere theoretical construct: the most that can be claimed for it is that it takes the written sources as far as they can be persuaded to go, and makes some kind of sense of them. This discussion will have achieved its aim if it has enlarged the basis for hypotheses about early Oxford; thereafter, archaeology takes over.

APPENDIX A: THE FIRST LIFE OF ST. FRIDESWIDE ('LIFE A'), PROBABLY WRITTEN c.1100–30

Life A is edited here from the one full text and the abridgements:

N = British Library MS Cotton Nero EI, part 2, ff. 156–7ᵛ (pencil foliation) (= *BHL* 3164)

Nero EI is a massive late Anglo-Saxon collection of *vitae*, written at Worcester.[66] The St. Frideswide text is not part of the original book, but among material written in a single 12th-century hand on twelve inserted leaves:
ff.156–7ᵛ: the text here edited.
ff.158–62ᵛ: Rhigyfarch's Life of St. David.[67]
ff.162ᵛ–5: Life of St. Margaret of Antioch.[68]
ff.187–8ᵛ: Life of Bede.[69]

It is possible that these leaves owe their present positions to Sir Robert Cotton's binder. However, the words '. . . dei gracia Wigo . . .' scribbled on f.165ᵛ indicate a Worcester origin, while alterations to the original text of the book in the hand of the addenda (e.g. on ff.95ᵛ, 151) imply that the leaves have always been associated with this volume. The material on them, written in two columns with red initials and headings, is in a book-hand of a distinctive Worcester type, current at the Cathedral Priory through the first half of the 12th century and associated with John of Worcester's circle.[70] The scribe has certain orthographic preferences: y for i ('paradysi'), n for m ('menbra'), h rather than ch ('nihil', 'mihi'), c rather than k ('caritatis').[71]

Following the words '. . . ingressa est in quodam nemore . . .' in section 12 is an erasure (Fig. 1). Under ultra-violet light the erased letters can be deciphered as 'qᵒd dcʳ B-n-sia'; this is confirmed by B's reading 'in nemore quod dicitur Benseya' and L's 'nemus de Beneseya'. In the present edition the name is reconstructed as 'Benesia'.

L = British Library MS Lansdowne 436 ff.101–3 (= *BHL* 3166)

Lansdowne 436, from Romsey Abbey, is a chronicle and collection of *vitae* in an early 14th-century hand.[72] Its abridgement of Life A follows N closely, though reduced to about half-length; it ends rather abruptly, leading

---

[65] Mr. David Wilson (pers.comm.) points out that up-river journeys would have been slower and more difficult than travel by road. Bampton may, however, have functioned as a loading-on point for sending Mercian produce down-stream towards London; note especially the Droitwich salt-rights attached to the manor in 1086 (*V.C.H. Oxon.* i, 400).
[66] *A Catalogue of the Manuscripts in the Cottonian Library* (Rec.Comm., 1802), 239–41; N.R. Ker, *Medieval Libraries of Great Britain* (2nd edn., 1964), 207.
[67] *BHL* 2107; edited J.W. James, *Rhigyfarch's Life of St. David* (Cardiff, 1967).
[68] Version of *BHL 5303–5*.
[69] *BHL* 1069; see T.D. Hardy, *Descriptive Catalogue of Materials Relating to the History of Great Britain and Ireland*. II (Rolls Ser. xxvi*a*, 1862), No. 985.
[70] See E.A. McIntyre, 'Early Twelfth-Century Worcester Cathedral Priory, with Special Reference to the Manuscripts Written There' (unpub. Oxford D.Phil. thesis, 1978), 29–51, where this group of hands is classified as 'Type B'. Mrs. Theresa Webber (pers.comm.) suggests a date in the second quarter of the 12th century for the Nero EI text; Dr. Patrick McGurk proposes (pers.comm.) that it was written by John of Worcester himself.
[71] In these respects the Frideswide text is consistent with the David text (James op.cit. note 67, p.xiv).
[72] *A Catalogue of the Lansdowne Manuscripts in the British Museum* (Rec.Comm., 1819), part ii, 121: Ker op.cit. note 66, 164; Hardy op. cit. note 69, No. 1000.

straight into an account of the later fortunes of the house, the rediscovery of Frideswide's relics and their translation in 1180 (below, Appendix C). The degree of abridgement varies from section to section:

(i) From the beginning to the building of the church (sections 2–4) is extremely brief, and omits Frideswide's upbringing: 'Tempore illo quo Anglia diversis regibus et subregulis erat subiecta, Cristianissimis parentibus regi Didano et Sefride regine beata virgo Friseuuida extitit orta. Huius regis dominium in Oxonifordia et partibus circumadiacentibus erat. Rex vero predictus construxit ecclesiam. . ."

(ii) Thence to '. . . imploransque Dei misericordiam' (end of section 6): a brief summary of N, omitting Didan's death.

(iii) The diabolic vision (section 7): essentially as N.

(iv) 'Quidam igitur rex Leiecestrensium. . .' to the healing of Algar's messengers (sections 8–10): substantially as N, but omitting Frideswide's long invocation on behalf of the messengers, and some shorter phrases.

(v) 'Repletus itaque rex furore. . .' to '. . . prope tribus annis in ipso nemore' (sections 11–13): essentially as N, though with the last phrase expanded to '. . . prope tribus annis in nemore illo, ieiuniis et orationibus intenta, miraculis clara'.

(vi) The miracle of the blind girl of Bampton (section 14): a brief summary of N.

(vii) The miracle of the young man of Seacourt (section 16): a slightly condensed version of N, omitting Frideswide's invocation.

(viii) The miracle of the demoniac fisherman (section 17): a brief summary of N, omitting Frideswide's invocation.

(ix) 'Quadam igitur die dixit . . .' (section 18) to Frideswide's death: essentially as N.

(x) The posthumous miracles (sections 22–4) are omitted, and the Life ends abruptly: '. . . valedicens omnibus, ad Dominum Iesum Cristum migravit, atque in loco ab ea designato honorifice sepulta fuit. In hora autem transitus eius, tanta lux effulsit per universam civitatem Oxenefordie, tanta etiam suavitas odoris trium horarum spatio fragravit, ut omnes mirarentur et glorificarent Deum.'

B = Oxford, Balliol College MS 228 f.300 (= *BHL* 3167)

A late 14th- or early 15th-century miscellany, including a kalendar, a *Legenda Aurea* and a collection of short *Vitae*.[73] The version of Life A is no more than a brief summary some 550 words long, but it includes all the main elements of the story, with these differences: Frideswide learns the psalter within seven months, not six; she is consecrated by Bishop Edgar, not Orgar; and the miraculous boat-journey to Bampton takes a moment, not an hour. After the curing of the leper (section 18) the text ends briefly, omitting the two posthumous miracles: 'Hiis gestis, precipit ei angelus domini diem obitus sui. Qua mortua, sepulta est in ecclesia beate Marie Oxonie, ubi per ipsius merita petentibus multa prestantur benficia.'

Although B, like L, omits the posthumous miracles, it is not derived from L but independently from a version of the full text. Phrases in N echoed by B but not by L include:

N	L	B
Transactis itaque quinque annis, . . . ita animum stabilivit ad discendas litteras ut intra sex menses totum sciret psalterium.	[whole passage omitted]	Cum esset annorum quinque, litteras discens, infra vij menses psalterium scivit.
. . . rogavit patrem suum, dicens, 'O dulcissime pater, concede mihi ut sanctimonialem habitum adipisci merear. . .' . Rex autem Didanus, audiens propositum filie, gavisus est valde.	Rex vero predictus construxit ecclesiam Oxonie . . . quam filie sue ab ipsa devote postulatus dedit . . .	Rogavit igitur patrem suum ut se sanctimonialem fieri permitteret in ecclesia Sancte Marie virginis quam Rex Didanus in Oxonia construxit, gavisus itaque rex de proposito suo . . .

---

[73] R.A.B. Mynors, *Catalogue of the Manuscripts of Balliol College, Oxford* (Oxford, 1963), 230–7.

Accidit etiam ut piscatores, . . . cum obdormissent in navi, unus eorum arreptus a demonio . . . tenensque unum e sociis suis suffocabat eum manibus, dentibusque dilaniare volebat. Ceteri vero, tenentes eum, ligaverunt manus a tergo, ducentes eum	Quadam etiam vice cum piscator quidam . . . a demonio arreptus, vinculisque ligatus, ad ipsam esset adductus . . .	Piscator quidam cum sociis suis in navi obdormientis a demone arripitur, apprehendens unum de sociis suis, suffocans, dentibus deliniare fecit. Ceteri vero, ligantes eum, duxerunt eum . . .

H, W and R = extracts in versions of the Hereford Breviary.[74]

H (Hereford Cathedral Library, MS P.9.vi: late 13th century)[75] contains a text of sections 2 to 4, essentially similar to N, ending at ' . . . omniumque Sanctorum in urbe Oxinefordia'. W (Worcester Cathedral Library MS Q.86: 14th century)[76] and R (printed version, Rouen, 1505)[77] contain extracts from sections 2 to 6 closely related to each other; they too are based on an N-type text, but often lapse into summary and paraphrase. H and W/R derive from a common exemplar, for they share one clear error ('volebat' for 'valebat', note 91). The textual authority of these extracts is low, and the agreement of any one of them with N must always overrule alternative readings within the group.

The Hereford extracts H, W and R are too brief to be useful for determining the development of the text, except that their exemplar was apparently close to N. But the summaries L and B, condensed though they are, contain suggestions that they derive from a text or texts independent of N, and in some respects superior to it. N has a slight tendency to drop minor words, six of which can be restored from I.[78] and one on the combined testimony of L and B.[79] Two phrases in L can also be interpreted as accidental omissions by N,[80] and L corrects two of N's implausible readings.[81] On the other hand, L and B agree on one apparent error. In N, Frideswide tells Algar's messengers that since she is betrothed to the King of all kings, she cannot leave the King to obey the commands of a slave (' . . . ut relinquens Regem, obediam mandatis servi'): L and B read *eum* for *regem* (note 113), thus destroying what is surely a deliberate antithesis between king and slave. From this it appears that L and B had a common exemplar (Y) which was independent of N. These inferences suggest the following stemma, with X the archetype and Z either N itself or N's exemplar:

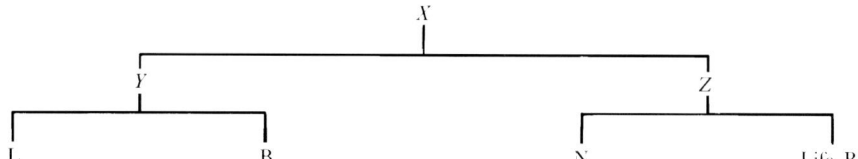

From this certain conclusions follow:

1. B's readings 'Edgarum' and 'in momento', which are contradicted by L and N, cannot reflect the archetype.
2. Since both L and B omit the two posthumous miracles but include all the others, and since miracles are more likely to have been added than excised, it may be that the posthumous miracles were not in Y or the archetype but introduced with Z.

---

[74] All variants are printed in *The Hereford Breviary*, eds. W.H. Frere and L.E.G. Brown, ii (Henry Bradshaw Soc. xl, 1911), 376–7.
[75] Described Ibid. iii (Henry Bradshaw Soc. xlvi, 1915), lv–lxi.
[76] Described Ibid. lxi–lxii.
[77] Described Ibid. liii–lv.
[78] Text footnotes 126, 138, 142, 145, 146, 152.
[79] Text footnote 112.
[80] Text footnotes 117, 144. (In the second case, the similarity of 'dies . . . recipiendi mercedem pro labore' to the devil's earlier statement that 'tempus est ut recipias mercedem laborum tuorum' supports the view that it belongs to the original text.)
[81] Text footnotes 128, 143.

3. Other material in N which is not attested by either L or B could also have been added at the Z stage. In fact, there are only two circumstantial details to which this applies: the year of Frideswide's death, and the location of her grave on the south side of the church. However, it is noteworthy that L completely omits Frideswide's long invocations of God to heal Algar's messengers, the young man of Seacourt and the demoniac fisherman in sections 10, 16 and 17 ('Deus invisibilis . . . infinita seculorum secula'; 'Adonay domine Deus . . . in secula seculorum'; ' . . . deprecabatur Deum patrem . . . generis prostratum'); and that none of these passages is echoed in B. Since L reproduces, or at least mentions, all other cases of Frideswide's reported speech, it seems possible that these rather distinctive passages (which are in collect form and employ a loose paraphrasing of the Vulgate not otherwise found in Life A) were also absent from Y, and thus probably from X.

The relationship between Life A and Life B is discussed more fully above (pp.3–11). Since the author of Life B re-worked Life A into a more elaborate Latin style, textual comparisons are difficult. However, his inclusion of the posthumous miracles and of Frideswide's invocations shows that his exemplar was closer to N than to the hypothetical Y; it very likely included the few circumstantial details which Life B itself omits, all of which belong to the common material of Y and N. Indeed, it is not impossible that the author of Life B used the N manuscript itself. The material peculiar to Life B must therefore be derived by its author from some other source, or from his own imagination, though it is conceivable that one small detail (Algar's attempted entry through the North Gate, section 13) reflects a passage in the archetype ignored by N, L and B.

The basic text of the present edition is of course N. Its chapter divisions are preserved as paragraphs, but punctuation, capitalisation and the usage of *u* and *v* are modernised, and contractions are expanded. Variant readings from L, B, H, W and R are noted when the differences seem likely to reflect the full texts underlying them, rather than to result merely from the process of abstraction. Direct quotations from the Vulgate are italicised. The section numbers, which are editorial insertions, correspond with the equivalent passages in Life B and on pp.4–10 above.

Incipit vita Sancte Fritheswithe virginis

(**2**) Igitur postquam populus Anglorum beati Augustini predicatione edoctus atque baptizatus est, constituti sunt presbiteri atque diaconi, ecclesieque constructe atque dedicate sunt per universam regionem illam. *Augebatur* igitur *credentium multitudo*,[82] et per universam terram Anglorum ecclesia nova prole fecundabatur. Post multum vero tempus fuit rex quidam Oxinefordie cui nomen erat Didanus. Hic accepit uxorem nomine Sefridam, colentem Deum atque prudentem in omni opere bono, cunque simul gauderent flore iuventutis, donavit eis[83] Dominus fecunditatem. Concepit itaque venerabilis Sefrida, et post peractum tempus idoneum peperit filiam. Cum hoc audisset supradictus rex, *gavisus* est *valde*,[84] iussitque earn regenerari ex aqua et Spiritu Sancto.

Baptizatam itaque vocaverunt[85] eam Fritheswitham. (**3**) Hec igitur regis filia diligenter enutrita est. Transactis itaque quinque annis, tradiderunt[86] eam cuidam matrone, Ælfgive[87] nomine, ad erudiendum[88] litteras. Virgo igitur, quam Deus iam providerat vas futurum Spiritus Sancti, ita animum stabilivit ad discendas litteras ut intra sex[89] menses totum sciret psalterium. *Proficiebat* igitur beata Fritheswitha virgo et *crescebat*,[90] omnique animo nitebatur omnibus se amabilem facere, semperque prout valebat[91] liminibus sancte ecclesie

---

[82] *Acts v.14*.
[83] ei *H, W, R*
[84] *II Joh.4, III Joh.3*.
[85] vocavit *W, R*
[86] tradidit *W, R*
[87] Eluine *H*, Eliue *W, R*
[88] erudiendas *H, W, R*
[89] intra sex] infra vij *B*
[90] crescebat *N, H*] crescebat in Domino, *W, R*. The passage echoes *I Chron. xi.9*.
[91] volebat *H, W*

adherebat. Sacrarum⁹² etiam scripturarum dicta in pectoris antro condebat, hanc sepe⁹³ orationem repetens, *ut inhabitare* valeret *in domo Domini omnibus diebus vite* ⁹⁴ sue, videretque voluntatem eius atque impleret. (**4**) Prefata igitur mater eius, infirmitate corporis detenta febreque gravi correpta, mortua est. Rex vero Didanus construxit ecclesiam, et dedicari⁹⁵ fecit in honore Sancte Trinitatis et intemerate Virginis Marie Omniumque Sanctorum, in urbe Oxinefordia.⁹⁶ Venerabilis igitur Fritheswitha petiit patrem suum, videlicet Didanum regem, ut daret sibi ecclesiam. Rex igitur dedit sibi ecclesiam.⁹⁷ Religiosa itaque virgo, post obitum matris sue, servire Deo studuit die noctuque vigiliis⁹⁸ et orationibus, semper intendens ita ut multotiens obliviseretur cibum corporeum, totisque nisibus anhelaret⁹⁹ cibum animarum.¹⁰⁰ Considerans virgo Fritheswitha transitoriam huius mundi pompam gloriamque, *quasi sterquilinium*¹⁰¹ omnia reputans, quicquid habere poterat pauperibus erogabat. Cilicio semper utebatur; modicum panem ordeiceum¹⁰² cum paucis oleribus et aqua pro cibo habebat. Omnis interea populus Anglorum mirabatur tantam in puerili etate virtutem, gaudebatque rex, considerans et cognoscens unicam filiam suam vas esse Spiritus Sancti. (**5**) Beata igitur virgo rogavit patrem suum, dicens, 'O dulcissime pater, concede mihi ut¹⁰³ sanctimonialem habitum adipisci merear et in templo Dei semper nomen eius laudare et benedicere.' Rex autem Didanus, audiens propositum filie, *gavisus* est *valde*,¹⁰⁴ et advocans quendam religiosum virum, Orgarum nomine, Lincoliensium pontificem,¹⁰⁵ fecit Deo filiam suam Fritheswitham consecrari. Sacrate sunt itaque cum ea duodecim virgines, omnes nobili progenie. Fecit itaque prefatus rex edificari domos que conveniunt sanctimonialibus, videlicet refectorium et dormitorium et claustra, virosque religiosos dedit ad serviendum eis. Dedit etiam rex Didanus predia et villas Sancte Marie, tertiamque partem civitatis Oxinefordie, ad victum sanctimonialium.

(**6**) Igitur beata Fritheswitha, bonis ornata moribus, studuit corpus domare, spiritumque vivificare, iuxta vocem apostoli dicentis, *'Mortificate menbra vestra que sunt super terram.'* ¹⁰⁶ Post non multum vero tempus, *decidit in lectum*¹⁰⁷ rex Didanus, gravi egritudine correptus. Distribuensque thesaurum suum pauperibus, communione corporis Cristi¹⁰⁸ confirmatus, Deo spiritum reddidit. Beata igitur Fritheswitha, sponsa Cristi, orbata utroque parente, magis ac magis se¹⁰⁹ commendabat Spiritui Sancto quem¹¹⁰ timebat. Statuit etiam in corde suo beata virgo ut centies per diem flecteret genua, centiesque per noctem affligens carnem, imploransque Dei misericordiam.¹¹¹

---

⁹² sanctarum *H, W, R*
⁹³ sepe *N, H*] semper *W, R*
⁹⁴ *Ps. xxvii.4.*
⁹⁵ dedicare *N, H, W, R*
⁹⁶ *H ends here*
⁹⁷ ecclesiam quam fecerat *W, R*
⁹⁸ noctuque vigiliis *N*] nocteque vigilans *W, R*
⁹⁹ anhelabat ad *W, R*
¹⁰⁰ *R ends here*
¹⁰¹ *Job xx.7.*
¹⁰² *sic N*
¹⁰³ *inserted above line N*
¹⁰⁴ *II Joh.4., Joh.3*
¹⁰⁵ Orgarum … pontificem] Edgarum episcopum Lincolnie *B*, Orgaro Lincolniensi episcopo *L*
¹⁰⁶ *Coloss. iii.5.*
¹⁰⁷ *I Macc. i.6 or vi.8.*
¹⁰⁸ X̄p̄i *etc. has been expanded throughout to* Cristi *etc.*
¹⁰⁹ se *W*] om. *N*
¹¹⁰ quem *W*] quod *N*
¹¹¹ *W ends here*

(**7**) Quadam igitur nocte, dum hec sola peragaret in oratorio quod sibi construxerat, dormientibus consodalibus suis, apparuit ei[112] diabolus ornatus auro et argento omnique lapide pretioso, constipatusque caterva demonum. Dixit ei, 'O mihi amabilis virgo, iam tempus est ut recipias mercedem laborum tuorum. Veni ergo adorare me: ego enim sum Cristus, daboque tibi coronam immortalitatis quam promeruisti.' Cui beata Fritheswitha dixit, 'O miser omniumque creaturarum fetidissime, cur non times Dei iudicium? Veniet enim dies quando et tu et magister tuus eternam recipietis penam. Quomodo ergo promittis quod non habes?' Hec dicens, venerabilis virgo consignavit corpus suum vexillo crucis, et statim diabolus, dans mugitum et ululatum, evanuit. Beata vero virgo, perseverans in oratione, persistensque in vigiliis, equo animo erat.

(**8**) Quidam igitur rex Leiecestrensium, vir nefandissimus et Deo odiosus, successit in regnum post obitum Didani regis, Algarus nomine. Hic misit legatos ad beatam Fritheswitham, ita dicentes, 'Misit nos ad te rex Algarus, Fritheswitha virgo, volens te habere in matrimonium. Quod si nolueris, faciet te trahi ad lupanar.' Quibus virgo Deo sacrata respondit, 'Desponsata sum Cristo, Regi regum omnium, et ideo nefarium videtur esse ut relinquens Regem[113] obediam mandatis servi. Quod autem dicitis me trahere ad lupanar, sciatis non posse contaminari animum nisi ex consensu mentis. Insuper omnia autem, *Dominus mihi adiutor, non timebo quid faciat mihi homo.*'[114] (**9**) Ministri ergo regis indignati dixerunt, 'Nisi adquieveris sponte preceptis regis, rapiemus te ducemusque ad regem Algarum, velis nolis.' Hec audiens, beata Fritheswitha, suspiciens sursum, clara voce dixit, *'Exurge, Domine, non confortetur homo: iudicentur gentes in conspectu tuo, sciant*que *quoniam homines sunt. Apprehende arma et scutum, et exurge in adiutorium mihi. Dic anime mee, salus tua ego sum.'*[115] Hec cum dixisset virgo sancta, excecati sunt oculi eorum, et *videre* non poterant *lumen celi.*[116] Videntes autem populi civitatis Oxinefordie, expavefacti corruerunt ad pedes sancte virginis, postulantes ut pro eis oraret. (**10**) Sanctissima igitur femina, volens bonum pro malo reddere,[117] flexis genibus cepit orare, dicens, *'Deus* invisibilis et incommutabilis, qui fecisti ce*l*um et ter*r*am*, mare, et omnia que in eis sunt*, quique formasti *Adam de limo terre*,[118] et seductum invidia diaboli eiectumque de paradysi amenitate[119] per mortem filii tui Domini nostri Iesu Cristi redemisti, redde his miseris lumen oculorum, ut cognoscat populus iste quia *tu es miserator et misericors, patiens et multe misericordie et verax,*[120] qui vivis et regnas per infinita seculorum secula.' Cunque omnes repondissent 'Amen', restituti sunt oculi eorum, currentesque provoluti pedibus beate virginis laudabant Dominum, magnificantes eius immensam clementiam. (**11**) Venientesque ad regem Algarum, narraverunt omnem eventum rei. *Repletus* itaque *rex furore et ira,*[121] dixit, 'Neque incantationes eius neque eius falsa dogmata neque ars eius magica eam liberabit de manibus meis, quin eam habeam.' In ipsa nocte, orante beata Fritheswitha, apparuit ei angelus Domini, dicens, 'O *vas electum*[122] Sancti Spiritus, noli timere minas funesti regis, quia *sub umbra alarum suarum proteget*[123] te Iesus[124] Cristus, et dextera sua sullevabit te. Pergens igitur ad amnem,

---

[112] ei B, L] *om.* N
[113] regem] eum B, L
[114] *Ps. cxviii.6.*
[115] *Pss. ix.19–20, xxxv.2–3.*
[116] *Echoes Tobias v.12, xi.8, xii.3*
[117] volens . . . reddere L] *om.*N
[118] *Paraphrase of Genesis ii.7, Tobias viii.7–8.*
[119] *inserted above line* N
[120] *Ps. lxxxvi.15.*
[121] *Conflation of Daniel ii.12, iii.13, iii. 19.*
[122] *Acts ix.15.*
[123] *Ps. xvii.8.*
[124] Ihī *etc. has been expanded throughout to* Iesus *etc.*

habe tecum quascunque volueris socias sanctimoniales,[125] inveniesque navem preparatam a Deo nautamque, intrantesque navim *deduc*et vos Dominus[126] omnipotens *in viam rectam*[127] ad glorificandum nomen suum.' Hoc dicto,[128] recessit ab ea. (**12**) Surgens igitur, beata virgo vocavit duas sanctimoniales secum virgines Deo dicatas, pervenientesque iuxta preceptum angelicum ad ripam Tamisie, invenerunt naviculam, sedentemque iuvenem fulgentem *angelico vultu*,[129] qui ita affatur virgines, 'Ingredimini in navim, virgines sacrate.' Ingresse itaque in navim, in unius hore spatio[130] venerunt ad villam que dicitur Bentonia,[131] ducente Domino. Egredientesque de navi, subito evanuit iuvenis ab oculis earum. Beata igitur Frithesuuitha cum suis virginibus, timens insidias nefandi regis, ingressa est in quodam nemore quod dicitur Benesia[132] non longe a supradicta villa, inveneruntque ibi semitam que ducebat ad mansiunculam quam quondam fecerant subulci custodientes greges porcorum, coopertumque erat ex omni parte edera. In quam introivit sanctissima virgo cum suis virginibus, muniens se signaculo sancte crucis. (**13**) Surgens itaque, rex impius cum satellitibus suis pervenit ad urbem Oxinefordiam, cupiens violare vasa Deo sacrata. Ex quo igitur cepit introire rex civitatem, excecati sunt oculi eius et videre non potuit. Inde creditur inolevisse reges Oxinefordiam non intrare. Permansit itaque rex impius cecus omnibus diebus vite sue, semperque insidiabatur et cogitabat quomodo nocere beate Frithesuuithe posset. Beata autem virgo Cristi semper gerebat vocem evangelii in pectore, et non cessabat diebus vel noctibus a colloquiis divinis et oratione. Mansit itaque venerabilis virgo prope tribus annis un ipso nemore.

(**14**) Puella itaque quedam erat in supradicta villa Bentonia,[133] que ante a diabolo obcecata erat prope septem annis. Hec cum quadam nocte dormiret, apparuit ei quidam in somnis dicens, 'Vade in nemore ubi sanctimoniales morantur, et stillam que de manibus beate Frithesuuithe ceciderit quando manus laverit tolle, et lini oculos tuos, et visum recipies.' Mane facto, narravit puella patri suo quod viderat. Pater vero, tenens manum eius, duxit eam secum usque dum veniret ad habitaculum virginis. Expectansque horam cum lavisset manus beata Frithesuuitha, recepta aqua linivit oculos filie sue, et visum continuo recepit. Benedicentes igitur Deum, reversi sunt ad propria, laudantes omnipotentiam Salvatoris, narrantes mirabilia que viderant fieri per sanctam Frithesuuitham.

(**16**) Erat etiam quidam adolescens nomine Alwardus in villa que dicitur Seuecordia, qui Dominica die incidebat ligna cum securi, parvipendens diem resurrectionis Dominice. Cum hoc ageret, adheserunt manus eius manubrio, ita ut extendere digitos penitus non valeret, sed clamans voce magna dicebat sibi manum incendi. Ductus usque ad sanctam virginem, provolutus eius pedibus, cepit eius implorare auxilium. Illa, ut erat miscericordia[134] visceribus repleta, mota pietate, flexis genibus cepit Domini clementiam rogare, ita dicens, 'Adonay Domine Deus, magne et mirabilis, qui *Moys*i *in igne flamme rubi apparu*isti, et ei in Syna legem dedisti, et filios Israel *de terra Egypti edux*isti, et per medium *mar*is *rubr*i[135] sicco vestigio transire fecisti, qui que Ionam prophetam de ventre ceti eduxisti illesum atque incolumem, et filium tuum Dominum nostrum Iesum Cristum pro redemptione mundi incarnari voluisti, queso ut per invocationem tuam huic viro pristinam sanitatem restituas, quia tu es Deus

---

[125] socias sanctimoniales] sanctimoniales feminas *L*
[126] Dominus *L*] *om.N*
[127] *Ps. cvii.7.*
[128] dicto *L*] audito *N*
[129] *Judges xiii.6*
[130] in . . . spatio *N, L*] in momento *B*
[131] villam . . . Bentonia] villam Bendonam *B,* villam que dicitur Bamtonia *L*
[132] ingressa . . . Benesia *N. last three words erased*] venit . . . in nemore quod dicitur Benseya *B*, ingresse sunt nemus de Beneseya *L*
[133] Bentonia] Bendonia B
[134] misericordie *N*
[135] *Paraphrase of Acts vii.30–40*

benedictus, Salvator omnium in te sperantium, permanens in secula seculorum.' Cunque astantes respondissent 'Amen', faciens virgo signum crucis tenensque manum adolescentis, fugato dolore liberavit eum. Reversusque ad propria, glorificabat Deum. Ad Domini igitur laudem divulgabatur nomen beate Frithesuuithe per totam region em illam.

(**17**) Accidit etiam ut piscatores, sicut mos est illius generis hominum, ascenderent in navim quadam nocte ut caperent pisces. Cum ergo misissent retia in navem, et obdormissent in navi, unus eorum arreptus a demonio cepitque cachinna falsa dare, tenensque unum e sociis suis suffocabat eum manibus, dentibusque dilaniare volebat. Ceteri vero, tenentes eum, ligaverunt manus a tergo, ducentes eum ad beate virginis oratorium. Videns igitur venerabilis virgo imaginem Dei illusam a diabolo, genibus flexis deprecabatur Deum Patrem omnipotentem, Filiumque eius Dominum nostrum, ut per virtutem Spiritus Sancti liberaret plasma suum ab inimico humani generis prostratum. Hec dicens, fecit signum sancte crucis in frontem eius, ita dicens, 'Recede, Satana, ab *imagine quam formavit Deus ad similitudinem suam.*'[136] Cum hoc dixisset, factus est velut mortuus, ceciditque in terram. Beata virgo iussit eum solvi. Cunque solutus esset, tenuit manum eius et dixit, '*In nomine Iesu Cristi Nazareni, surge*[137] incolumis.' Et surrexit sanus, cepitque[138] glorificare Deum, qui eum liberavit per merita sancte Fritheswithe. Erat autem nomen eius Leowinus.[139] (**18**) Hec et alia multa miracula operatus est Dominus per beatam Fritheswitham.

Quadam igitur die dixit consodalibus suis, 'Revertamur ad cenobium[140] nostrum.' Preparata igitur navicula, beate virgines intraverunt in eam, venientesque ad civitatem Oxinefordiam, honorifice a civibus et ab omni clero[141] suscepte sunt. Cum autem ingrederetur beata Fritheswitha in supradictam urbem, occurrit ei quidam iuvenis plenus lepra, dixitque ei, 'Adiuro te, O Frithesuuitha virgo, ut des mihi osculum in nomine Iesu Cristi.' Illa, ut semper erat repleta Sancto Spiritu, faciens signum crucis dedit ei[142] osculum in nomine Domini, et statim mundatus est a lepra. Videntes autem populi urbis illius omnisque clerus que fiebant per sanctam Fritheswitham virtutes et miracula, gaudebant[143] in adventu eius. (**19**) Beata itaque Cristi virgo omnipotenti Deo servire non cessabat, affligebatque corpus ut vivificaret spiritum. Unde cum hec per multa tempora continuaret, et dies retributionis a Domino recipiendi mercedem pro labore appropinquaret,[144] quarto idus Octobris apparuit ei angelus Domini, dixitque ei,[145] 'Quartodecimo kalendas Novembris erit dies Dominicus, recipiesque a Domino coronam immortalitatis quam semper desiderasti. Preparata enim tibi est aula celestis, luxque immarcescibilis, quia despexisti terrenum palatium patris.' Hoc dicto, angelus ab ea recessit. Beatissima igitur virgo Fritheswitha correpta fortissima febre, ingravescente egritudine corporis, cepit omnibus menbris dissolvi. Unaquaque igitur die veniebant ad eam omnes cives illius urbis. Beata vero virgo monitis salutaribus non cessabat eos reficere. (**20**) Sabbato igitur quo in crastinum recessura erat a[146] corpore, rogavit ut ei sepultura aperiretur in ecclesia beate Dei genitricis Marie, dicens, 'Crastina die erit dies Dominicus, et nolo ut aliquis laboret propter me. Hac enim in nocte post tertium cantum galli, munita corpore et

---

[136] 'Recede . . . suam'] 'Precipio tibi, Sathana, in nomine Iesu Cristi, ut recedas ab hac ymagine Dei' *L. The N text is a conflation of Genesis i.26–7, ii.7 and v.1.*
[137] *Acts iii.6.*
[138] cepitque *L*] cepit *N*
[139] Leowinus] Leswinus *L*
[140] cenobium *N, B*] monasterium *L*
[141] clero *N, L*] clero nobilium *B*
[142] ei *L*] *om.N*
[143] gaudebant *L*] gaudebat *N*
[144] Unde cum hec . . . appropinquaret *L*] *om.N*
[145] ei *L*] *om.N*
[146] a *L*] *om.N*

sanguine Cristi, vadam ad Dominum[147] meum. *Bonum* enim *certamen certavi, cursum*que iustitie *consummavi,* mundum et omnem pompam eius contempsi, ideoque *reposita est mihi corona iustitie.*'[148] Hec dicens, ingravescente molestia egritudinis, iussit sibi afferri eucharistiam Cristi. Quam gaudenter suscipiens, omnipotentem Deum benedicere cepit. (**21**) Cunque infirmitatis mole nimium opprimeretur sicut antea predixerat,[149] post multas predicationes,[150] respiciens sursum, clara voce dicebat,[151] 'Bene, sancte virgines, bene veniatis.' Interrogaveruntque eam astantes cum quibus loqueretur. At illa respondit, 'Nunquid non videtis beatas virgines Dei, Katerinam atque Ceciliam?' Cunque iterum loqueretur ad eas, dixit audientibus cunctis, 'Modo veniam, Domine mee.' Post tertium itaque galli cantum, sicut predixerat, valedicens omnibus, migravit ad Dominum Iesum Cristum. In illa hora tanta lux effulsit per universam civitatem Oxinefordiam, tantaque suavitas odoris trium horarum spatio fragravit,[152] ut omnes mirarentur et glorificarent Deum. (**22**) Quidam etiam vir paralitico morbo percussus, vir dives valde, iussit famulis suis ut eum deportarent ad sepulchrum sancte virginis. Cunque detulissent eum usque ad sepulchrum, ilico meritis sancte Frithesuuithe incolumitatem recepit, et qui iam per biennium fuerat mutus et claudus, aliorumque manibus deportatus erat, propriis pedibus remeavit laudans Deum ad propria.

(**23**) Alius quidem nomine Athelwoldus, vir nobilis, qui erat contractus ab umbilico deorsum, cum sepelirent corpus beate Frithesuuithe, venit ad fores ecclesie, trahens corpus suum duobus scabellis. Volens igitur introire in ecclesiam, pre multitudine populorum non poterat. Cepit autem ad fores ecclesie clamare, 'O sponsa Cristi electa, virgo Fritheswitha, libera me ab infirmitatibus meis. Scio enim quia si vis subvenire mihi, potes.' Hec dicens, ita sanus factus est, quasi nunquam aliquid habuisset infirmitatis. Surgens itaque et exiliens, et quasi *cervus sali*e*n*s,[153] viriliter introivit in ecclesiam portans elevatis manibus scannulos cum quibus corpus suum trahere solebat, laudans Deum omnium redemptorem. (**24**) Migravit igitur beata Fritheuuita virgo ad Dominum quartodecimo kalendas Novembris, anna ab incarnatione Domini septingentesimo vicesimo septimo. Sepultaque est in ecclesia sancte Marie in australi parte, ubi fiunt multa miracula propter merita eius a Domino nostro Iesu Cristo, qui cum Patre et Spiritu Sancto vivit et regnat per omnia secula seculorum. Amen.

APPENDIX B: THE SECOND LIFE OF ST. FRIDESWIDE ('LIFE B'),
PROBABLY WRITTEN BY MASTER ROBERT OF CRICKLADE *c*.1140–70

Life B is edited here from the three manuscripts of the full text:

M = Bodleian Library, MS Laud Misc. 114 ff.132–40 (= *BHL* 3162)

Laud Misc. 114 is a collection of *vitae* written at Pershore in a careful, regular hand of *c*.1160–80.[154] The Frideswide text is divided into chapters, with rubricated initials, and is preceded by a list of chapter-headings. Other 12th-century English items are Osbert of Clare's Life of St. Eadburh (f.85ᵛ) and Prior Robert of Shrewsbury's Life of St. Winifred (f.140).

C = Cambridge, Gonville and Caius College, MS 129 ff.167–77ᵛ

This is a miscellaneous collection of tracts in several 12th- and 13th-century hands, from an unknown monastic provenance.[155] The Frideswide text is written in a rather scrappy mid 13th-century hand, with minor corrections

---

[147] Dominum] Deum *L*
[148] *II Tim. iv*.7.
[149] sicut . . . predixerat] *om.L; N alters* dixerat *to* predixerat
[150] predicationes] devotas exhortationes *L*
[151] dicebat] cepit dicere *L*
[152] fragravit *L*] *om.N*
[153] Echoes Isaiah *xxxv*.6.
[154] H.O. Coxe (ed.), *Laudian Manuscripts* (1858, repr. as *Bodleian Library Quarto Catalogues* II, 1973), 122–3; Ker op.cit. note 66, 150.
[155] M.R. James, *A Descriptive Catalogue of the Manuscripts in the Library of Gonville and Caius College,* i (1907), 137–8.

by a contemporary reviser. It does not observe M's chapter divisions.

G = Gotha, Forschungsbibliothek, Mm. I81, ff.225v–30[156]

The Gotha collection, from an unknown but probably western English provenance, is written in an early 14th-century hand with rubricated initials.[157] The *vitae* are entirely those of English saints: martyrs (Nos. 1–20), confessors (Nos. 21–49) and holy women (Nos. 50–64), with Frideswide the last (No. 64). The Frideswide text has the same chapter divisions as M.

Collation shows that M and G are related, for they often agree on demonstrably false readings where C appears to be correct (e.g. text notes 222, 243, 249, 310, 318, 345, 357). The combined testimony of M and C is often correct against G, and that of C and G against M; whereas there seems to be no case where M clearly overrules C and G, or G clearly overrules C and M.[158] This indicates the following stemma, with *P* the archetype and *Q* the stage which produced the errors common to M and G:

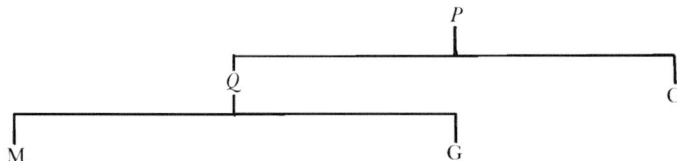

The basic text of the present edition is M. Its chapter divisions are preserved as paragraphs, but punctuation, capitalisation and the usage of *u* and *v* are modernised, and contractions are expanded. The footnotes record all variant readings, except for some trivial inversions of word-order which only occur in G and therefore cannot reflect the archetype. C/M readings have always been chosen in preference to G, and C/G readings in preference to M; where C disagrees with M/G, the reading which seems to make the best sense has been chosen. The C reviser's amendments are indicated in the notes thus ⌜ ⌝, but since these readings bear no relationship to the other manuscripts, and probably have no textual authority, they are never adopted. Direct quotations from Life A are italicised. The section numbers, which are editorial insertions, correspond with the equivalent passages in Life A and on pp.4–10 above.

De[159] patre et matre Sancte Fridesuuide,[160] et de nativitate eius et disciplina.

De morte matris eius, et de provectu eius in sancta conversatione, et de constructo a patre eius monasterio, et quomodo monacha facta est, et de morte patris eius.

Quomodo post mortem patris de die in diem virtutibus crescebat, et qualiter ab ea confutatus abscessit diabolus.

De nuntiis regis Algari obcecatis, et precibus illius sanitati restitutis.

Quomodo ab angelo instructa regis Algari vitavit vesaniam.[161]

De regis Algari obcecatione, et quare non intrant reges in Oxinefordiam.[162]

De puella sanata per stillam cadentem ex manibus eius.

Quomodo in predio quod Beneseia dicitur habitavit, et fontem precibus impetravit.

Quomodo relaxavit precibus manum hominis a manubrio securis.

De piscatore a demonio liberato.

Dc leproso osculo eius sanato.

Quomodo morienti apparuerunt sancta Caterina atque Cecilia, et de luce et odore refuso.

Quomodo paraliticus quidam et contractus alius sanati sunt ad eius exequias.

---

[156] Collated from a microfilm kindly lent by Dr. Michael Lapidge.
[157] P. Grosjean, 'De Codice Hagiographico Gothano', *Analecta Bollandiana* lviii (1940), 90–103.
[158] The only exceptions arc three trivial grammatical points (text footnotes 225, 267, 268), where the superior M and G readings could result from scribal correction.
[159] *M and G texts begin here.*
[160] Frideswythe *G*
[161] vitavit vesaniam] visitavit insaniam *both MSS*
[162] Oxinefordiam *G*] Oxenefordiam *M*

Incipit prologus in vita Sancte Frideswide virginis[163]

(**1**) De vita et virtutibus beatissime et omni veneratione dignissime virginis Frideswide, fratres karissimi, que addiscere potui in chronicis, et preter hec in quibusdam autenticarum hystoriarum voluminibus sive in cathalogis[164] sanctorum Anglie, in unum cohartare volumen curavi. Ubi liquido apparet quia longe ab errore in pluribus declinavit, quisquis ille fuit vite virginis sacratissime scriptor, licet quorumdam supercilio contempnendus videatur, qui stili simplicitate in improbandum adducti fastidium, florum probant se magis attendere speciem, quam fructus utilitatem.

Incipit vita[165]

(**2**) *Anno*[166] itaque[167] *ab incarnatione Domini* nostri Iesu[168] Cristi[169] Regis omnium seculorum *septingentesimo* circiter *vicesimo septimo,* cum in effera gente Anglorum, que Brittanniam insulam invaserat, depopulaverat, dominatuique[170] suo cruenta manu subiugaverat, verbum Dei[171] effloruisset fructumque plurimum produxisset, subregulus *quidam Didanus* nomine, vir catholicus et omni morum honestate prestantissimus, civitatem que lingua Saxonica Oxinefordia[172] denominatur, quod nos Latine Boum Vadum dicere possumus, incolatus sui frequentatione[173] honestabat. *Hic* nutu divino *uxorem* moribus suis congruam, *Safridam nomine, accepit,* de qua morum magis quam prediorum heredem suscepit,[174] unicam videlicet *filiam,* quam fonte sacri baptismatis ablutam *Fridesuuidam* appellari precepit. (**3**) *Transacto*[175] quinquennio *diligenti* educatione, *litter*arum studiis *erudienda trad*itur sub *matrone cui*usdam admodum religiose disciplina, cui *nomen Algiva.* Felicis quidem posteritatis quoddam quasi felicissimum presagium, in ipso eius discipline primordio adeo[176] enituit, ut perspicuum foret omnibus quoniam mentem illius iamiam sibi habitaculum[177] preelegerat *Spiritus Sanctus.* Quis etenim[178] non obstupesceret quinquennem[179] virgunculam in quinque fere mensibus psalmos Daviticos, qui centum quinquaginta sunt, didicisse, memorieque commendasse? Nec hinc sibi consodalium ascivit invidiam, sed fervore quo replenda erat caritatis attacta, cunctis *se* prebuit *amabilem.* Humilitatis namque simul[180] et mansuetudinis tanta extunc prepollebat[181] gratia, ut non regiam[182] esset videre iuvenculam, sed servilem in tali etate personam, omnibus obsequium, omnibusque[183] compassionis exhibentem affectum. Non erat plane verbi divini auditrix obliviosa facta, sed factrix operum.[184] Quamque de *scripturis*

---

[163] *heading only in* M
[164] cathalogis G] catholicis M
[165] *heading only in* M
[166] C *text begins here*
[167] *om.* C
[168] Ihū *etc. has been expanded throughout to* Iesu *etc*
[169] Xp̄i *etc. has been expanded throughout to* Cristi *etc*.
[170] ⌈et⌉ dominatui C
[171] verbum Dei C, G] verbumque M
[172] Oxinefordia C, G] Oxenefordia M
[173] frequentationem G
[174] suscepit C, G] accepit M
[175] Transacto C, G] Transacto quippe M
[176] primordio adeo discipline C
[177] *om.* C
[178] Quis etenim C, G] Quisenim M
[179] quinquennem C, G] quinqucnnam M
[180] simul C, G] *om.* M
[181] pollebat C
[182] *om.* C
[183] omnibus G
[184] *based on James i.25.*

audiebat, armario[185] *pectoris*[186] pie re*condebat,* dans operam sedulo, creditam sibi cum usura reportare Domino[187] pecuniam. Propterea diebus assidue et noctibus piis lacrimarum rivulis, suspiriis quoque et gemitibus, cordis mactabat hostiam in holocaustum acceptabile Domino, supplicans iugiter *ut inhabitare* mereretur *in domo Domini omnibus diebus vite sue,* et contemplari vultum eius.

(**4**) Nec adultam adhuc etas eam proprio consignabat viri, cum iam *mater eius* de medio discessit.[188] Altero igitur carens virgo[189] solatio, patri protegenda relinquitur. Quem saluberrimis quoad[190] potuit impellebat monitis, ne pigritaretur iturus hinc in brevi quo precessit thori socia, anime sue remedia querere. At ille, ut assolet coniugis nuper amisse dolore perculsus, et assiduis[191] dilectissime filie precibus compulsus, *ecclesiam* infra urbis ambitum *construxit,* et *in honore sancte* ac sempiterne *Trinitatis,* semperque *virginis* Dei genitricis *Marie, Omniumque Sanctorum, dedic*atam, filie commendavit poscenti. Ipsa vero ecclesiam ingressa, divinis se studiosissime mancipabat[192] operibus, suam Domino pudicitiam sedulis commendans precibus, pietatis viscera aperiebat petentibus, larga prebens manu que poscebant egentibus. Mundi etiam fertur sic postposuisse gloriam, sic ad supernam hanelare[193] patriam, ut iam propemodum carnis cerneretur deposuisse sarcinam, et immortalitatis tunicam induisse.[194] Non enim corpus alebat escis, sed spiritum protrahebat. Non mollibus vestiebatur, sed asperrimis setis vigilans, nec[195] mollioribus dormiens, si tamen aliquotiens dormitabat, pungebatur. Quid de lectisternio illius loquar, cum nullum illi preter humum durissimam fuerit? Super illam somno victa[196] recumbebat, nature solvens debitum, illam assidue prostrata petebat genibus, quando orationes Domino fundebat. Stuperes regiam regiis puellam epulis educatam, vilium *oler*um incondito pulmento *modic*o*que pane ordeiceo*[197] famis expugnare proterviam, *aque* vero sorbitiuncula sitis ardentissime imminentem superare dissolutionem. Quid plura? Arctam et arduam viam que ducit ad vitam[198] ita aggressa est, ut nichil supra. O infelices huius temporis homines, 'quorum deus venter est, et gloria in confusione illorum, qui terrena sapiunt',[199] qui religionem habitu pretendunt, moribus et vita contradicunt. Vili veste intuentium in se convertunt oculos, sed pretiosorum ciborum crapula, intestina confundunt. Si quando ieiunant, terra marique queritur, unde ieiunii dampnum restituatur. Sed non est hoc ieiunium quod elegi dicit Dominus. Stupet *Angh*a, *mir*antur universi, infirmum cernentes sexum *in etate* tenera robur excessisse virile. Pater vero[200] virguncule hilaris admodum effectus tripudiabat, quia heredem quem terrenarum rerum putabat prestari superstitem, iam ad celestia cernebat hanelantem.[201] (**5**) Et quidem ut omnem spem corruptibilis posteritatis eam plene[202] postposuisse constaret, exegit a patre,

---

[185] ⌈in⌉ armario *C*
[186] pectoris *C*] cordis *M, G*
[187] Domino reportare *C*
[188] discessit *C, G*] decessit *M*
[189] Virgo carens *C*
[190] quoad *C, G*] quoat *M*
[191] assiduis *C, G*] assidue *M*
[192] mancipabat studiosissime *C*
[193] anelare *G*
[194] induisse tunicam *C*
[195] *om. G*
[196] *om. C*
[197] ordeaceo *C*
[198] *Based on Matth. vii.14.*
[199] *Philipp. iii. 19.*
[200] vero *C, G*] *om. M*
[201] anhelantem *G*
[202] eam plene] *om. G*

monacharum ut *mer*eretur *habitum* suscipere, prudenti[203] proculdubio precavens consilio, ne forte defuncto patre cuiusquam cogeretur inire conubium, et virginale usquequaque fedare[204] propositum. Tedebat preterea virginem beatissimam corporali decorari purpura, que se noverat Cristi sanguine redemptam, dum a perfidis morte turpissima condempnaretur. Anulo fidei subarrata, aurum gemmasque velud mercimonium contempnebat[205] vilissimum. Hoc *proposito filie rex Didanus,* inestimabiliter *gavisus,* accersiri iubet proxime[206] diocesis episcopum, filieque karissime habitum dari monacharum impetravit. Emulatione profecto beatissime virginis *duodecim* ferme *nobili*bus orte natalibus puelle, relictis omnibus secute sunt Dominum, incedentes in omnibus mandatis et iustificationibus eius iuxta exemplum Deo dilecte Fridesuuide. Et si ei equari[207] non potuerunt meritis, consortes tamen eius fieri nitebantur participatione regni celestis. Ex regis itaque munificentia diversoria religioni aptissima secus ecclesiam construuntur, ubi dulciflua diebus ac noctibus mente[208] virginum cum voce consona psalmorum et hymnorum modulata resonabat suavitas.

(**6**) Interim *rex* ipse, *gravi*ssima tactus febre, *decidit in lectum,* atque ad extrema perductus, *corporis Cristi* munitus viatico, dormivit cum patribus suis, complens dies in senectute bona. *Beata igitur Frideswida, utri*usque *parentis* destituta solatio, ad Patrem qui in celis est ardentius hanelabat,[209] quibus potuit gressibus ad eum properabat. Protelabat enim ieiunia, orationibus instabat continuis, et preterea *per diem centies, centiesque per noctem, flex*is *gen*ibus quesivit quem dilexit anima illius. (**7**) Sed quis in mundo prevalet esse bonus, cui non invideat qui singulariter est malignus? Omnes namque conatur deicere, qui primum hominem a paradisi gaudiis potuit propellere. Et quia Fridesuuide animum nullius stimulo suggestionis potuit evertere, ad dimicandum comminus corporeis eius oculis corporalem speciem exhibuit. Elatusque in antique vesanie sue presumptionem, qua se Altissimo fore similem promittebat, Cristum se esse mentitur. Magnaque *demonum constipatus caterva,* angelorum lucis speciem mentientium, his virginem aggreditur: 'Veni, dilecta mea, veni, quia *tempus est ut per*cipias immarcessibilem glorie *coronam quam promeruisti. Veni,* et ad pedum meorum provoluta vestigia, quem diu desiderasti, *adora.* Apparere quippe tibi ob[210] hoc volui, ut me, ad quem tanta aviditate suspiras, in hac etiam vita mortali conspiceres, et me adorato ad perpetue vite commodum, absque corporis incommodo prevaleres ingredi.' *Cui* virgo, Sancto edocta Spiritu, cuius instinctu humani generis hunc fuisse deprehendit inimicum, ita infit, 'Quid, miserrime, *quod* nec[211] *habes,* nec habere pre superbia vales, aliis *promitt*ere presumis? Quid tibi cum vita immortali, qui vivens mortuus es,[212] et manens semper in interitum vergis? Sed et ego, infelix et miserrima peccatrix, interitus tui particeps fuissem, ni me[213] Redemptoris mei Cristi, quem tu te esse nefandissime mentiris, misericordia prevenisset. Ipse enim[214] "spes mea a iuventute mea."'[215] Hec humillima virginis verba superbus ille non sustinens spiritus, *evanuit,* et aerem *ululatu* horribili fetoreque pestifero implevit. *Beata* quidem Frideswida *in oratione perseverans, persistensque in vigiliis, equo erat animo* et permansit intrepida.

---

[203] prudenti *C, G*] prudente *M*
[204] federa *G*
[205] mercimonium contempnebat *C, G*] mercennarium tempnebat *M*
[206] *om. G*
[207] ei equari] *om. G*
[208] ⌜in⌝ mente *C*
[209] anhelabat *G*
[210] tibi ob *C, G*] ad *M*
[211] nec *C, G*] non *M*
[212] *om. G*
[213] ni me] mi ne *G*
[214] enim ⌜est⌝ *C*
[215] *Ps. lxxi.5.*

(**8**) At non commentor impietatis, tametsi victus et confusus abscesserit, ab impugnationis sue arte quievit. *Regem* namque *Algaru*m satis superque *nefand*um aggreditur, et virginis Frideswide iam amore tactum impudico inflammat, et, ut a[216] sanctimonialis habitu deiciat,[217] suggerit iniustum non esse nefariumve interminans regis filiam licet monacham ad thorum regium evocare, sed magis optimum prolem suscipere et ad spem regni educare, quam inertem et plenam desidia ducere[218] vitam. His suggestionum stimulis rex furibundus concitatus,[219] quasi amens prosiliit:[220] nuntios accelerare precipit, qui summa cum festinatione Frideswidam adducant, et nolentem eque ut volentem properare compellant.[221] Nec mora, nefandissimi regis nefandi[222] evolant nuntii, et emenso celeriter multo terrarum spatio, ante conspectum Frideswide assistentes, his eam aggrediuntur compellare[223] sermonibus. '*Rex*,' inquiunt, '*Algarus ad te*, O *Frideswida, nos* direxit, legationis siquidem tibi[224] profuture causa. Tu autem sapienti utere consilio, et voluntati regis consenti[225] honorem proponentis. Nam contradictio tua expers pene esse non poterit. Te sibi thori sociam rex vehementissime affectat, et matronali vinculo[226] coniungere, et partipicem efficere regni.' Quibus virgo, mitissimo ut erat semper animo, summissa humiliter voce,[227] 'Si me,' inquit, 'hominis conubio sociare disposuissem, nequaquam regis Algari postulationi contradicere haberem. Nunc, quia *Regi* immortalitatis *Cristo desponsata sum, nefa*ndum sane arbitror ut eo contempto assensum mortali prebeam peritura cum ipso, et fructu immortalitatis despecto posteritatem[228] mortalem cum detrimento integritatis queram.' Et illi, 'Hec te,' inquiunt, 'versutia iuvare non poterit, quoniam *si* acquiescere ac obtemperare regis voluntati *nolueris,* tuam cupientis honorare ingenuitatem, *ad lupanar tra*cta multas sustenebis integritatis tue iniurias vel invita, lenonibus ludibrium facta. Et ignominiose corrupta sic tandem edoceberis sani capitis non esse regiam huiuscemodi repulsa fedare dignitatem.' Ad hec[229] virgo, 'Mine siquidem,' inquit, 'vestre oppido timende fuissent, ni Dominus continere impiorum manus valeret, uti complere non possint[230] opere quod conari animo nefando proponunt. Preterea[231] nullis pollutionum contagiis *contaminari* potest corpus,[232] *nisi ex consensu mentis*. Et[233] profecto quemadmodum corporis integritas Deo grata non est, quam mentis corruptela fedavit, ita prorsus, si violentia impudicorum claustra signaculi pudicitie vexaverit, voluntatis contradicente arbitrio, ab inspectore Deo ad integritatis sue premium mente[234] illibata dupplicato reducetur merito.' (**9**) His[235] iniquitatis *ministri* puelle responsis, velud solis meridiani aspectu hebetati, in[236] amentie tamen sue obstinatione perseverantes, cum pre stupore tante constantie eius quid amplius opponerent non haberent, vim inferre

---

[216] in *G*
[217] deicterat G
[218] deducere *C*
[219] *om. G*
[220] prosiliit *C*] prosilit *M, G*
[221] compellatur *G*
[222] regis nefandi *C, G*] *om. M*
[223] *om. C*
[224] *om. G*
[225] consenti *G*] consentire *M, C*
[226] matronali vinculo *C, G*] matrimonio (*with* –imonio *written over an erasure*) *M*
[227] voce ⌜respondit⌝ *C*
[228] potestatem *G*
[229] hoc *G*
[230] Possunt *G*] possunt *amended to* possint *C*, possint *M*
[231] propterea *G*
[232] contaminari potest corpus] puto contaminari corpus *G*
[233] Ex *G*
[234] mente *G*] mente *altered to* mens *C*, vite *M*
[235] Hiis *G*
[236] *om. G*

parabant. At Frideswida, confugiens ad protectorem suum Deum, preces cum lacrimis in excelsum porrexit, clamans *voce* magna atque dicens, '*Exurge, Domine, non confortetur homo: iudicentur gentes in conspectu tuo, sciantque quoniam homines sunt. Apprehende arma et scutum, et exurge in adiutorium michi. Dic anime mee, salus tua ego sum.*' O altitudo sapientie tue, Domine[237] Deus, quam incomprehensibilia sunt iudicia tua, et investigabiles vie tue![238] Vere nemo speravit in te[239] et derelictus est![240] Ecce homines pessimi, qui noluerunt audire vocem tuam et[241] ancille tue ut beneagerent, prius animi nunc corporis amisso lumine, ab iniuriis suis[242] desistere compelluntur vel inviti. Ac experimento discunt, quod[243] doctrina salutari neglexerunt. Nec mora, miraculi magnitudine impletur *civitas*. Concurrunt undique, stupent universi,[244] *pave*ntque, ac *ped*ibus *virginis* pro excecatorum compassione provoluti suppliciter *postulant,* quatinus hominum insensatorum et iccirco miserrimorum non attendat facinora, sed *pro eis* intercedere dignetur[245] propitia et lumen pia restituat supplicatione, quo destituti sunt miseri[246] propria protervitate. (**10**) At non sustinuit pietatis vasculum diuturnum impiorum cruciatum, vel populi in postulatione singultum. Ad preces convertitur, Deum *genibus*[247] deprecatur. '*Deus,*' inquit, '*invisibilis et incommutabilis,* Deus universe Conditor creature, cuius nutu que non sunt fiunt, cuius voluntate cuncta subsistunt, qui hominem sua culpa perditum reformasti ad vitam, hominibus istis *miser*rimis *lumen* restitue, *ut cognoscat populus iste quia tu es miserator et misericors, patiens et multe misericordie et verax,* reddens unicuique[248] iuxta opera sua, *qui vivis et regnas per infinita seculorum secula.*' Ad hanc vocem beate virginis,[249] *cum* astantes *respondissent 'Amen',* lumen redditur miseris. At illi corde[250] salubriter[251] compuncti, corruerunt ad *pedes* eius, veniam commissi huius flagitantes. Quibus illa, 'Non hoc meis,'[252] inquit, 'actum esse meritis estimetis, sed clementia Salvatoris, et fide populi ipsi supplicantis. Vos autem horum que passi estis memores estote,[253] et ancillas Cristi deinceps infestare nolite.'

(**11**) Repedantes itaque viri, que gesta sunt regi[254] ex ordine nuntiant. Ille vero, 'Nequaquam,' inquit, '*incantationes eius, falsa*v*e dogmata,* aut *ars magica,* a *meis* eam eripient *manibus.* Sed quoniam me contempnere ausa est, prius quam[255] illa ut libuerit abusus fuero, lenonum siquidem tradetur polluenda ludibrio.' Hec dixit, et furore agitatus inpreceps equos poscit, iterque ad urbem[256] qua virgo manebat nefanda urgente libidine aggreditur. O quam magna est multitudo miserationum tuarum, Domine, qui non derelinquis sperantes in te! *In ipsa nocte,* dum *Frideswida* horum inscia more solito *ora*tioni incumberet, astitit ei *angelus*[257] tuus sanctus, *dicens,* 'Ignoras, o virgo, quia profanissimus rex Algarus cras pre foribus urbis istius

---

[237] *om. C*
[238] *Based on Rom. xi.33.*
[239] in te *C, G*] *om. M*
[240] *Based on Eccli. ii.*11–12.
[241] tuam et *C*] om. *M. G*
[242] suis *C*] illius *M. G*
[243] quod ⌜in⌝ *C*
[244] stupent universi, concurritur undique *C*
[245] dignetur intercedere *C*
[246] *om. C*
[247] genibus *C*] gemitibus *M, G*
[248] reddens unicuique *C, G*] unicuique reddens *M*
[249] vocem beate virginis *C, G*] beate virginis vocem *M*
[250] *om. G*
[251] salubriter corde *C*
[252] meis hoc *C*
[253] estote memores *C*
[254] *om. C*
[255] prius quam] postquam *MSS*
[256] urbem ⌜in⌝ *C*
[257] angelus ei *C*

aderit libidini sue satisfacturus, si detur possibilitas irrumpendi in pudicitiam[258] integritatis tue?' Audiens hec, sancta 'vehementer expavit',[259] nec adeo tamen ex visione angelica tam subita, quantum ex immanissime impietatis acceleratione, et[260] ignara quid ageret stabat stupefacta. Cui angelus, 'Ne timeas,' inquit, 'Frideswida: Dominus *Iesus Cristus* iocundum quod in tua virginitate habitaculum ipsi preparasti custodiet, illususque rex et malignitatis sue spe frustratus redibit, ac penas cecitatis perpetue solvet. Tu autem propera, et semitam que ducit ad fluvium Thamesis[261] cum quibuslibet tuarum ingredere, repertura scapham *a Deo paratam* et in ipsa ducem itineris *nautam*'. Hec fatur, et ab aspectu virginis subito[262] eripitur. (**12**) Frideswida vero, gratias agens[263] Deo, hylaris ab oratione surrexit, *dua*sque de sororibus suis *secum* assumens, *ad Thamesi*m[264] usque *pervenit,* et *iuxta* verbum *angeli naviculam* secus *ripam* repperit. Quam *ingresse,* vident *iuvenem* in parte[265] *sedentem,* habitu splendido *vultu*que venustissimo,[266] *qui* eas[267] dulci demulcens *affatu* in naviculam[268] collocavit. Mira res, mirus impetus spiritus. Sub *unius hore spatio*[269] decem miliaria[270] transferuntur, et sub *villa que Bentona dicitur* exponuntur. Exposite vero, nec navem nec itineris ducem uspiam conspiciunt. Inventam ilico secus villam[271] semitam pergunt, et silvam *non longe* ab ea distantem *ingre*diuntur. Sequentes autem *semitam* in profundum *nemoris*[272] se protendentem, tandem mapale[273] conspiciunt ad *porcorum* tutamen contra aeris intemperiem constructum, sed multo iam tempore ab incolis derelictum, adeo ut *hedera* succrescente *ex omni parte* contectum, occultato[274] aditu ingredi volentibus, negare videretur introitum. Quod *virgo cum suis* ingressa sodalibus primum *signo crucis munivit,* ac deinde qualiter ibidem Deo disponente manerent prout sibi oportunum[275] videbatur statuit.

(**13**) Interea *rex impius ad Oxinefordiam*[276] veniens, minis precibusque ac premiis propositis conabatur ab incolis addiscere, quonam Frideswida divertisset. Sed quoniam non erat occulta Dei nosse, sicut nullius eorum[277] hoc actum erat consilio, ita nec revelari poterat eorum eloquio.[278] Hinc iratus rex et amentium more intolerabili permotus furore, civitatem terribiliter intuens, in eius subversionem coniuravit. Cumque appropinquaret porte que[279] ad aquilonem recluditur, iturus quo se vesanie sue propellebat impetus, luminibus ilico amissis didicit quam nichil est quod molitur humana perversitas, cui contrastat divina potestas. Expavit itaque stultus repentinam in se divine potestatis ultionem, nec a malignitatis sue desistens obstinatione, cor Pharaonis ad propria revehens, plagas Egypti cernentis et in

---

[258] in pudicitiam] impudentiam *M,* impudicitiam *C,* in pudiciam *G*
[259] I. Macc. xvi.22.
[260] *om. G*
[261] 'Thamesis *C*] Tamesis *M,* Thamensis *G*
[262] subito *C, G*] *om. M*
[263] agens gracias *C*
[264] 'Thamensem *G*
[265] *Either a corruption, or* in parte *meaning 'on one side'; cf. below, note 415.*
[266] *Echoes Mark xvi.5.*
[267] eos *C, G*
[268] navicula *C, G*
[269] spatio ⌜per⌝ *C*
[270] milia *G*
[271] villam *C, G*] villa *M*
[272] *om. G*
[273] mapale *altered to* magale *C*
[274] occulto *C*
[275] *om. C*
[276] Oxinefordiam *G*] Oxenefordiam *M,* Oxonefordiam *C*
[277] *om. C*
[278] consilio *G*
[279] que *C, G*] qua *M*

promerita obcecatione perdurantis, *omnibus diebus vite sue*[280] sicut a presumptionis[281] sue protervitate non destitit, luminum amissorum solatio caruit. Ob huius[282] equidem tyranni crudelissimi[283] iustissimum supplicium, innatus est horror re*g*ibus Anglie, ut ne[284] unus profecto successorum eius civitatem O*xinifordie*[285] presumat[286] *intrare*. Frideswida vero iam quasi in heremum promota, soli Deo vacare studuit, solum Cristum pre oculis, solum in mente, solum in animo semper habebat. Non *diebus* aut *noctibus* vacabat de eo loqui, ipsum venerari, et assiduis interpellare precibus. *Mansit* autem *tribus* ferme *annis* in prefati *nemoris* solitudine, sed non incolis ignota. Neque enim poterat lucerna Dei diutius abscondi, cuius odor luxque virtutum usquequaque diffundebatur.

(**14**) Fuit sane *in predicta Bentona puella* generis stemate nequaquam ignobili, que cecitatis incommodo ab hoste antiquo percussa, sibimet oneri et parentibus dolori extitit. At miseratio divina insultantis inimici proterviam in femine dampnum ulterius non sustinuit. *Dormi*enti etenim, astitit *ei quidam in sompnis*[287] *dicens,* '*Vade,*' inquit, '*in* lucum[288] ad habitaculum virginum, et *stilla de beate Frideswide manibus* manante, dum *manus* abluerit, *oculos tuos lini*to*, visum*que *recipies.*' Expergefacta mulier et leta admodum effecta, ubi se primum dies terris apparuit, que in sompnis *viderat* parentibus indicare non distulit. Illi *vero,* congratulantes filie,[289] ac si iam[290] visum recuperasset, iter ilico arripientes, ad virginum incessu celeri perveniunt mansionem, et astantes pre foribus pulsantesque obnixe postulant, quatinus adesse mereantur Frideswide manus suas lavanti. Quod cum non negaretur petentibus, et si vix unquam sustinuisset ab aliqua sibi sororum aquam effundi manus abluenti, verumtamen istis adesse non[291] abnuit, veluti non eam[292] lateret, cur affore tantopere[293] postulassent. Stillam itaque puella[294] decidentem, quam primam[295] potuit avidissime rapuit, qua cum *oculos lini*visset, dicto citius recuperavit obtutum. O quam innocens manibus et mundo corde virgo, cuius e manibus quod immundum putabatur, ad tante salutis profuit ministerium! Desinant, queso, qui contra Redemptoris promissa garriunt, in evangelio dicentis, 'Capillus de capite vestro non peribit.'[296] Desinant, inquam. Pretiosior etenim est capillus qui ad munimentum capitis et ornamentum prebetur, qui de carne nascitur et in carne radicatur, quam sordes ex sudoris coagulo constipate seu ex rebus quibuslibet contrectatis superficiem cutis fedantes. Et ecce, quia nec ille in Dei servis et ancillis a virtutum officio vacant,[297] igitur, qui per ancille sue sordium ablutionem potuit excecate puelle visum restituere, potest redivivos in resurrectione capillos[298] capiti vel cetero ut libet corpori apponere. Stupendum sane[299] miraculum, stupenda virtus! Melior est plane acquisitio talis argento et auro[300] ac lapidibus

---

[280] diebus vite sue *C*] vite sue diebus *M,* vite diebus sue *G*
[281] apresumptionis vite *G*
[282] huius *C, G*] cuius *M*
[283] *om. C*
[284] ne *C, G*] nec *M*
[285] Oxinefordie *G*] Oxenefordiam *M,* Oxonie *C*
[286] presumat *C*] ⌜pre⌝ sumat *M,* presumant *G*
[287] in sompnis] *om. C*
[288] in lucum inquid *C*
[289] *om. C*
[290] iam *C, G*] eam *(with* m *erased) M*
[291] non adesse *C*
[292] eam non *C*
[293] tanto opere *G*
[294] puella *C, G*] *om. M*
[295] primam *M, C*] primum *G*
[296] *Luke xxi.18.*
[297] vacant *C, G*] vacabat *M*
[298] capillos *C, G*] *om. M*
[299] sane *C, G*] valde *M*
[300] argento et auro *C*] auro et argento *M, G. Based on Prov. iii.14.*

quantumvis pretiosis. Hinc quoque exclamare libet spei plena dictante letitia. O 'Domine, Dominus noster, quam admirabile est nomen tuum in'[301] omnibus operibus tuis! *Rever*tentes autem cum gaudio, factum hoc diffamaverunt per omnia confinia sua.

(**15**) Sed non virgo prudentissima[302] sustinuit quoad adulationis procellosus favor vas olei e suis excuteret manibus, ut veniente Sponso non haberet unde lampadum[303] suarum lumen informaret.[304] Unde et hominum pro facti magnitudine cum inmani[305] eam admiratione visere cupientium, laudes neuticam sibi profuturas, fugere iudicavit utilius. Convocatis *igitur* solitudinis sue *consodalibus,*[306] 'Arbitror,' inquit, 'iam oportunum esse ut proprio appropinquemus *cenobi*o. Sorores namque nostre aut sollicite[307] pro nobis, ut assolet, aut in absentia nostra in tristitie[308] abyssum corruentes, a bono, quod absit, proposito fortasse[309] destiterunt.' Sic fatur, et *naviculam preparata*m cum sororibus conscendens, prepeti valde[310] cursu ad predium civitati propinquum quod Buneseia dicitur, ope navigantium perducitur. E navi quippe[311] progressa, locumque pervidendo permetiens, utile duxit tantillum a civitate defore, et dilecte quieti operam dare. Quo et virginibus quas in cenobio dimiserat venire non esset onerosum, et civibus semper quod pro novitate stupeant querentibus minus aptum. Erat in predicto predio locus multigenis arboribus consitus, qui pro multitudine diversi generis spinarum lingua Saxonica Thornbiri[312] nuncupabatur,[313] solitarius[314] siquidem et religioni aptissimus. In quo extimplo construxit oratorium, et quam plurima edificia sanctorum usibus competentissima. Et quoniam fluminis alveus longius aberat, inoportunumque sibi videbatur quod sorores illuc usque ad hauriendum aquam[315] procederent, fontem precibus impetravit qui nunc usque superest, plurimis prestans beneficia sanitatum potantibus.[316] Hic latere, hic dilecte[317] quieti operam dare et hominum vitare frequentiam sperabat.[318]

(**16**) Quid est quod conaris, Deo dilecta virgo, quid inquam? Latebras queris,[319] at latere diu non prevales. Dominus in evangelio dicit, 'Non potest civitas abscondi supra montem posita.'[320] Tu prorsus civitas es regis omnium Cristi, turribus virtutum et propugnaculis operum bonorum constructa, et supra Montem illum fundata, qui 'lapis abscisus de monte sine manibus,'[321] universum implevit orbem. Sed tu te grandi premis humilitate, et 'qui se humiliaverit,' inquit idem[322] Dominus, 'exaltabitur.'[323] Esto. Nequaquam hominum te perquiret curiositas, quia mundo crucifixa es, sed non ob hoc ab inquisitione tui desistet

---

[301] *Ps. viii.* 2 *or 10.*
[302] Sed virgo prudentissima non *C*
[303] lampadarum *G*
[304] *Echoes Matt. xxv.*
[305] inmani *C, G*] inmanu *M*
[306] consodalibus *C, G*] sodalibus *M*
[307] sollicite *C*] sollicitudine *M, G*
[308] in tristicie] inercie *G*
[309] *om. C*
[310] valde *C, G*] *om. M*
[311] igitur *C*
[312] Thornberi *G*
[313] nuncupatur *C*
[314] solitariis *C*
[315] aquam *C*] *om. M, G*
[316] potantibus *M, G*] petentibus *C*
[317] dilectam *C*
[318] superabat *G*
[319] Latebras queris] *om. C*
[320] *Matt. v.14.*
[321] *Dan. ii.34.*
[322] idem *C, G*] *om. M*
[323] *Matt. xxiii. 12.*

miseranda[324] invalidorum et[325] anxia necessitas. Ecce prope te infortunatus iuvenis *in villa que dicitur Seuecordia,* dum *securi die Dominica ligna incid*eret, nullam diei *Dominice resurrectionis* reverentiam prestans, cuius *manus* – sed horreo referens – ilico *manubrio adhe*rens, adeo *incendi*tur, ut pre doloris intolerantia terribiliter *clamans* vicinos vel invitus ad sui cogat spectaculum accurrere. Nec enim laxare manum valet[326] pre dolore, aut *digitos* a manubrio solvere. Stat igitur miser[327] clamans et eiulans, stant parentes eius flentes et semetipsos pugnis cedentes, necnon et vicini pavidi ire Dei vindicantis usque ad mortem tormenta metuentes. Quidni? Enimvero cernunt penam in homine[328] intolerabilem, nec unde ferant[329] opem. Tandem ad se invicem conversi, 'Nunquid non potest,' inquiunt, 'beatissima virgo Frideswida ab hoc tormento filium nostrum piis absolvere meritis, cuius e manibus stilla decidens, cece puelle visum restituere valuit? Ducamus et hunc ad habitaculum ipsius, ut miserta nostri liberet filium nostrum.' Apte sane. Fidem quippe vestram cum exempli propositione vehementer approbabo. Abstraite[330] queso latitare volentem, abstraite inquam, et impetrantes[331] quod pre pietate negare non poterit,[332] palam omnibus[333] facite.[334] Quantum apud Deum valent[335] merita, que non propriam, sed illius querunt gloriam![336] Nec mora, amne transito, sistitur iuvenis ante habitaculum virginis. Clamatur ad ipsam, et vocem interrumpente singultu salutis petitur remedium. 'Beata,' inquiunt, 'Frideswida, miserere iuvenis, ob proprium[337] delictum tormenta patientis. Novimus enim, et valde novimus, quoniam si volueris, et illius noxa tuis relaxabitur precibus, et salus pristina redonabitur.' Ad hanc vocem tam luctuosam, pre tam grandi miseria eiulantem, quid facies,[338] virgo? Numquid redibunt[339] miseri misericordia frustrati? Nunquid non erogabit pietas, quod denegare parabat latendi voluntas? Ecce infelices parentes precibus instant, et iuxta vocem Salvatoris querentes pulsant, ut intercessione tua noxa[340] filio suo dimittatur, et salutis remedium conferatur. Tandem igitur *pietate* victa procidit[341] Frideswida, et lacrimis *ita* precatur obortis:[342] *'Adonay, Domine Deus,* pater omnipotens *magne et mirabilis,* qui per legis latorem *Moyse*n populum tuum *Israel* iugo servitutis oppressum liberasti, et Ninivitas per *Ionam* in *ventre ceti illesum* ab impietatis errore revocasti, te precor, Domine pie et misericors, per Unigenitum tuum Redemptorem nostrum horum virorum actibus prefiguratum, ne elonges misericordiam tuam[343] ab his[344] famulis tuis, sed presta quod petunt, ut cognoscant *quia tu es* potens in omnibus operibus tuis, *permanens in* omnibus *seculis.'* Hoc dicto, *sign*oque salutifere *crucis*[345] impresso, manus a manubrio solvitur, et pristine saluti restituitur.

---

[324] merenda *C*
[325] etiam *G*
[326] valet laxare manum *C*
[327] *om. C*
[328] in homine] *om. C*
[329] ferat *G*
[330] abstraite *C, G*] abstruite *M*
[331] inprecantes *C*
[332] poterat et *G*
[333] hominibus *C*
[334] *Sense unclear: a word such as* ostendere *or* revelare *perhaps omitted.*
[335] valeant *G*
[336] *Echoes John vii.18.*
[337] ob proprium] obprobium *C*
[338] facis *G*
[339] redibit *G*
[340] noxa a *G*
[341] procidit *C*] procedit *M, G*
[342] precatur obortis] precabatur abatis *C,* precatur abortis *G*
[343] *om. C*
[344] hiis *G*
[345] *om. G*

(**17**) Modico profecto intercedente tempore, dum intempesta *nocte piscatores* quidam insidentes navicule laxatis in *cap*turam *reti*bus predam expectarent, et sompnolentia urgente *obdo*rmirent, *unus eorum a demonio* repente *cor*reptus volutabatur, et post paululum facto[346] impetu in[347] quendam consodalium, *dentibus laniare* et *manibus* illum prefocare parabat. *Ceteris* hinc horroris et meroris causa fuit. Attamen reliqui prevalentes ei, *man*ibus post *terg*um revinctis, *du*c*unt*[348] *ad* habitaculum *virginis*. Quem cum fuisset intuita, condolens miserie hominum qui ob proprium[349] delictum ad tantam devenere miseriam, ut demonum insolentie traderentur, ingemuit, et ab alto vocem revocans suspirio, lacrimis habundantissime perfusa, preces prius ad Dominum et abinde manum[350] porrexit ad miserum, salutiferum *crucis* adversus demonem depingens *signum*. Ac deinde, 'Adiuro te,' inquit,[351] '*Sathana,* per nomen magnum Filii Dei vivi et Domini nostri Iesu Cristi, *recede ab* hoc homine ad ipsius *imagine*m *form*ato, et abhinc amplius ne presumas vexare illum.' Ad hanc vocem virginis, quasi letali percussus vulnere, corruit homo, et auctore mortis eiecto, quo male fortis fuerat, *factus est velud mortuus,* ut qualis fuerit in anima, tali obsessus ab hospite, corporis hoc indicaretur specie.[352] Quod cernens virgo accessit, et *manu* iniecta, '*Surge,*' inquit, 'homo, *in nomine Iesu Cristi Nazareni.*' Qui statim *surrexit,* mentis et corporis incolumitati restitutus. Nec ille reticuit factum, sed quocunque procedebat in auditu omnium predicabat, quam potenter curatus fuerit *per merita* Deo dilecte *Frideswide.*

(**18**) His *et aliis* quam plurimis virgo *bea*tissima refulgens *miracul*is*,* dierum succedentium alternatione, ad extremam vite temporalis communi[353] urgente necessitate decedebat horam. Et quoniam tantarum virtutum quantitatem[354] per illam Salutis Auctor[355] operatus est Deus,[356] vix scriptori credula foret mortalis infirmitas. Pluribus admodum intermissis, unum opus eius,[357] mirificum Dei inestimabili virtute consummatum,[358] reticere indignum valde iudico. Quod revera pro caritate magnifica et constantia pietatis, nequaquam minus obstupendum esse arbitror, quam pro magnitudine miraculi. Instante iam[359] die luctuoso quidem hominibus, angelis autem letabundo, quo Frideswida e corpore fuerat migratura, ad proprium redire *cenob*ium equum duxit, quatinus illic ultimum Deo commendatum spiritum redderet,[360] ubi primum in religionis habitu ipsi servire studuit. Repedanti ergo sacrosancte virgini, tota ilico in obviam ruit civitas, et ecce inter *cler*i populique utriusque sexus congratulantium turbas, adest *iuvenis lepra* immanissima[361] adeo tabe et pustulis[362] toto deformatus corpore, ut de forma hominis nichil fere inesse videretur preter exteriora liniamenta, velut in trunco ad formam humani corporis desecto, antequam artifex menbrorum ac sensuum, convenientiam distinctam imprimat arte magistra. Sic enim ulcera, sic tumores, sic iniquus color cuncta obduxerant, ut monstrum potius putaretur quam homo. Iste profecto non modo miserabilis verum extra modum horribilis, cum appropinquaret ad sanctam, quanta potuit voce horribiliter quidem

---

[346] *om. G*
[347] *om. G*
[348] ducunt ⌈eum⌉ *C*
[349] obprobrium *amended to* ob proprium *C*
[350] manus *C*
[351] inquid te *C*
[352] hoc indicaretur specie *C*] hec indicaretur species *M*, hoc indicaret species *G*
[353] *om. C*
[354] quantitatem *C*] quantas *M, G*
[355] salutis auctor *om. C*
[356] deus ⌈q⌉ *C*
[357] opus eius] est opus *C*, eius opus *G*
[358] consummatum ⌈quod⌉ *C*
[359] autem *G*
[360] spiritum redderet *C, G*] redderet spiritum *M*
[361] immanissima lepra *C*
[362] pistulis *G*

rauca³⁶³ emisit sonitum satis confusum, verba tamen exprimentem, dicens, *'Adiuro te, virgo Frideswida,* per Deum omnipotentem, *ut des mihi osculum in nomine Iesu Cristi* Filii eius Unigeniti.' O durum omnino sermonem, O dura sane postulatio! Petis, iuvenis leprose, virginem³⁶⁴ natura uti³⁶⁵ regiam³⁶⁶ sed, quia Cristi ancillam, non moribus delicatam, tibi dare osculum, in quem mares animo³⁶⁷ prorsus duriores figere abhorrent obtutum? Plane postulatio tua, ni fides eam magnifica proferri compulisset, forte³⁶⁸ putaretur insanientium improbitate prolata. Quidni? Homines, ut dixi, te intueri pre horrore nequeunt, pro sanie profluente tangere, pro fetore intolerabili tibi³⁶⁹ appropinquare, et osculum petis a regia virgine? Esto. Nisi³⁷⁰ leprosus fueris, attamen masculus, num tibi porrigere poterit osculum, que virilem ab ineunte etate non novit attactum? Sed inquis, 'Morbi mei intolerabilis estus, et non quem tu commemoras sexus, hoc me petere compellit.³⁷¹ Credo enim quod ad tactum oris eius mundissimi, fugiet morbida immunditia corporis mei.' O res miranda et seculis inaudita preteritis! Caritatis igne succensa virgo, contra opinionem omnium ilico accessit, et *signo crucis* prius impresso, leproso contulit *osculum*. Facile etenim³⁷² proculdubio sit quod a caritate vera procedit. Abhorrent intuentes, et cum admiratione non modica rei exitum expectant. Stupendum plane miraculum! Non enim minus quam Naaman Siro septena et mistica iuxta sermonem Helisei in Iordane ablutio,³⁷³ quantum ad corporis sanitatem spectat, huic una pia cum humili devotione puelle sacratissime deosculatio contulit. Ore etenim virginis os leprosi tangitur, et continuo toto corpore *mundatur*. Cutis aspera ad³⁷⁴ squamarum modum³⁷⁵ solvitur et velud exuvie colubrine deponitur, ac statim fit caro ipsius sicut caro pueri parvuli. Quis tanto presens non expavit miraculo? Quis a laude Cristi os continere potuit? Repletur letitia civitas. Exultant omnes, congratulantur universi, et *in* tante patrone *adventu* se nequaquam pre gaudio capiunt. Sed non his³⁷⁶ virgo extollitur, immo in dies quanta amplioribus virtutibus augebatur, tanto semetipsam et corpore et spiritu castigabat humilius.

(**19**) Die tandem pretiose dissolutionis eius instante, ecce *angelus Domini* astitit oranti, dicens, '*Quartodecimo kalendas Novembris,* in ipsa nocte que *Dominice* aurora terminabitur, finis tibi, Frideswida, agonis a Deo³⁷⁷ decernitur, et merces sempiterna preparatur.³⁷⁸ Et quoniam *terrenum patris palatium* contempsisti, Regis eterni introibis thalamum, ubi *lux*³⁷⁹ *immarcessibilis, et vita nescia mortis.*' *Hec dic*ens, discessit, et Fridesuuidam *febr*is gravissima *corripuit,* unde³⁸⁰ et viribus *corporis cepit* ilico destitui. Quod cum *civ*ibus innotuisset, quasi ad nutricem et matrem con*veniunt ad* illam, *monita salut*is cum gemebunda exigentes devotione. Quos pio ut erat pectore a desiderio non fraudabat, set singulis egritudinis sue diebus conamine quodam quasi contra³⁸¹ ius nature verbum salutis in commune disseminabat. Etenim caritas

---

³⁶³ rauca *amended to* ⌈et⌉ rauc ⌈e⌉ *C*
³⁶⁴ virginem ⌈teneram⌉ *C*
³⁶⁵ *om. G*
³⁶⁶ regiam *C, G]* regiam *amended to* regia *M*
³⁶⁷ omnino *G*
³⁶⁸ forte *C]* fore *M, G*
³⁶⁹ *om. C*
³⁷⁰ Nisi] Non *MSS*
³⁷¹ petere compellit *C, G]* copellit petere *M*
³⁷² enim *C*
³⁷³ *Ref. to IV Kings v.*
³⁷⁴ ab *G*
³⁷⁵ nodis *G*
³⁷⁶ hiis *G*
³⁷⁷ a Deo *om. C*
³⁷⁸ preparabitur *C*
³⁷⁹ lux ⌈est⌉ *C*
³⁸⁰ inde *G*
³⁸¹ contra *C, G] om. M*

impendebat, quod virium destitutio denegabat. (**20**) Cum vero *Sabbati* dies illucesceret, et nox instaret iam proxima qua e *corpore* virgo erat migratura, secus se assidentibus inquit, 'Hodie mihi fodite sepulchrum in basilica *beatissime semperque virginis Marie genitricis Dei et Domini mei Iesu Cristi*, cuius munita presidio, securior spirituum malignorum insidias contempnere, securior ante tribunal eiusdem Domini mei Filii eius valeam assistere. Et quoniam eius cras solennis et solita resurrectionis celebrabitur[382] memoria, et ego *hac nocte post tertium gallicinium de presenti seculo migrabo, nolo pro me* quemquam in tanta et tam illustri feria fodiendo fatigari.' Hec[383] *dixit, et sibi eucharistiam afferri* precepit. *Quam* cum gratiarum actione *suscipiens, benedic*ebat Dominum. (**21**) Et intentis ad superna luminibus, aspexit inde venientes ad se virgines, quas in veneratione maxima semper habebat, quoat inter homines in terris degebat. Et advenientibus suppliciter[384] inclinans, letabunda *voce* proclamabat, '*Bene venitis,*[385] *virgines* beate.' O 'quam magna multitudo dulcedinis tue, Domine, quam abscondisti timentibus te, perfecisti autem eis qui sperant in te'.[386] 'Quis non timebit te, Domine, et magnificabit nomen tuum, quia tu solus pius?'[387] Ne ancilla tua ad te migratura[388] Sathane paveret occursum, qui etiam victus et confusus victoribus victricibusque a castris suis[389] ad te redeuntibus occursare et fallatie sue calumpnias assolet apponere,[390] munivisti[391] semitas gradientis munimine quo nosti, et dedisti ei beatas iam[392] virgines in decessu suo cernere, quas ante dederas quadam quasi familiari veneratione in vita diligere. Hinc[393] quippe constare arbitror quoniam tuorum mentibus fidelium inseris, ut quidam hos alii vero illos famulorum famularumve tuarum qui iam ad te[394] meritorum evaserunt gratia, quodam speciali pre ceteris venerentur honore. Ad vocem itaque[395] proclamantis, commote que assistebant[396] sorores quas alloquatur *interrog*ant. Quibus *illa,* '*Num,*' inquit,[397] '*non* cernitis sacratissimas adventare *virgines, Katerinam atque Ceciliam?*' Et ad illas denuo conversa, *dixit,*[398] '*Modo veniam, Domine mee,* modo veniam.' Et *valedicens* astantibus, hora quam[399] *predixerat migravit ad Dominum*. Ipsa quidem *hora* migrationis eius, *lux* celitus emissa habitaculum quo sacratissimum ipsius iacebat corpus subito illustrans, ita totam replevit urbem subsequente[400] *odore* inestimabiliter *suav*issimo, quatinus non dubitaretur Unigenitum affuisse Patris luminum cuius nomen unguentum effusum[401] universum implevit orbem.

(**22**) Et ut eam vivere post mortem non esset ambiguum, ecce *paralitic*us, etiam lingue destitutus officio, *vir* admodum *dives, famul*orum manibus defertur ad feretrum super quod repositum erat sanctissime corpus virginis. Quod cum tetigisset, confestim sic solidatus est, ut exiliens in *laud*em *Dei* et sancte Frideswide magno cum clamore prorumperet.

---

[382] celebratur *C*
[383] Hoc *G*
[384] simpliciter *C*
[385] veniatis *G*
[386] *Ps. xxxi.20.*
[387] *Rev. xv.4.*
[388] migratura ad *MSS*
[389] suis *C*] tuis *M, G*
[390] apponere *C, G*] opponere *M*
[391] munivisti *C*] minuisti *altered to* munisti *M*, munisti *G*
[392] beatas iam *C, G*] iam beatas *M*
[393] Huic *G*
[394] *om. G*
[395] *om. C*
[396] astabant *C*
[397] Num inquit] Numquid *C*
[398] dixit *C, G*] ait *M*
[399] quam *C, G*] quam *altered to* qua *M*
[400] subsequente *C, G*] subsequentem *M*
[401] *construction unclear*

(**23**) *Cum*que *corpus* illud castissimum[402] cum magna frequentia utriusque ordinis et sexus deferretur ad sepulchrum, accidit ut *quidam* ab *umbilico deorsum* vitio nervorum ita constrictus, ut officio quoque gressuum destitueretur, scannulis nitens quia pedibus non potuit, et manuum[403] iuvamine miserabile *trahens corpus,* exequias virginis subsequeretur. Sed quoniam *non potuit* feretrum preciosissimi oneris aut gradiendo assequi, aut ad illam cum *in*[404] *ecclesiam* perventum fuit *pre* constipatione intrare *populi,* fecit quod potuit, magnis vocibus tanquam ad vivam, ad iam defunctam proclamavit, dicens, 'O inestimabilis virgo pietatis, O *sponsa* Fontis misericordie, quamdiu est ex quo[405] desideravi venire ad te? Sed me miserum cum vitio corporis vitium quoque impedivit male sane mentis. Peccatis etenim meis id promerentibus, nec te mihi vivam[406] nec cernere concessum est defunctam. Veruntamen, domina mea, converte nunc ad me viscera misericordie tue, et sana me ab hac invalitudine. Enimvero[407] certe credo quia hoc tibi facillimum est, quoniam ad Illum iam pervenire meruisti cui nichil esse potest difficile.' Hec proclamans, omnium[408] secus astantium in se convertit oculos, cum ecce crepans vehementer nervorum contractio solvitur, et iuncture gressuum solidantur. Itaque con*surgens* repente prosilit homo, et immunis a dolore letabundaque cum vociferatione proclamans, in *manibus* sustulit *scannulos,* proruensque per turbas ad sepulturam prorupit virginis. Et proiectis ibi scannulis, gratias agit[409] Deo et gloriose famule sue Frideswide. Tunc meror omnium in congratulationem[410] conversus est, quoniam cernebant quanta pro meritis famule sue post huius etiam vite decursum, et dum celebrabantur[411] exequie, faciebat Deus mirabilia. (**24**) *Sepulta est* beata virgo in basilica intemerate semper virginis Dei genitricis *Marie in parte australi* prope ripam fluminis Thamesis.[412] Sic enim se tunc habebat situs basilice usque ad tempus regis Athelredi, qui, combustis[413] in ea Dacis qui confugerant illuc, basilice ambitum sicut ante voverat[414] ampliavit. Hinc nimirum actum est, quia sepulchrum, quod ante fuerat in parte,[415] medium extunc esse contigit. Inibi[416] quippe tot tantaque per illius merita facta sunt mirabilia, ut nec hominum ea fides capere, nec scriptorum posset colligere sollicitudo, prestante *Domino nostro Iesu Cristo,* cui est honor et imperium in *secula seculorum, Amen.*

---

[402] illud castissimum corpus *C*
[403] manum *G*
[404] ad illam cum in] cum ad illam *G*
[405] ex quo] ex exquo *G*
[406] te mihi vivam *C, G*] vivam te mihi *M*
[407] Et enim vero *G. From this point the C text has flaked off.*
[408] omni *G*
[409] egit *G*
[410] congratulatione *G*
[411] celebrabantur *G*] celebrantur *M*
[412] Thamensis *G*
[413] combustis *G*] combussis *M*
[414] voverat *G*] noverat *M* (voverat *is supported by extract in* Cart. St. Frid. *op.cit. note 23, i, 9*).
[415] *Sic M, G and frags. of C. Unless* australi *is omitted,* in parte *evidently means 'on one side'; cf. above note 265.*
[416] In ibi que *G*

APPENDIX C: THE INVENTION AND FIRST TRANSLATION OF ST. FRIDESWIDE'S BONES

The production of Life B by Prior Robert of Cricklade suggests an intention to promote the cult. If so, the logical next step would have been a solemn translation of Frideswide's bones into a raised shrine. While it is inconceivable that such a scholar as Robert, with wide contacts and hagiographical interests, did not contemplate this, it was not achieved during his priorate. The canons were faced with the problem that they were not completely sure where the relics lay. According to Life A, Frideswide had originally been buried on the south side of St. Mary's church. Life B adds that after the 1002 fire, King Æthelred enlarged the church in such a way that the grave was thereafter central. The story is taken up by a narrative (Text I), of unknown source, which survives as a continuation of Life A in its abbreviated 14th-century version L (above, pp.23–4). This describes how Abingdon Abbey had held the church and its possessions between the expulsion of the secular clerks and the installation of the Augustinians (in other words at some date between 1086 and 1122), a fact which aroused fears that the monks had stolen the precious corpse.

An investigation was therefore initiated, presumably to be identified with the 'invention' of St. Frideswide later celebrated on 15 May.[417] It cannot be dated more precisely than to between the regularisation of the house and the translation of the relics, in other words between 1111×22 and 1180. It is likely enough that the Augustinians wanted to reassure themselves of Frideswide's presence as soon as their community was established: similar 'inspections' of Edward the Confessor's and St. Cuthbert's bodies occurred in 1102 and 1104.[418] On the other hand, it may have been an immediate prelude to the events of 1180: clearly it was essential to avoid the embarrassment of staging a solemn translation from what might prove to be an empty grave.

After fasting for three days, the canons entered the church secretly at dead of night and began to excavate the grave by torchlight. Finding an empty stone coffin, they almost despaired, 'but urged by an astute man amongst them they set about digging deeper. For he said that it had once been a common practice to put empty coffins over the bodies of saints, so that if thieves came intent on stealing the body they would go away deluded.' Thus encouraged, the excavators continued until they found a skeleton, whereupon all their torches were miraculously extinguished and re-kindled. Convinced by the heaven-sent sign that they had indeed found Frideswide, they closed the grave and left the corpse in peace.

'Thereafter', continues the narrative, 'miracles started to come thicker than before, and the virgin's grave was visited more diligently by people from many parts.' Prior Philip, elected during 1174×9, organised the translation. The ceremony is described (Text II) in the prologue to a miracle-collection which Philip wrote soon afterwards (Bodl. MS Digby 177); a transcript of the same passage continues the narrative in L. The Digby manuscript, of *c*.1200, contains an erasure of three words which are completely omitted by L, suggesting that the latter derives from Digby; on the other hand, L expands Digby's *in feretro* to *in feretro ad hoc decenter ornato*. It is at least clear that the L scribe had a copy of Prior Philip's book, for he goes on to give a statistical summary of the miracles and to quote one verbatim.

According to Philip the translation took place in 1180 on 12 February, the day on which its feast was later celebrated.[419] In January Henry II had held a council at

---
[417] C.R. Cheney, *Handbook of Dates for Students of English History* (1970), 51.
[418] F. Barlow, *Edward the Confessor* (1979), 268–9.
[419] Philip evidently uses the year beginning on 1 January: in other words 1180 by modern reckoning, not 1181. Henry II's presence in Oxford is consistent only with 1180, and John was only 'elect' of St. Andrew's until June 1180. The feast of the translation appears as 12 February in R.Stanton, *A Minology of England and Wales* (1892), 63, but wrongly (as 11 February) in Cheney, *Handbook,* 51. For this point I am grateful to Miss L. Dennison.

Oxford,[420] bringing together a suitable collection of notables including the archbishop of Canterbury, the bishops of Winchester, Ely, Norwich and St. David's, the bishop-elect of St. Andrew's and the papal legate to Scotland. Presumably the translation was timed to follow the council, though Prior Philip did not miss the opportunity of recognising God's providence in so distinguished a gathering to honour Frideswide. The party came into the church, and the archbishop 'opened with the greatest reverence the grave in which her most blessed corpse had rested for some 480 years. With a great crowd of clergy and people standing around and rejoicing, he took the virgin's glorious bones from the grave and laid them in a feretory fittingly embellished for this purpose, so that so precious a pearl, who proclaimed her life in heaven by such glorious miracles, should lie no longer hidden in the earth. Then the bystanders were filled with a most delightful scent which refreshed them like spices, so that it seemed not inappropriate to say of her, 'The smell of thine ointments is above all manner of spices.''

I: *The rediscovery of St. Frideswide's bones, 1111 × 79*

(British Library, MS Lansdowne 436, ff. 103–3ᵛ)

Iacuit autem beata virgo Frideswida, miraculis clara, in eodem quo sepulta fuit loco, videlicet in ecclesia sua in honore Sancte Trinitatis, beate Virginis Marie et Omnium Sanctorum dedicata, ferme quadringentis octoginta annis. In cuius temporis spatio, varii fuerunt illius monasterii status. Nam processu temporis, monialibus de loco illo recedentibus, monasterium cum possessionibus optinuerunt clerici seculares. Quibus ob eorum insolentiam exclusis, monachi Abyndonienses per aliquot tempora omnia habuerunt. Finaliter vero canonici regulares, viri religiosi, illuc introducti, pro maiori parte omnia recuperantes, usque hodie ibidem inhabitant. Qui post eorum adventum ad dictum monasterium, hesitantes an monachi predicti corpus virginis a sepulture sue loco abstulissent, indicto triduano ieiunio, secrete de nocte cum lumine copioso sepulchrum effodientes, sarcofagum lapideum vacuum invenerunt. Et cum iam quasi desperantes ab inceptis desistere proposuissent, cuiusdam discreti inter illos usi consilio profundius fodere conati sunt. Dicebat autem quod quandoque sic fieri consuevit super sanctorum corpora poni sarcofaga vacua, ut fures, si forte venirent et corpus furari vellent, sic delusi recederent. Diligenter igitur fodientes ad corpus virginis pervenerunt, quod cum fieret omnia luminaria que habebant subito extincta sunt. Unde illi admirantes, cum non corpus virginis sed alicuius alterius se invenisse putarent, omnem dubitatem a cordibus eorum evidenti miraculo omnipotens Dominus misericorditer effugavit. Nam omnia luminaria prius extincta igne de superveniente divinitus sunt reaccensa, quod cum vidissent miraculum repleti gaudio magno Dominum collaudabant.[421] Certioresque de veritate affecti, corpus gloriosissimi[422] in eodem loco in pace dimiserunt.

Ceperunt autem extunc crebrius solito ibidem miracula fieri et a populis diversarum partium sepulchrum virginis devotius visitari. Inter hec multis revelationibus diversis super hoc preostensis, innumeris etiam precedentibus miraculis evidentibus, decretum est unanimi assensu, regis videlicet Henrici secundi illo tempore regnantis et in palatio suo extra Oxoniam tunc existentis, cleri etiam et populi, virginis corpus e terra elevari, et in locum eminentiorem debere transferri. Ad preces igitur et instantiam Philippi tunc prioris et totius conventus[423] . . .

---

[420] R.W. Eyton, *Itinerary of Henry II* (1878), 230.
[421] *written* collaubant *with* da *inserted MS*
[422] gloriosimi *MS*
[423] *from here the text continues as in (II) below*

II: *The translation of the relics in 1180*

(Extract from the preface to Prior Philip's miracle collection, Bodleian Library, MS Digby 177ff. I^v–2, printed *Acta Sanctorum: Octobris: VIII* (1853), 568–9; variants from incomplete version in British Library, MS Lansdowne 436, ff.103^v–4.)

Scripturus itaque miracula que temporibus nostris per merita beatissime virginis Frideswide Dominus operari dignatus est, ab eius translatione inchoandum duxi, que facta est anno ab incarnatione Domini m°c°lxxx°, regnante illustrissimo rege Anglorum Henrico secundo. Que quidem eo gloriosior apparet, quod eam non sub modio abscondi sed super candelabrum poni Dominus voluit, ut lucerna super candelabrum posita lucis sue radios ubique diffunderet. Eo nempe tempore idem gloriosus rex propter maxima et ardua regni negotia, reverendissimum patrem nostrum Ricardum Cantuariensem archiepiscopum, domnum quoque Ricardum Wintoniensem,[424] Galfridum Helyensem, Iohannem Norwicensem, Petrum Menevensem episcopos, et copiosam cleri multitudinem, proceres quoque et magnates regni sui ex omnibus Anglie partibus apud Oxenefordiam convocaverat, Deo nimirum id agente, ut pretiosa margarita, que tanto tempore terra iacuerat operta, gloriosius omnibus ostenderetur, cum ipsius revelationi terrena negotia, et cleri et populi tanta multitudo Domino quasi latenter id instigante ad hoc convocata, deservire viderentur. Predicto igitur invictissimo rege votis favente, suumque benignissime prebente consensum, ad preces et instantiam[425] Philippi tunc prioris et totius conventus, pridie idus Februarii idem[426] venerabilis archiepiscopus,[427] convocatis secum domino[428] Ricardo Wintoniensi, Galfrido Helyensi, Iohanne Norwicensi, Petro Menevensi episcopis, presente venerabili viro magistro Alexio tunc temporis ex delegatione domini pape Scotie legato, et magistro Iohanne tunc quidem electo, post modum autem episcopo,[429] Sancti Andree, ad eiusdem gloriosissime virginis[430] ecclesiam accedens, prius quidem indicto ieiunio, sepulcrum maxima cum devotione aperiens, ubi[431] per quadringentos et lxxx^a circiter annos beatissimum eius corpus requieverat, astante et congaudente copiosa cleri et populi multitudine, gloriosa virginis ossa de sepulcro transtulit, et in feretro ad hoc decenter ornato[432] ea collocavit, ne tam pretiosa margarita terra diutius operta iaceret, que celebri miraculorum gloria se in celis vivere protestabatur. Odor denique suavissimus astantes replevit et aromatum more refocillavit, ut non inmerito de ea dictum videretur, 'Odor unguentorum[433] tuorum super omnia aromata.'[434] Precesserant sane translationem eius commonitiones creberrime, visiones plurime, revelationes gloriosissime, de quibus aliqua presenti inserere libet opusculo, ut beate virginis sanctitas posterorum memorie arcius inprimatur.

APPENDIX D: THE FRENCH CULT OF ST. FRIDESWIDE

No less enigmatic than the Oxford legend of St. Frideswide is its French counterpart: the cult of 'Ste. Fréwisse' long observed in a small village named Bomy in the Pas-de-Calais.

---

[424] Witoniensem MS
[425] L text begins here in continuation from (1) above
[426] Idem] *om. I.*
[427] archiepiscopus] pater dompnus Ricardus archiepiscopus Cantuariensis L
[428] domino] dominis venerabilibus L
[429] post . . . episcopo] *erased Digby, om. L*
[430] virginis] *om. L*
[431] ubi] ubi ut dictum est L
[432] ad . . . ornato L] *om. Digby*
[433] unguentorum L] ungentorum *Digby*
[434] *From here L summarises the contents of Prior Philip's book and repeats one of the miracles.*

Despite the Bollandists' lengthy discussion of it in 1853,[435] historians of Oxford have never given it more than a passing glance. At first sight it deserves no more, for much of the 'tradition' was clearly acquired from English sources in the late 16th or 17th century. Yet there is enough evidence to show that 'Ste. Frèwisse' was venerated at Bomy by the 12th century, and that her cult there was strikingly similar to St. Frideswide's at Binsey. Even though little new evidence has come to light since 1853, it seems appropriate here to provide an account in English of the Bomy cult, and to take speculation a little further.

Bomy (Fig. 4) lies 4½ miles (7 km.) south of the Roman town of Thérouanne, where a bishopric was re-established in the 7th century. The Roman road from Boulogne through Thérouanne to Amiens and Arras passes 4 miles (6 km.) north-east of Bomy, which thus lay on one of the main early medieval routes from England to many parts of Europe. Later in the middle ages it had a large parish, and was the centre both of a rural deanery and of a substantial lay *seigneurie*.[436]

Except for some tenuous archaeological data, and one crucial document to be discussed later, evidence for the cult derives essentially from three printed books of the 17th and 18th centuries:

(i) A 'Life of Ste. Frèwisse' by R.D. le Heudre, *curé* of Bomy in the mid 17th century. The Bollandists were unable to obtain a copy and none can be traced now, so this is only known from brief extracts in the later works of Malbrancq and de Neufville.

(ii) J. Malbrancq, *De Morinis* (3 vols., Tournai, 1639–54). A notoriously unreliable compilation on the history of the Thérouanne district, which nonetheless provides the only record of many ancient texts and traditions.

(iii) R.D. de Neufville, *La Vie de Sainte Frèwisse, Vierge, Religieuse Bénédictine, Honorée dans une Chapelle de son Nom au Village de Bomy* (Saint–Omer, 1720).[437] A primarily devotional treatise written by the *curé* of Bomy for the benefit of his flock, drawing heavily on le Heudre and Malbrancq but adding some local information.

It must be said at once that the hagiographical material in these sources is utterly worthless: a garbled version of the Oxford 'Life B', with Bomy substituted for Bampton as the place of Frideswide's three-year exile.[438] In a revealing passage, Malbrancq praises the faithful of Bomy for keeping alive the cult so shamefully suppressed in Oxford since the 1560s, and notes that le Heudre had obtained much of his information from the English Catholic establishment in Saint-Omer.[439] Evidently le Heudre found himself presiding over a cult with no adequate tradition of its own, and made good the deficiency by adopting the Oxford story wholesale. Thus there is no reason to think that the legend in which Ste. Frèwisse comes from Oxford to Bomy in the 8th century is anything other than a late fabrication.

The topographical evidence is more interesting (Figs. 4–5).[440] The village and parish church of Bomy lie in a small valley, flanked on its eastern side by a wooded slope. Immediately west of the church is a motte,[441] presumably a predecessor of the late- and post-medieval seigneurial *château* further east. By the roadside half a mile (1 km.) south of

---

[435] *Acta Sanct.* op. cit. note 57, 560–4.
[436] *Mémoires de la Société des Antiquaires de la Morinie,* xiii (1864–9), 44–5, and map reproduced Ibid. xxvi (1898), frontispiece.
[437] The only copy of this work I have been able to trace is an incomplete one in the Bibliothèque Municipale at Saint-Omer, shelfmark 3412/83A2. A Xerox has now been deposited in the Bodleian Library.
[438] This is obvious from the accounts in Malbrancq i, 574–7, 582–3 and de Neufville 1–63; the sources which they cite (Matthew Paris, Polydore Virgil, Mabillon and le Heudre) all go back to 'Life B', with elements from William of Malmesbury's story.
[439] Malbrancq i, 583.
[440] The topographical observations in this section were made by Mr. Edward Impey during his visit in August 1987.
[441] Mr. Impey's observation.

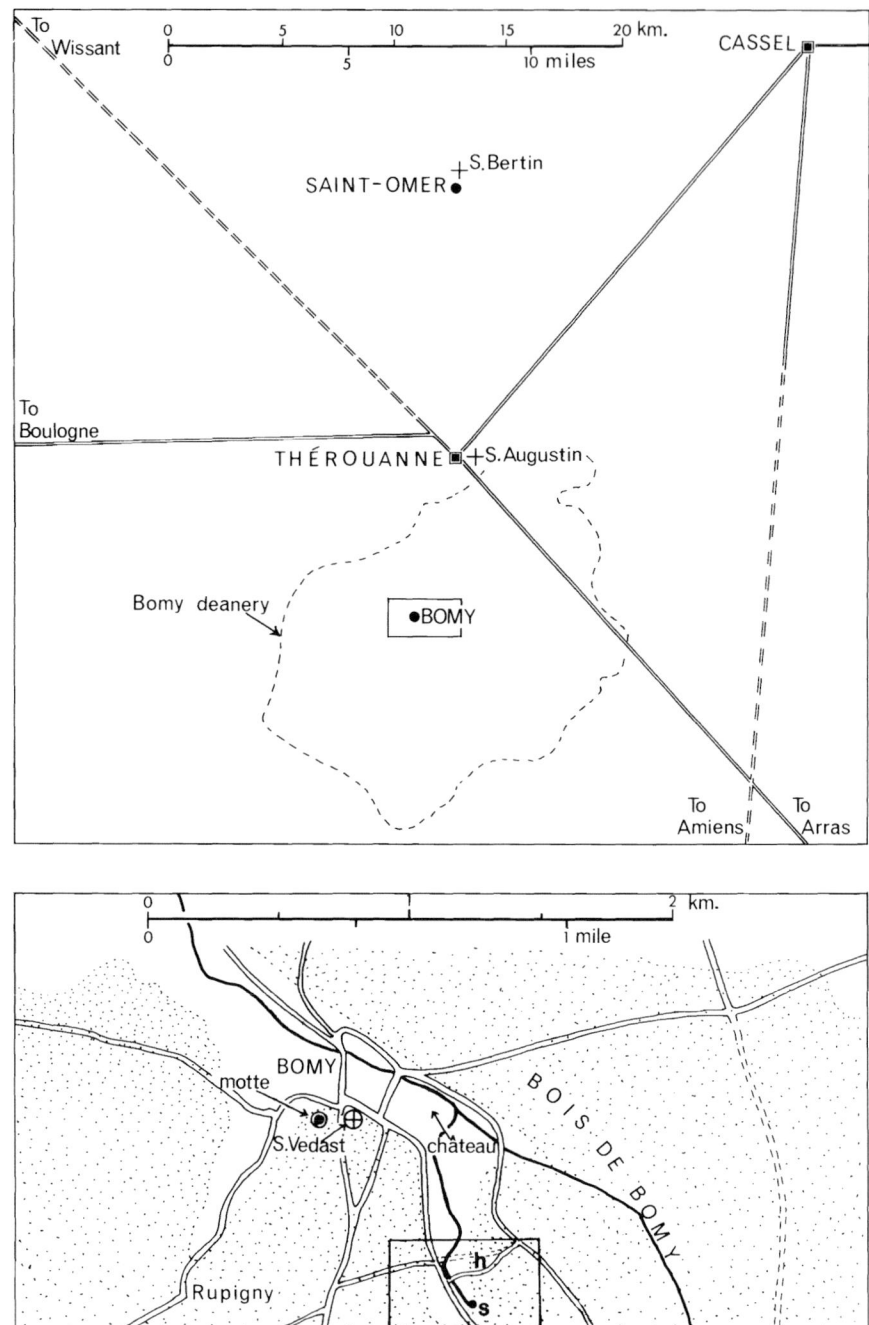

Fig. 4. The location and local topography of Bomy (land above 105m. stippled). **h** = hermitage site, **s** = St. Frideswide's spring.

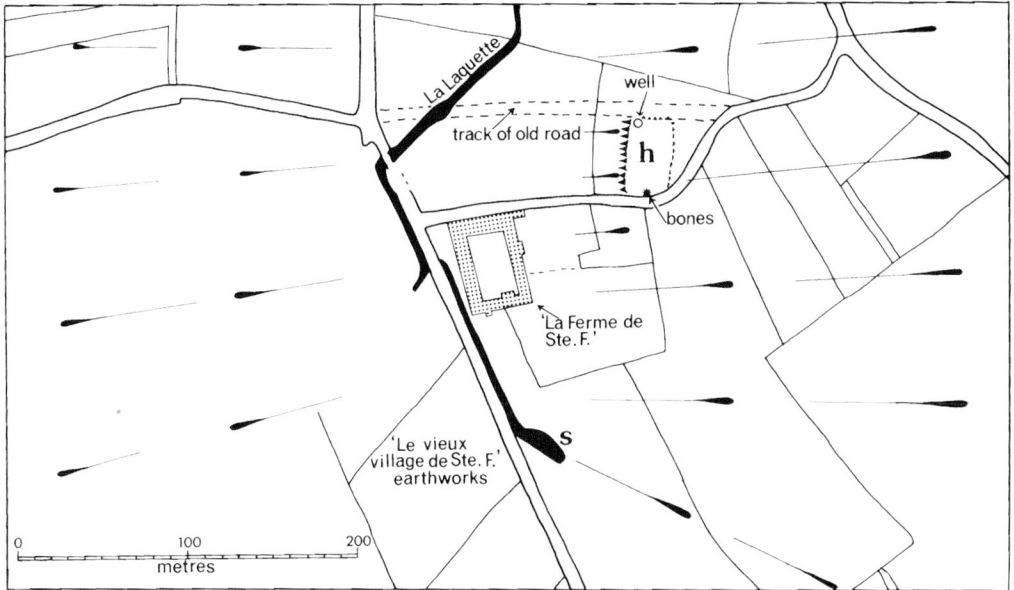

Fig. 5. The context of St. Frideswide's's spring and hermitage, Bomy: for location see lower map in Fig. 4. **h** = hermitage site, **s** = St. Frideswide's spring. (After Carte Cadastrale de la Commune de Bomy, 1973, 2ⁿᵈ edn. 1983, and fieldwork by Edward Impey.)

the village is a powerful natural spring (Fig. 6A), gushing from a deep cleft in the chalk at the foot of the slope, which is still called 'la Fontaine de Sainte Fréwisse'. From the spring a stream, normally called la Laquette but sometimes known in the 19th century as 'le fleuve de Sainte Fréwisse',[442] runs northwards down the valley towards the village.

Near the spring there stood, until the Revolution, a small chapel and hermitage. In the 18th century this was under the *curé* of Bomy's jurisdiction, but was served and occupied by a succession of hermits appointed by the lords of the manor.[443] Its exact site (Fig. 5) is unfortunately the subject of some confusion. Malbrancq says that it lay 'below' *(subtus)* the spring,[444] while de Neufville locates the spring on the east side of the hermitage.[445] These references suggest either a very restricted site *(c.*8 m. square) between the spring and the main road, or three meadows immediately west of the spring on the other side of the road; the latter, which contain indistinct earthworks *c.*30 m. square opposite the spring, are believed locally to be the site of 'l'ancien village de Ste. Fréwisse' which preceded the modern village of Bomy.[446] On the other hand, neither site is consistent with Malbrancq's statement that the hermitage was 'under an overshadowing wood',[447] or de Neufville's that it stood on 'a little hill at the foot of a wood, a place most appropriate for retreat and

---

[442] De Neufville, 101; *Acta Sanct.* op.cit. note 57, 564.
[443] De Neufville, 96: 'Dans cette Chapelle, il y a un espece de Benefice avec assignation de certains revenus pour decharger quelques messes toutes les semaines. Les Seigneurs de Bomy, qui l'ont fondé, s'en sont reservé la nomination.' The 18th-century hermits are discussed by P. Doyère, 'Ermites et Ermitages au Diocèse de Boulogne', *Bulletin Historique de la Société Académique des Antiquaires de la Morinie,* xviii (1952–7), 386–7. Cf. below, note 464.
[444] Malbrancq i, 684: 'necnon in proximo adsideat sacrariolum cum cella eremitica, hactenus culta ab anachoretis, subtus scaturiente lympha, desuper obumbrante sylva.'
[445] De Neufville, 101; 'Cette Fontaine est auprés de l'Hermitage de Bomy du côté de l'Orient . . . Cette source se nomme communement *La Fontaine de Sainte Fréwisse*. Elle est ainsi appellée d'un têms immemorial.'
[446] Mr. Impey's observation, and statement from M. Devaux.
[447] Loc. cit. note 444.

seclusion':[448] both imply a location further up the valley-side towards the wood, and thus north or north-east of the spring.

In fact, a site *c.*200 m. north of the spring provides what seems to be conclusive archaeological evidence (Fig. 5). It lies south of an old west-east road, now disused but traceable as a hollow-way, and north of the modern 'chemin rurale dit de l'Hermitage'. A flat terrace between the two road-lines is bounded west by a line of old trees, beyond which the ground falls away steeply towads la Laquette. The southern part of the terrace has produced several inhumations, some cut by the modern lane;[449] this accords with de Neufville's statement that hermits of his own day often found human bones in the chapel garden.[450] In the north-west corner of the terrace is a stone-lined well, into which the chapel bell is reputed to have been dropped at the time of the Revolution. Recent excavation failed to find the bell, but produced instead a quantity of 15th- to 18th-century pottery and several small terracotta statuettes of the Virgin and Child, probably thrown into the well when the chapel was destroyed;[451] the statuettes are presumably relics of the post-medieval cult of the Infant Jesus mentioned by de Neufville.[452] The excavator claims to have found remains of the chapel and hermitage nearby, but no plan is available. It can hardly be doubted that the hermitage stood here in at least the post-medieval period; the inconsistencies in the texts could perhaps be resolved by translating Malbracq's *subtus* as 'downstream' and assuming that de Neufville wrote 'orient' in mistake for 'occident'.

At all events, le Heudre judged the chapel 'one of the oldest holy places of Artois',[453] and Malbrancq and de Neufville followed him in thinking it extremely ancient. All three authors believed that Ste. Fréwisse herself had dwelt at the chapel and spring, imbuing them with her holiness.[454] She was honoured there especially on two feasts, the anniversary of her death on 19 October and that of the chapel's dedication on the first Sunday after Easter, when the *curé* of Bomy sang vespers and mass there;[455] le Heudre also reports that the canons of Thérouanne celebrated her festival.[456] Pilgrims were believed to have come from time immemorial to invoke the saint and drink the waters of her spring, which were thought especially useful for curing fevers.[457] A 17th-century *curé* reported a local legend

---

[448] De Neufville, 96: 'Cette Chapelle fait partie d'un Hermitage, qui est situé sur une petite colline au pied d'un bois, lieu fort propre à la retraite, et à la solitude. Elle est nommé, d'un têmés immemorial, *La Chapelle de Sainte Fréwisse*'.

[449] Recent discoveries of burials are noted by M.M. Devaux, 'Note Préliminaire sur les Découvertes de Ste.-Fréwisse à Bomy', *Bulletin Historique du Haut-Pays,* iv.21 (1er semestre 1981), v–vii. In 1987 Mr. Impey observed skeletons in shallow graves protruding from a tree-hole on the edge of the modern road, in the position marked on Fig. 5.

[450] De Neufville, 106: 'Les Hermites modernes, commis pour le soin de cette Chapelle, assurent que bechant la terre de leur jardin, ils y ont trouvé plusieurs fois des ossemens humains: preuve certaine que cet entroit étoit cet ancien cimetière de l'Eglise Paroissiale de Sainte Fréwisse.'

[451] Devaux op.cit. note 449. Mr. Impey interviewed M. Devaux, and examined the photographs and finds in his possession.

[452] De Neufville, 96.

[453] Quoted de Neufville, 98: 'Saint lieu des plus anciens de l'Artois'.

[454] Le Heudre (quoted de Neufville, 98): the antiquity of the chapel 'le faisont entrer en conjecture, toute vrai semblable, que cette Sainte aurait marché sur cette terre, y aurait respiré l'air, et laissé devant nos yeux de grands traits de sa bienveillance, et des témoignages évidens de sa Sainteté et de sa vertu'. De Neufville, 64, boasts that the suppression of the English cult 'n'a servi qu'à faire augmenter ce culte dans la Chapelle de Bomy, où cette Sainte étoit en particuliere veneration depuis un têms immemorial'.

[455] Malbrancq, i, 684: 'Cum vera Bomyensis ille vicus omni memoria templum illi [i.e. in the parish church] Divae sacrum gerat, quotannis 19. Octobris festam ejus diem recolens; . . . [Nearby are the chapel and well] ubi etiam quotannis, prima post Paschalem solemnitatem dominica, celebris loci dedicatio recurrit'; De Neufville, 96: the chapel 'est sous la jurisdiction spirituelle de Mr. le Curé de Bomy, qui y chante ordinairement les premieres Vêpres et la Messe deux fois l'année; sçavoir, le Dimanche *de la Quasimode,* jour de la Dedicace de ce lieu, et le 19 d'Octobre, jour de l'heureux Trépas, et de la Fête de nôtre Sainte'.

[456] De Neufville, 92–3: 'les venerables Abbés et Religieux de Saint Augustin de Terrovane font chaque année memoire solemnelle de nôtre Sainte, selon le raport de Mr. le Heudre dans son Histoire'.

[457] Malbrancq, i, 684 (quoted *Acta Sanct.* op.cit. note 57, 561, and de Neufville, 102–3). Le Heudre (quoted de Neufville, 102) writes of the water: 'Laquelle n'a été éprouvée apporter peu de soulas à ceux et celles qui en goûtent, venans Pelerins par

Fig. 6A : 'La Fontaine de Sainte Fréwisse', Bomy. B : Bomy parish church: statue of 'Sainte Fréwisse' by F.P. Savary, 1755. *Phh. Edward Impey, 1987.*

that the saint had obtained the spring by striking the earth with her staff, and his successor of 1847 believed that it never dried up.[458] The cult survived the demolition of the chapel, and in 1847 the Bollandists found an image (Fig. 6B) and even relics of Ste. Fréwisse in Bomy parish church.[459]

From all this it is clear that, whatever hagiographical material le Heudre may have obtained from the English Jesuits, the chapel, spring and cult cannot have been his invention. Some suspicion must rest on the observance of the main Oxford feast of St. Frideswide (19 October), but that a long-established tradition associated the chapel with a holy woman named Fréwisse, and that healing powers were ascribed to the water from her well, can hardly be doubted. And luckily, a document survives which takes the cult much further back: an episcopal charter of 1187 ratifying an exchange between the Premonstratensian canons of Thérouanne and Walter Butri, lord of Bomy. The text is only known from Malbrancq's transcript,[460] but internal evidence makes its authenticity almost certain.[461] In translation it reads:

---

sincere devotion et affection en ladite Chapelle.' See also de Neufville, 64, 93–4, and *Acta Sanct*. op.cit. note 57, 564.
[458] Both reported *Acta Sanct*. op.cit. note 57, 564.
[459] Ibid, 564.
[460] Malbrancq, iii, 520; reprinted *Acta Sanct*. op.cit. note 57, 562, and (in French translation) de Neufville, 104–5.
[461] The text is vindicated by an exhaustive analysis in *Acta Sanct*. op.cit. note 57, 562–3, and is accepted without question by O. Bled, *Regestes des Évêques de Thérouanne*, i (Saint-Omer, 1902), No. 918.

Didier bishop of Thérouanne: Whereas the Abbot of St. Augustine of Thérouanne has persuaded the lord Walter Butri to allow his court of Fréwisse to be transferred within the same parish to the valley of Wigelm and Walter Butri *(ut curtem suam de Fredesuide transferret in eadem parochia ad vallem Wigelmi et Gualteri Butri);* the Abbot, with the Chapter's consent, has granted in my presence to Walter Butri all his right in his mill, and the whole court of Ste. Fréwisse *(totam curtem Sanctae Fredeswidis)* with the orchard and with the adjoining land. The Abbot further grants that, within a year after Ste. Fréwisse's chapel *(capellam Sanctae Fredeswidis)* has been moved by the lord Walter Butri, he will transfer it to Wigelm's valley, rebuild it, and institute a priest ministering there forever at the Abbot's expense. He will transfer the corpses of the dead from the old site [to] the new chapel at Walter Butri's pleasure. In exchange, Walter Butri has given to St. Augustine's church ten measures of land next the new court on whichever side they choose, and 120 measures of new land to cultivate and marl, without seed and all [. . . ? . . .] excepted. They shall possess and cultivate freely whatever land they buy or receive in alms in Bomy parish, and all common roads, especially to Ste. Fréwisse's spring *(et maxime ad fontem Sanctae Fredeswidis)*, and likewise all pastures; and the brethren shall remain free from all multure charges. Given in the year 1187.

It is possible that this transaction merely involved shifting Ste. Fréwisse's *curia* from the meadow west of the spring to the later hermitage site; but it is hard to see how a move up the slope from the valley-bottom could be said to be *ad vallem Wigelmi et Gualteri Butri*. De Neufville assumed, rather, that the effect was to transfer parochial functions from Ste. Fréwisse's chapel to the later parish church in the village, further down the valley,[462] and he was probably right. The earliest part of the parish church is evidently its axial tower, which could well date from the 1180s or 1190s.[463] The graves in the *curia,* and their (evidently not very thorough) removal to a new site, suggests the replacement of an old parochial cemetery by the one which remained in use into modern times. The seigneurial family's later patronage of the hermitage[464] is consistent with its acquisition by Walter Butri; the point of the final clause is presumably to safeguard the canons' access to a spring which would now no longer be on their land. In short, the likelihood is that Ste. Fréwisse's chapel was the mother church of Bomy until 1187, but was then superseded by the present parish church of St. Vedast; because of its holiness it survived, but merely as a humble hermitage.

To explain the cult, and to determine what, if any, connection it had with Oxford, is another matter. There seem to be four possibilities, none of which can be either substantiated or eliminated:

1. Ste. Fréwisse of Bomy originally had nothing whatever to do with St. Frideswide of Oxford, whose legend was attached to her in the 17th century or slightly earlier. Against this is the presence of a feature common to both Bomy and Binsey: a spring which sprang up at the saint's request and which heals those who drink from it. Holy springs are of course numerous, but the association between saints with identical names and springs with identical attributes seems an unlikely coincidence. If it could be shown that the 19 October feast was observed at Bomy from an early date, this would be conclusive evidence for the identity of Ste. Fréwisse with St. Frideswide.

---

[462] De Neufville, 106.
[463] Mr. Impey's observation.
[464] Cf. above, note 443. De Neufville's dedication to the Marquis de Trazegnie, *seigneur* of Bomy, includes (prelims. pp.iii^v–iv): 'Si nous passons de cette Ville à vôtre Terre de Bomy, nous y trouverons que vos Predecesseurs ne s'y sont pas moins distingués, et pour m'arrêter uniquement a la Chapelle de Sainte Frewisse, que je dois avoir particulierement en vûe, outre qu'on ne peut leur contester la qualité de Fondateurs, depuis un têms immemorial ne l'ont-ils pas toûjours gratifié de leurs bienfaits, pour témoigner la pieuse affection qu'ils lui portoient. Ils y ont attaché un Benefice qui se donne aujourd'hui à votre Nomination. Ne puis-je pas dire avec justice que cette pieté exemplaire, qui leur faisont avoir ce lieu en veneration, se trouve transmise en vous, Monsieur, qui par le même esprit prenez cette Chapelle de Sainte Frewisse sous vôtre protection . . . . Vous avez orné cette Chapelle d'un Clocher, la mettant dans le même état qu'elle étoit dans le X siècle.'

2. The cult was exported from Oxford to Bomy after the re-foundation of St. Frideswide's minster as an Augustinian priory, in other words in the early to mid 12th century.[465] Since the chapel and well belonged before 1187 to the Premonstratensian canons of St. Augustine at Thérouanne, it would be necessary to postulate a link through the international community of canons regular. There is, however, no evidence that St. Frideswide's had any connection with St. Augustine's, which was founded in 1131 by Bishop Miles I of Thérouanne and colonised from Sélincourt in the Low Countries.[466] Its dedication to St. Augustine of Canterbury, which probably commemorates the ancient links between the Pas-de-Calais and the Gregorian mission to Kent, can scarcely explain the adoption of a minor Mercian cult. But the biggest obstacles to this view are the facts that the first site of the cult was already being down-graded and deprived of parochial status in 1187, and that Fréwisse eventually gave way to St. Vedast as the main patron of Bomy.[467] Traditions can become 'immemorial' with disconcerting speed, but it is hard to believe that this obscure and wholly extraneous saint was installed as patron of a large parish, complete with her holy spring and a cemetery, only to be demoted within two generations.

3. The cult was exported from Oxford to Bomy through one of the many links between English and Flemish churches in the 10th and 11th centuries.[468] From Alfred's time onwards there was regular contact between the West Saxons and St. Bertin's monastery at Saint-Omer, which was visited by many English pilgrims. Some Englishmen brought relics with them into Flanders, such as those of St. Oswald and St. Eadburh which the abbey at Bergues obtained in 1038.[469] The merit of this hypothesis is that it allows a plausible interval between the establishment of the Bomy cult and the 1187 charter, and on balance it is perhaps the most likely. The links between St. Frideswide's minster and Abingdon Abbey (above, pp.46–7) make it a tempting possibility that St. Æthelwold, who was abbot of Abingdon (954–63) before becoming bishop of Winchester (963–84), had a hand in transmitting the cult.

4. The cult at Bomy results directly from Frideswide's own activities, or from those of her companions or followers. The relationships between the English and Gallic church hierarchies in the 7th and 8th centuries, the connections and similarities between 'double monasteries' on both sides of the Channel, and the unifying influence of Irish missionaries[470] would provide a context, and some 7th-century English princesses certainly went to Gallic monasteries.[471] Alternatively, the cult could have been transmitted slightly later but still in the pre-Viking period: the Englishman Fridegis, abbot of St. Bertin's during 820–34,[472] is one possible link. It can only be said that none of this is impossible, but neither can it be used as evidence for events in Frideswide's lifetime.

---

[465] This explanation is preferred by the latest French commentator: G. Coolen, 'Sainte Fréwisse ou Frideswide', *Bulletin Historique de la Société Académique des Antiquaires de la Morinie*, xviii (1952–7), 363–4.

[466] *Sacri et Canonici Ordinis Premonstratensis Annales,* i (Nancy, 1734), 224; H. Piers, 'L'Abbaye de S. Augustin-lez-Thérouanne', *Mem. Soc. Antiq. de la Morinie* ii(2) (1834), 199–203; E. de Moreau, *Histoire de l'Eglise en Belgique,* iii (2nd edn., Brussels, 1945), 19. Bled op.cit. note 461, No. 586, says that Bishop Miles gave 'la cure de Sainte-Fréwisse' to St. Augustine's in c.1140, but this seems to be based on nothing more than Malbrancq's conjecture.

[467] De Neufville, 95–6: 'Il est vrai qu'elle n'est point la premiere Patronne de la Paroisse, puisque depuis la fin du XII siècle ce titre est attribue à Saint Vaast, Evêque d'Arras; mais pour n'y être depuis lors que la seconde, elle n'y est pas moins honorée et respectée, non seulement des habitans de ce Village, mais encore des peuples voisins.'

[468] For these contacts see P. Grierson, 'The Relations between England and Flanders before the Norman Conquest', *Trans. Roy. Hist. Soc.* 4th ser. xxiii (1941), 84–95; F. Barlow, *The English Church 1000–1066* (2nd ed., 1979), 17–20; J. Campbell, 'England, France, Flanders and Germany', in his *Essays in Anglo-Saxon History* (1986), 201–5.

[469] Grierson op.cit. note 468, 101.

[470] For all of which see Campbell, 'First Century', op.cit. note 29, 49–67.

[471] Ibid., 55–6.

[472] Grierson op.cit. note 468, 83.

If the cult at Bomy was old by 1187, and if its object of devotion was indeed our St. Frideswide, it is not impossible that it reflects forgotten aspects of the Oxford cult. In particular, it adds a little weight to the view that the holy site at Binsey was not invented for the convenience of the 12th-century canons, but perpetuates older traditions associating Frideswide with a hermitage and a healing spring. Further speculation is pointless; but it is pleasant to record that pilgrims are still attracted to St. Frideswide's spring in this second Binsey 150 miles from Oxford.[473]

The Society is grateful to the W.A. Pantin Trust for a grant towards the publication of this paper.

---

[473] Doyère op.cit. note 443, 387: 'Aujourd'hui il ne reste aucune trace de l'ermitage, mais la tradition d'un pèlerinage à la fontaine de Sainte Fréwisse s'est maintenue.'

Part Two – Thornbury, Binsey: A Probable Defensive Enclosure associated with Saint Frideswide

With a contribution by MAUREEN MELLOR

Reprinted with permission from *Oxoniensia* 53 (1988), pp 3–20.

SUMMARY

A large sub-oval earthwork enclosure at Binsey, associated with St. Margaret's chapel and its graveyard, is identified with Thornbiri ('thorny fortress'), named in the late 12th-century Life of St. Frideswide as one of her places of refuge. It was regarded as a holy spot from the 12th century onwards, and the canons of St. Frideswide's may have maintained a cell there. Until 18th-century changes in the road-pattern it lay directly on the main route between Eynsham and Oxford. Excavations in 1987 identified a series of boundary features. A ditch on the N. W. side, its fill containing material dated by a radiocarbon determination to the Roman or sub-Roman period, was either preceded or succeeded by a revetted rampart. On the S. W. side, the earliest identified ditch had an early Anglo-Saxon potsherd stratified under its primary fill. The earthwork seems to have remained conspicuous until the early 18th century, and is still defined by an eroded bank and field-ditch. It remains uncertain whether the original enclosure is of Iron Age or post-Roman date; it may possibly belong to the series of small Iron Age forts on terrace-edge and island sites on the Thames gravels. The stratified sherd, however, suggests that the ditch was being kept clean at some date in the early Anglo-Saxon period. The legend of Frideswide at Binsey, and the fact that it was an old-established possession of her monastery by the early 12th century, suggest a possibility that the earthwork may have been used during her life as an ancillary monastic enclosure or retreat-house.

ACKNOWLEDGEMENTS

The excavation, by kind permission of Christ Church and its tenant Mr. D.J. Parris, was carried out in 1987–8 by Roger Ainslie, Michelle Armstrong, John Blair, Richard Hornsey, Edward Impey, Joszef Laszlovszky, Sally Oatley, Nicholas Palmer, Christine Peters and Christopher Whittick. Radiocarbon dating was financed by the Historic Buildings and Monuments Commission for England, and carried out at the Isotope Measurement Laboratory, AERE Harwell. I am also very grateful to Maureen Mellor for her contribution; to George Lambrick for advice on valley-forts; to David Haddon-Reece and Tony Fleming for help with the radiocarbon samples; to Bruce Levitan for identifying the bones; and to Mark Robinson for examining a soil sample.

HISTORICAL EVIDENCE

The early 12th-century Life of St. Frideswide relates how the princess, fleeing from the lecherous King Algar, hid at Bampton in 'a wood called Binsey', where she worked miraculous cures on a blind girl of Bampton, a young man of Seacourt and a demoniac fisherman. Although Binsey is in fact near Oxford, and nowhere near Bampton, the reference to its neighbour Seacourt suggests that the author had access to older material associating Frideswide with miracles in and around Binsey.[1]

When Robert of Cricklade, prior of St. Frideswide's, came to re-write the Life of his Monastery's founder-saint around 1160, the confusion perturbed him.[2] In his own version he resolved it by inserting, between the first two miracles, a new chapter which transports

---

[1] Above, pp.14–6.
[2] Above, p.11 for Robert's authorship of the second Life.

Frideswide from Bampton to Binsey in time to cure the young man of Seacourt. Frideswide and her companions set out for Oxford, but when their boat reaches 'the possession called Binsey near the city' they decide to stay there for a further spell of solitude:

> On that possession *(predium)* was a place *(locus)* entangled with various kinds of trees, called *Thornbiri* in the Saxon tongue because of the many different species of thorns there, lonely and most suitable for devotion. Here she straightway built an oratory, and many buildings well-suited to the needs of holy people. And since the branch of the river was some way away, and she felt it inconvenient for the sisters to go there to draw water, she obtained by her prayers a well which remains to this day, and performs healing works for many who drink from it [*or* who pray there]. Here she hoped to hide, here devote herself to sweet tranquillity and shun the crowds.[3]

Beyond the existence of some sort of traditional link between Frideswide and Binsey, it is impossible to say how much of this story is based on anything other than Prior Robert's imagination. There is, however, independent evidence that Binsey was regarded in the early 12th century as a holy place, appropriate for the religious life. The foundation narrative of Godstow nunnery recounts that in Henry I's reign there lived a lady of Winchester named Edith, wife of Sir William Lancelin. After her husband's death

> a vision often came to her that she should go near the city called Oxford and wait there for a sign from the Almighty King, by which she would know how to do God's service. She came, as a vision commanded her, to Binsey, where she dwelt in prayer and lived a most holy life. One night she heard a voice which told her what to do: 'Edith', it said, 'arise, go without delay to the place [i.e. Godstow] where a light descends to earth from heaven, and establish nuns there to serve God.' Thus in truth was this Abbey first founded.[4]

Binsey is not mentioned in Æthelred II's charter for St. Frideswide's minster (1004), which does not, however, claim to list all properties.[5] In Domesday Book (1086), the canons' 'four hides near Oxford', which never paid geld nor belonged to any hundred, probably included both Walton and Binsey; it is even possible that the 8 ac. of 'thorn-scrub' or 'spinney' *(spineti)*, a rare item of Domesday terminology, represents the placename *Thornbiri*.[6] Henry I's re-foundation charter (*c.*1122) includes 'the whole place *(locus)* called Binsey'; this text may have been tampered with, but 'the possession *(predium)* called Binsey' appears in the more reliable confirmation of Pope Honorius II (1124x30).[7] Property returned to the canons by Roger of Salisbury in 1139 included the 'whole place *(locus)* called Binsey', and in the same year the burgesses of Oxford acknowledged that 'from the land which pertains to one hide in Walton and from the land which pertains to Binsey the said canons have yearly rent and service of their peasants and their hundred in all things'.[8] In 1279 St. Frideswide's was said to have a hamlet *(hamelot)* called Binsey in the suburbs of Oxford, assessed at half a hide.[9] The Priory's 15th-century cartulary asserts that 'the possession *(predium)* called

---

[3] Above, pp.15–6, 40.

[4] The narrative survives as a late 14th-century French verse version (P.R.O. EI64/20, f. 1 of main text): '... Souent luy vient par avisiun/ Ke ele alast pres de la citee/ Que Oxenford fust apele,/ E la demorast desk' ataunt/ Quele veit signe del Rey pusaunt/ Desk'ele eit oy en quele guise/ Estoit fere la Dieux service./ A Benseye est pus ale/ Cum en auisiun fut maunde,/ Entes oraisuns iluske demora,/ E mult seinte vie demena./ Une voiz oist par un nuit,/ La quele dist quy fere luy estust./ 'Ediz', fet il, 'fus levez,/ E saunz demorance yalez/ Au lu qu lumer desent/ Au tere del firmament,/ E la fetes ordeynir/ Noueines a Dieu servir.' / En ceste manere par verite/ Fust cest albeie primes trouve./ ...' This may well be a translation of an earlier Latin narrative. The Middle English version *(The English Register of Godstow Nunnery*, ed. A. Clark, i (E.E.T.S. orig. ser. cxxix, 1905), 26) is simply a translation of the French.

[5] *Cart.Frid.* i, 2–9

[6] Domesday Book f. 157a. This was evidently the belief of the later medieval canons, who rubricated their transcript of the Domesday entries as 'faciens mensionem de Wynchendon' et Bunseye': *Cart. Frid*. ii, 206.

[7] *Cart.Frid.* i, II, 14.

[8] Ibid. i, 18, 20; *Regesta Regum Anglo-Normannorum* iii, No. 640.

[9] *Oxoniensia*, xxxvii (1972), 173.

Binsey, with the hundred and its other liberties, was given to the said monastery from the time when St. Frideswide was alive in the body', and lists the customary dues of the tenants as *sant'* (sandgavel?), landgavel, ingavel, churchscot and tollsester.[10]

The impression conveyed by these texts is not only that Binsey was an ancient, presumably pre-Augustinian, possession of St. Frideswide's monastery, but also that the house's proprietorship of it was of a somewhat unusual character. The 'four hides near Oxford' are the only holding in the Oxfordshire Domesday which is claimed to be extra-hundredal, a claim evidently re-asserted in 1139 and again in the 15th-century cartulary passage.[11] The Binsey men seem to have been unique among the Priory's tenants in the exotic customary renders which they owed, notably churchscot with its connotations of ancient parochial jurisdiction. And the terms 'possession' *(predium)* and 'place' *(locus),* if commonplace enough in themselves, are not standard legal designations like *manerium, terra, hida* or *acra*: the persistence with which they are applied to Binsey is curious. There may be an implication that Binsey was a *special* place: small and part of a larger entity, yet worth mentioning because it had some significance of its own.

The original Binsey ('Byni's island') which gave the estate its name was presumably the small gravel outcrop on which the village now stands. Since Prior Robert attributes to Frideswide the chapel and holy well, both of which still exist, he clearly identified *Thornbiri* with the area around the chapel, as distinct from the village site (Fig. 1). Binsey chapel is mentioned in the cartulary texts of Henry I's foundation charter and later royal confirmations, but there are strong reasons to suspect a systematic interpolation;[12] an episcopal confirmation of 1203x6 may provide the first genuine charter reference.[13] Nonetheless, the fact that Prior Robert could claim so ancient an origin for the chapel must mean that by *c.*1140–70 it had existed from beyond living memory. The absence of any references to it in the 12th-century charters may be precisely because it was bound so closely to its mother house as to be regarded as an extension of the Priory.

Binsey had no burial rights, bodies being taken to Oxford for burial as late as 1552.[14] In 1341 the chapel was said to be attached to St. Edward's parish, which had absorbed St. Frideswide's parish in 1298 on the suppression of its altar in the Priory church;[15] a direct parochial dependence on St. Frideswide's before 1298 is therefore likely. Although post-medieval sources generally speak of St. Margaret's chapel, a reference in 1323 to 'the chapel built at Binsey in honour of St. Frideswide and St. Margaret' makes this the only reliably-attested dedication to Oxford's patron saint.[16]

Whether the Priory ever had a monastic cell at Binsey is uncertain. Edith Lancelin, who must have stayed there soon before or soon after St. Frideswide's was re-founded *c.* 1122, may have lived as a recluse, but the narrative does not actually say so; it is equally possible that she chose Binsey because there was a cell of canons, or even nuns, which could house her. In the 17th century, Anthony Wood believed that the Augustinian canons

---

[10] *Cart.Frid.* ii, 18.

[11] Binsey was, however, said to be part of Northgate hundred (probably a 12th-century creation) at various times from the late 13th century onwards: see *V.C.H. Oxon.* iv, 265, 270; *Oxoniensia,* i (1936), 122.

[12] The suspicious fact is that although Binsey chapel is mentioned, along with immunity from episcopal visitation, in charters of Henry I and Matilda (*Cart.Frid.* i, 10, 23), both are conspicuously absent from the otherwise comprehensive lists in papal and episcopal confirmations of 1124x30, 1141, 1158, 1154x9 and *c.*1155x60 (Ibid. 13–15, 20–22, 27–9, 29–30, 31–2). It looks as though a shameless tamperer with royal charters has baulked at falsifying papal bulls.

[13] *Cart.Frid.* i, 46.

[14] *V.C.H.Oxon.* iv, 270–1.

[15] *Inquisitiones Nonarum* (Rec.Comm., 1807), 142; J. Blair, 'St Frideswide's Monastery: Problems and Possibilities', *Oxoniensia* 53 (1988), 221–58, at p.256.

[16] Lincoln Archives Office, Bishops' Reg. V, f.340. Pre-Victorian evidence for the dedication of Frilsham church (Berks.) to St. Frideswide has not been found.

> instituted and ordained it to be a cell or place of retirement ... , and therin not only at some times enjoyed themselves in great repose and devotion, but also sent their stubborn monks to be punished for crimes committed against the prior or his brethren, and that commonly was either by inflicting on them confinement in a dark roome or else by withdrawing from them their usuall repast and the like. Here it was alsoe that several priests appointed by the prior of St. Frideswid's had habitation, purposely to confesse and absolve pilgrims of all sorts that flocked hither to receive remidy for their malidies from the water of St. Margarett's Well.[17]

Given Wood's habit of extrapolating beyond his sources this should probably not be taken too seriously, though he may have seen documents now lost. Firmer evidence that Binsey was a place of resort for the community comes with the temporary seizure of St. Frideswide's by the Crown in 1374: the prior and one fellow-canon were allowed to retain as their dwelling a place near Oxford called Binsey chapel.[18] There was no formal vicarage, and no medieval curates are recorded (with the possible exception of one 'Simon chaplain of Thornbury' mentioned in 1293); in 1423 a canon of St. Frideswide's served Binsey, and apparently lived there with one servant.[19] These intimations that the canons controlled Binsey directly, and perhaps maintained a cell or rest-house there, reinforce the impression conveyed by the land-holding records that it was a place to which they ascribed special significance.

TOPOGRAPHY AND COMMUNICATIONS[20] (FIG. 1)

Much of Binsey township consists of poorly-drained alluvium, and human settlement has probably always concentrated on the three small gravel islands in the floodplain: Langney to the S., the area around Binsey village and Green, and the northernmost island on which the chapel stands. The edges of these islands have not been defined exactly, but the chapel probably marks the N. edge of an oval gravel outcrop encircled by the recently-discovered earthwork.[21] Seen from the air, the land thus defined appears slightly raised above the old enclosures, bounded W. by Shire Lake Ditch and E. by Swift Ditch, which surround it.

Binsey Green is now approached from the Botley Road causeway (built in the 16th century) by a lane crossing a branch-stream at Wyke Bridge,[22] or from North Oxford by a footpath across Port Meadow. From the Green a lane running north-westwards, laid out in 1821 to replace an earlier field-path,[23] provides the only access to St. Margaret's chapel. For modern visitors it is a place of almost perfect seclusion, disturbed only by the traffic on the western bypass.

In the middle ages Binsey may have been much less remote. Until the 18th century, the normal routes into Oxford from Eynsham and the Berkshire villages around the foot of Wytham Hill crossed the Seacourt and Shire Lake streams near the chapel. One came by the now-deserted village of Seacourt, which Anthony Wood believed to have been 'a thorough fare towne from Einsham and the westerne parts to Oxon (long before the other way by Botley was thought upon)', with a bridge at the crossing of the Seacourt stream indicated by stones 'lying in great abundance in the river'.[24] Thomas Hearne wrote of Seacourt in

---

[17] Wood, *City*, ii, 42–3.
[18] *Cal. Close Rolls* 1374–7, 48.
[19] *V.C.H.Oxon.* iv, 271.
[20] See also Ibid. 268–9.
[21] Geological Survey Map 1", drift, sheet 236 (1972 edn.). The 1982 edition of this map shows the gravel island as much smaller, but observations of natural gravel at several points within the enclosed area indicate that the earlier map is more correct.
[22] *V.C.H.Oxon.* iv, 284, 268.
[23] Ibid.
[24] Wood, *City*, i, 324–5 (with editorial note that 'the ruins of this bridge are still seen in the water, 1888').

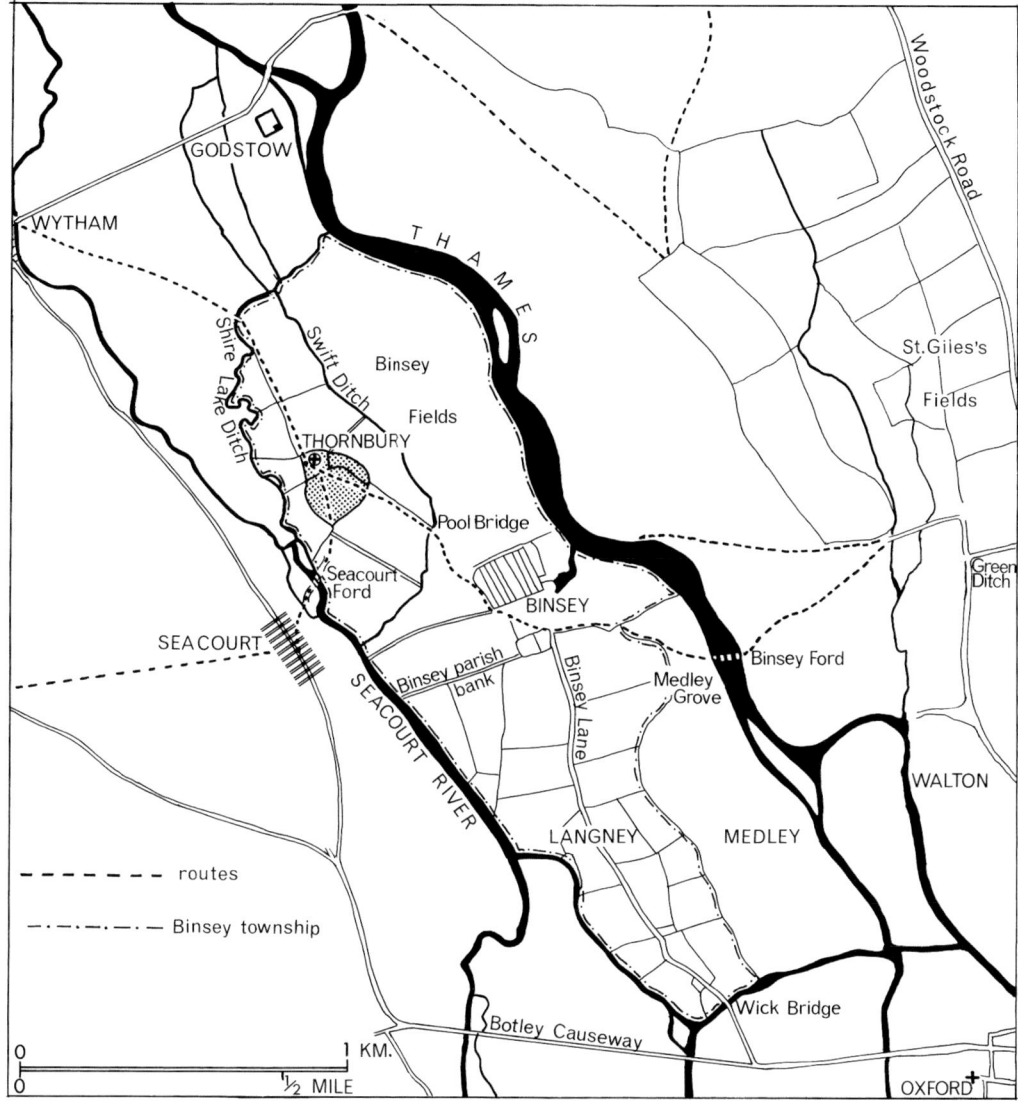

Fig. 1. Sketch-map of the environs of Thornbury, incorporating detail from the 18th-century maps (Christ Church Maps Binsey 1 and 2). The paths across Port Meadow are as shown on Cole's map of 1695 (Bodl. (E)70 Oxford (121)).

1728: 'The highway passed through it, and so over the water through Binsey Ford, and so to Oxford. There is a hardway now to be seen, and at Binsey the said way (which comes over the ... [Seacourt stream]) is called in one or two Places the King's Swarth.'[25] Prior Robert must have had this in mind when he pictured distraught suppliants from Seacourt crossing the river and beating on Frideswide's door at Binsey.[26]

---

[25] *Hearne's Collections,* ix (O.H.S. lxv, 1914), 399.
[26] Above, p.41.

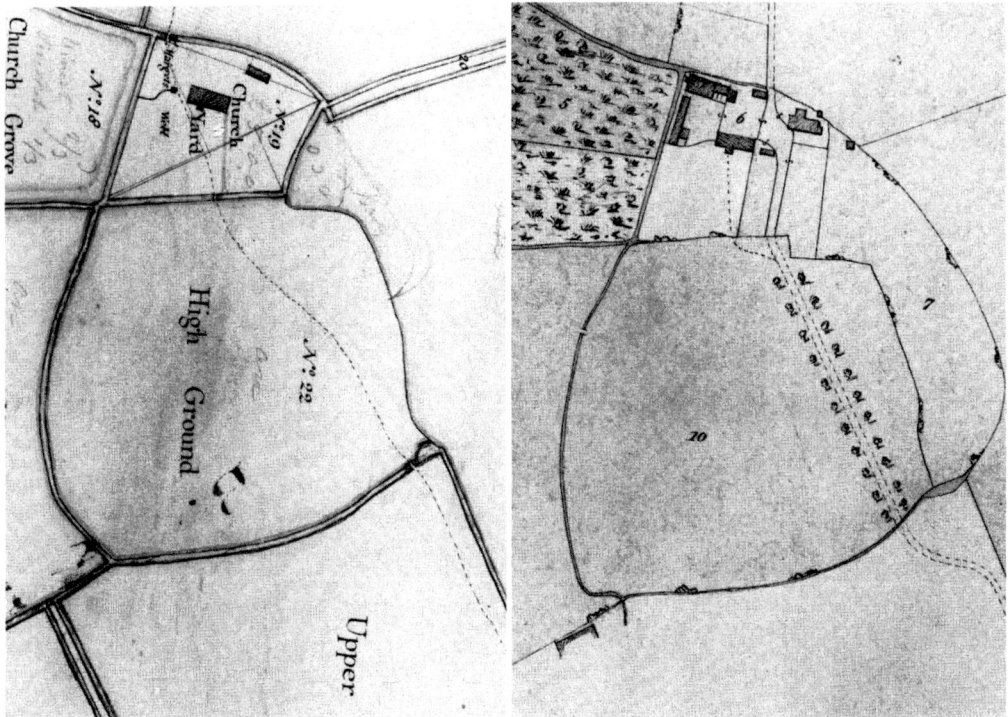

Fig. 2. Thornbury in 1792 and *c*.1850 (Christ Church Maps Binsey 2 and 5).

A more northerly route from Wytham was used by Hearne in 1716: 'From Wightham I went to Oxford by Binsey. But the Bridge, before we come to Binsey, being broke down lately by some Young Scholars ... I was forced to be carried over upon a Man's Back. I stop'd in Binsey Church Yard on purpose to read the Inscriptions.'[27] This route appears on a map of 1792 (Fig. 2): a footpath runs north-westwards from Binsey Green, over Swift Ditch at Pool Bridge, into the graveyard, between the chapel and well, and across the N. boundary ditch of the graveyard by a small bridge; from there it continues northwards to meet Shire Lake Ditch (presumably where the bridge had been broken by the 'young scholars'), and its onwards direction is labelled 'to Wytham'. At one point S.E. of the chapel, this line is still marked by a hollow-way (Fig. 4).

The most direct line to Seacourt from Binsey Green would run due W., avoiding the chapel; but the road did not in fact follow it. In 1783, Thomas Warton described what he imagined to be a minor Roman road:[28]

> [It] perceptibly slants from the brow of Shotover-hill near Oxford, down its northern declivity; bisects Marston-lane, crosses the Charwell north of Holywell-church with a stone-pavement, is then called KING'S SWATH, or Way, goes over saint Giles's field, and Port-meadow, has an apparent trajectus over the Isis, now called Binsey-ford, being a few yards north of Medley-grove, runs through Binsey church-yard, in which are the signatures of large buildings, winds up the hill towards the left, where stood the antient village of Seckworth [i.e. Seacourt] ... ; and from thence either proceeds to Gloucester, or falls into the AKEMAN about Witney.

---

[27] *Hearne's Collections*, v (O.H.S. xlii, 1901), 188–9.
[28] T. Warton, *Specimen of a History of Oxfordshire: Kiddington* (2nd edn., 1783), 57n.

The only possible interpretation of this account is that the Seacourt road from Binsey Green was identical with the Wytham road as far as the graveyard, and then turned sharply south-westwards to enter Seacourt on its N.E. side. Archaeological support for this circuitous route comes from the excavations at Seacourt in 1958–9, which identified a track and sunken way fording the river and entering the village in exactly the position required. From there the road would have continued up Seacourt Hill to join the Eynsham coach-road 1 km. W. of Seacourt.[29]

The road E. from Binsey Green across Port Meadow, which formed the main approach to Oxford via the Woodstock Road, seems to have continued as a through-route towards Shotover. It was evidently known both at Binsey and in St. Giles's Fields as the 'King's swath' (i.e. 'way' or 'track'), and may have been identical with the 'green ditch' (now St. Margaret's Road) which formed the N. boundary of the City liberty.[30]

Far from being isolated, Binsey chapel stood at a junction of routes between Oxford, Wytham and Seacourt. The late medieval traveller from Oxford or Headington to Eynsham, Witney or Bampton would have passed the chapel and well (perhaps actually between them), and would have deviated from the shortest route in order to do so. This accords ill with Prior Robert's description of *Thornbiri* as *solitarius*; it may be that the road via the chapel was established in the 12th century or later as a consequence of the cult, replacing a more direct route from Seacourt to Binsey Green along 'Binsey parish bank'.[31]

THE CHAPEL AND WELL

The chapel and graveyard, together with the farmhouse to the N.E. and farm buildings to the N., occupy a rectilinear enclosure (Figs. 2–4) defined by wide boundary ditches (noted by Hearne in 1718).[32] The site has all the appearance of a moated manor-house, and must surely represent the establishment of the later medieval canons. A 'court' with the chapel and well is pictured in the 15th-century metrical Life of St. Frideswide:[33]

> *Thre ȝer with hir' felawes. heo bilevede there,*
> *And to servy Ihesu Crist. a chapel heo let rere.*
> *Ther is ȝut a vair court. and a chirche vair and suete,*
> *Arered in honour of hir'. and of S' Margarete.*
> *..................*
> *So sprong ther up awel vair welle. crer inouȝ and clene.*
> *That fond hem alle water inouȝ. that hi ne dorste noȝt hem bymene.*
> *That biside the chirche ȝut is. alute in the west side,*
> *That mony man hath bote ido. and that many man sech' wide.*

The chapel itself is a simple rectangular building, its earliest datable features the S. door and porch of *c*.1180–1200.[34] Irregularities in the external face of the N. wall suggest that the present square E. end may have replaced an apse, which implies a date rather earlier than the late 12th century for the oldest standing fabric. Fifteenth-century glass in the

---

[29] M. Biddle, 'The Deserted Medieval Village of Seacourt, Berkshire', *Oxoniensia*, xxvi/xxvii (1961/2), 75, 77 n.35, 78 and n.44, Pl.IIA.
[30] For the crossing from Binsey to Port Meadow, and its use by Binsey commoners, see *V.C.H. Oxon.* iv, 281–2. The main medieval exit from the Meadow on the Oxford side was not, as now, at Walton Well Road, but at Brooman's well near the line of Green ditch (Ibid.). The names 'King's swath' and 'Green ditch' both suggest a track running along a grassy baulk.
[31] So named on the early 18th-century map (Christ Church Maps Binsey I).
[32] *Hearne's Collections*, vi (O.H.S. xliii, 1902), 264; *Guilielmi Neubrigensis Historia*, ed. T. Hearne, iii (1719), 762.
[33] Bodl. MS Ashmole 43 ff.156ᵛ–157.
[34] *R.C.H.M. Oxford*, 148; *V.C.H.Oxon.* iv, 271.

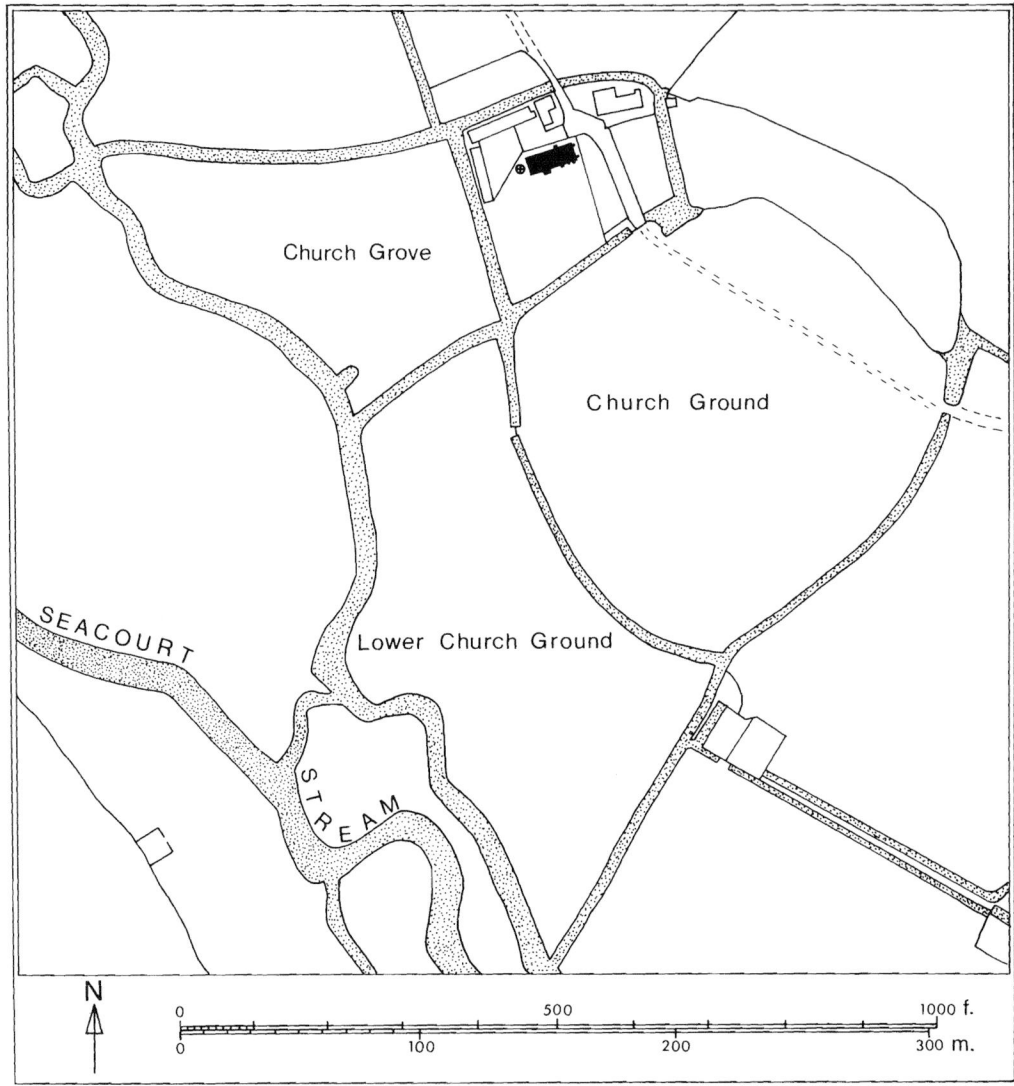

Fig. 3. Thornbury in the late 19th century (after O.S. 25" 1st edn.).

E. window may include fragmentary figures of St. Margaret and St. Frideswide;[35] Wood believed that the tabernacle in the S. wall of the chancel contained Frideswide's image, with the pavement before it worn hollow by 'those superstitious people that came somtimes barefoot to this place, using cringes and adorations on their knees.'[36]

Wood also notes an 'old and small building joyning to the north side of the chapple', which 'doth [not resemble] (as formerly it did) a court'; in another place he describes it as a 'house with arched windowes and arched dore, joyning to Binsey Chapel, pulled downe

---

[35] Cf P.A. Newton (ed.), *Corpus Vitrearum Medii Aevi: the County of Oxford* (1979), 35–7.
[36] Wood, *City,* ii, 43; cf. Ibid. i, 578.

July 1678'.[37] In 1718 Hearne wrote: 'tho' there be no Houses now by the Chapell, yet in those Times [i.e. Frideswide's] there were several .... I have heard of Foundations of Buildings which confirm this Assertion';[38] Warton saw 'signatures of large buildings' in the churchyard in 1783 (above, p.62). The windowless N. wall of the chapel, with various joints and scars still visible in its outer face, suggests that buildings were indeed 'joined' to it. The traditions of the place, the residence there of regular canons, and Wood's use of the word 'court' (by which he probably meant 'courtyard' or 'cloister') all suggest the possibility of a simplified claustral layout, created perhaps in the 12th century.

The well is, as noted by Wood, 'at the west end of this chappel about three yards distant',[39] though now in a Victorian setting. According to Wood it was 'almost to the last frequented by superstitious people, and especially about 100 years before the dessolution. Soe much that they were forced to enclose it (as in old time before, they had defended it) with a little house of stone over it, with a lock and a dore to it'.[40] This building had 'on the front the picture of St. Margaret (or perhaps of St. Frideswyde)', and was pulled down in 1639; by Wood's time the well was 'overgrowne with nettles and other weeds and harbouring froggs snails and vermin'.[41] Wood probably knew the characteristics of late Perpendicular architecture, so his description suggests that the well-house was indeed of the late 15th or early 16th century.

THE OVAL EARTHWORK ENCLOSURE (FIGS. 2–4)

A large, roughly oval area defined by narrow drainage ditches, with Binsey chapel and graveyard on its N.W. perimeter, appears on estate maps of 1792 and *c.*1850 (Christ Church Maps Binsey 2 and 5) and on late 19th-century Ordnance Survey maps. On the S.W. and S.E. sides of the enclosure the ditches were filled in during the 1960s, but the boundary remains conspicuous as a spread and eroded bank now *c.*15–20 metres wide, standing well above the low-lying field on the S.W., with traces of a ditch around its outer side.

There are no clear remains of the bank on the N. and E. sides of the enclosure, and its position must be inferred from field-boundaries. Skirting the area around the N.E. are two curving ditch-lines, either of which may reflect the original perimeter. The outer ditch is rather more substantial, and connects the two straight field-ditches which drain into the Shire Lake ditch on the N.W. and the S.W. The 1792 map creates an unfortunate ambiguity (Fig. 2): the outer ditch is omitted from the scale drawing in ink, but is indicated by a very sketchy pencil line. An early 19th-century copy of this map (Christ Church Map Binsey 3) also shows the ditch in pencil, but much more clearly and accurately, the area enclosed by it being labelled 'garden'. The only other boundary which the 1792 map treats in this way is the wall dividing the graveyard from the farm to its N.E. The ditch looks most unlike a 19th-century boundary, and if the pencil lines are intended to record changes after 1792 it is odd that none of the other new inclosures are shown in this way. It is therefore a reasonable hypothesis, though no more, that the ditch was omitted accidentally by the original surveyor and added as a correction.

---

[37] Ibid. i, 329, 324n; cf ibid. i, 577, 578 and ii, 42.
[38] *Guil.Neub.* op.cit. note 32, iii, 757–8.
[39] Wood, *City,* i, 323.
[40] Ibid. 328–9. Cf ibid. 577: 'The inhabitants here will tell you that there have bin many miracles wrought at this well and people hung up their crutches.'
[41] Ibid. 324n, 329.

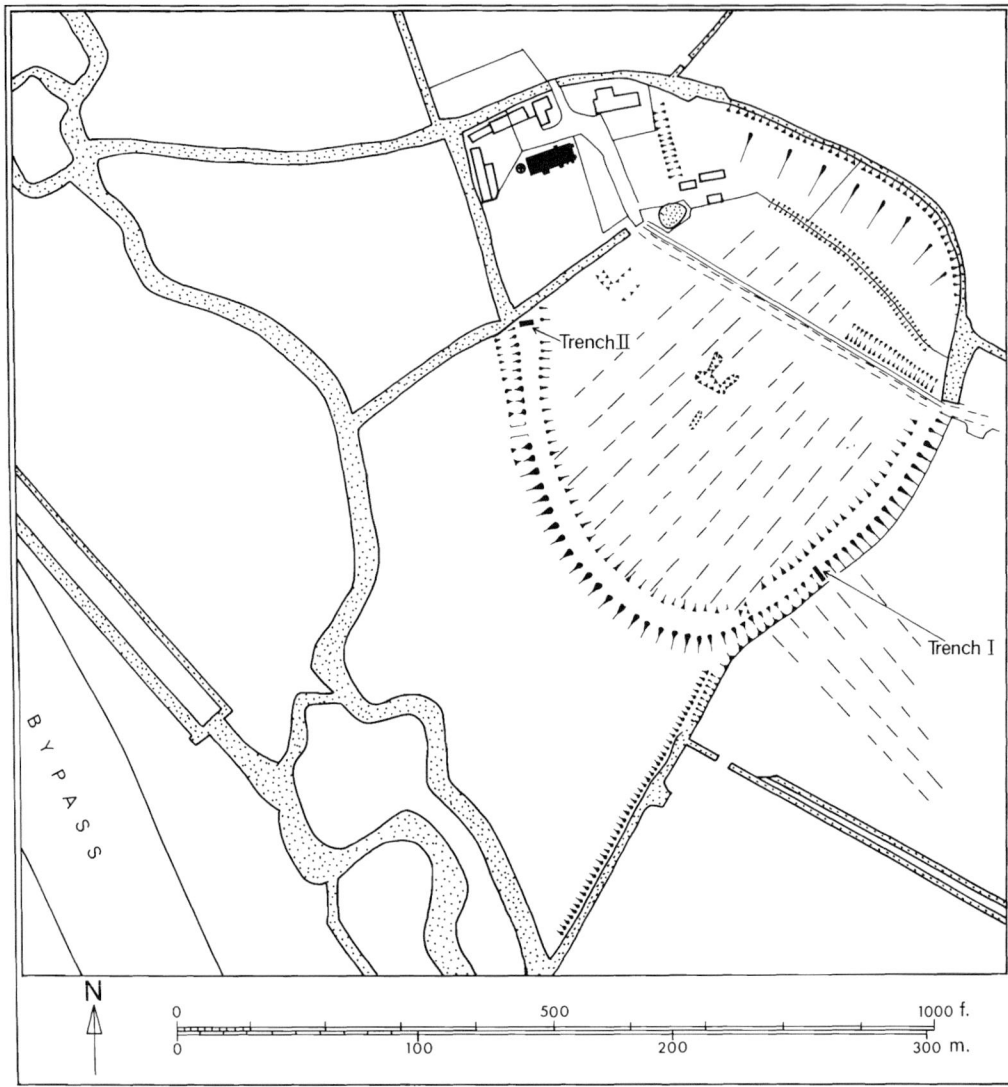

Fig. 4. Thornbury: earthworks as remaining in 1987.

This interpretation of the map evidence suggests the reconstruction shown in Fig. 5A: a large oval enclosure with the rectilinear moated area containing the chapel and farm superimposed on its N.W. sector, the original perimeter ditch having presumably been straightened out to form the N. and W. sides of the moat. Fig. 5B shows the alternative reconstruction, required if the 1792 map is accepted as reliable: a smaller oval excluding the chapel enclosure, which appears as a later addition to its N. side. Further excavation is needed to decide between these alternatives.

Ridge-and-furrow, crossed by the 1821 path to the chapel, occupies much of the interior. The hollow-way of the old road to Binsey Green only survives to the S.E., beyond the limits of the ridge-and-furrow (Fig. 4); the obliteration of the rest by ploughing had probably occurred by 1792, when the route was a mere footpath across the field (Fig. 2).

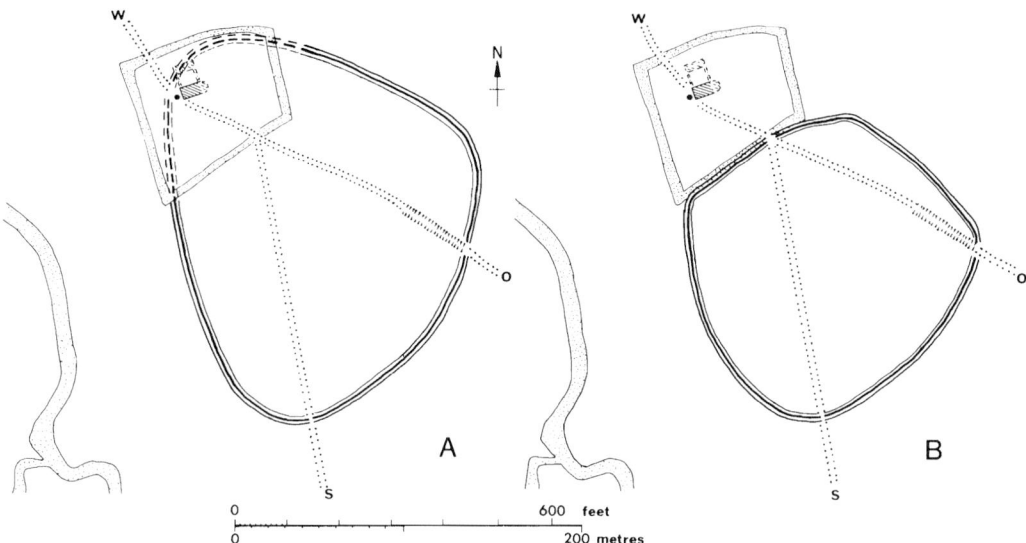

Fig. 5. Thornbury: alternative reconstructions of the early enclosure and routes leading into it. (W Wytham, S = Seacourt, O = Oxford.)

THE EXCAVATION

Trench I (Fig. 6)

A trench 7.5 by 1.5 m. was excavated on the S.E. perimeter of the enclosure (see Fig. 4), bisecting the course of the field-ditch shown on the first edition of the 25" O.S. map. The outer edge of the present low bank proved to overlie a sequence of shallow, gravel-cut ditches, evidently moving progressively outwards from the interior of the enclosure, and a phase possibly involving a stone wall. Successive layers sloping down from the inner (N.W.) end of the trench are interpreted as bank material, and the existence of substantial, continuously eroding banks seems the most likely explanation for the outwards advance of the ditch line.

The first ditch contained fill layers of grey clayey gravel (L11c) and dark-grey silt (L11b). A grass-tempered sherd lay on the clean ditch floor under L11c, securely sealed by the clayey gravel; L11b contained a sandy sherd. A wedge of dark-grey silt (L9c), left isolated by the cutting of the second and third ditches, is likely to have been part of the fill of the first ditch and identical with L11 b, though it could also be interpreted as the

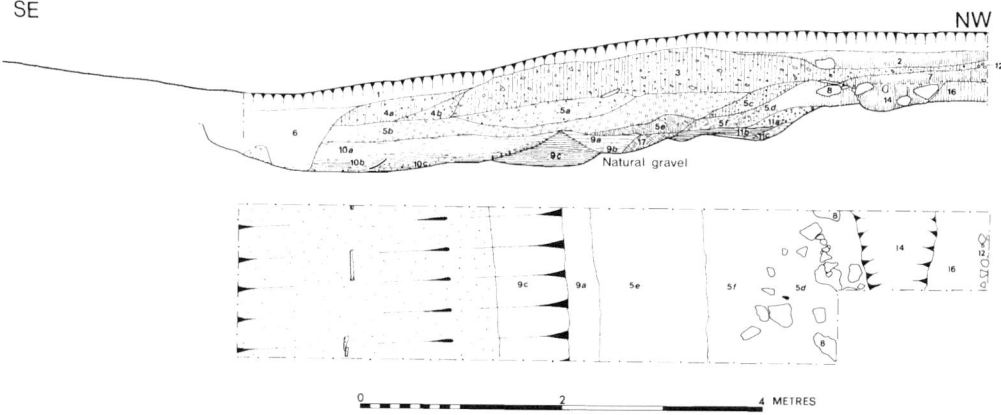

Fig. 6. Thornbury, Trench I, plan and S.W. section.

fill of an independent re-cut. Layers of brown sandy gravel (L11a) and sticky brown clay (L5f) overlay L11b. A deposit of brown silty clay loam with manganese flecking (L5d) formed an ambiguous interface with L5f, but certainly overlay LL11a–c. L16 was identical with L5d and may have been part of the same layer, though it could also be interpreted as old ground-surface (L5d being the same material redeposited). Bedded in L5d were two rows of small blocks of corallian ragstone rubble (F8, F12), running on the alignment of the ditch, which might have been the remains of a footing. A grass-tempered sherd was found among the stones of F8. Under L5d, a small patch of orange-brown subsoil (L13) survived on the inner (N.W.) lip of the ditch, showing that the natural surface of the gravel was intact at this end of the section. LL5d/16 and F8 were cut by a pit (FI4), perhaps created by robbing of the footing, containing brown silty clay loam (L7) and several stone lumps, and were overlain by a layer of brown silt loam with $c.40\%$ gravel (L5c); one sandy sherd was found in F14, and bones (7 cattle, 1 sheep or goat) in L7.

TABLE 1: RADIOCARBON DETERMINATIONS

Site Reference	Harwell Reference	Years b.p.	Calibrated ranges (data of Stuiuer & Reimer 1.986)	
			68% confidence	95% confidence
L32	Har-8921	1740±90	AD 190–390	AD 80–530
L10c	Har-8922	220±60	–	–
L5a	Har-8923	960±70	AD 1000–1140	AD 900–1220
L3	Har-8935	590±90	AD 1290–1430	AD 1260–1470

The surviving stratigraphy left the order of the second and third ditches uncertain, but the outermost, which was evidently open into modern times, must be the later of the two. What is therefore interpreted as the second ditch cut L11b, L9c and L5f. It had fill layers (involving at least one re-cut) of grey silty gravel (L17), grey silt with preserved organic material (LL9a–b), and brown silty clay loam (L5e); there were bones in L9b (2 cattle, 1 pig) and 5e (1 horse, 3 probably cattle).

The third ditch, which cut L9c, contained fill layers of very dark-grey silt with preserved organic material (LL10c–b), and grey silt with $c.3\%$ gravel (L10a). L10c contained bones (2 of cattle and 5 of cattle or horse, mostly butchered or dog-gnawed), some lying on the bottom of the ditch; this material produced a radiocarbon date of AD 1670–1790, indicating that the third ditch remained open until the 18th century.

Over L5c, L9a, L5e and L10a were layers of brown clay with yellowish-brown mottling (L5b) and light-grey silty clay with $c.3\%$ gravel (L5a), possibly derived from the slighting and spreading-out of the bank in the 18th or 19th century. A bank of brown silt loam with $c.50\%$ gravel (L3), containing limestone rubble and large pebbles, overlay L5b, L5a and L7; it produced 3 sheep or goat and 2 dog bones. Calibrated radiocarbon dates were obtained from bone material in L5a (AD 900–1220) and L3 (AD 1260–1470) (Table 1). It is possible that the high proportion of rubble in this deposit represents the robbing of a substantial footing (i.e. F8) incorporated in the pre-existing bank.

Later layers (L2, L4a–b) contained modern pottery, as did a final re-digging of the boundary as a narrow field-ditch (F6). The topsoil (L1) post-dated the filling-in of this ditch during the 20th century.

Trench II (Fig. 7)

A trench 5.0 by 1.5 m. was excavated on the W. perimeter of the enclosure (see Fig. 4), bisecting the bank just inside the line of the late field-ditch. This revealed a sequence of boundary features comparable to those in Tr. I, except that the outermost and latest major ditch lay outside the trench area.

The earliest ditch was shallow, flat-bottomed, and cut the natural gravel. A straight baulk of gravel $c.0.8$ m. wide (F37), running transverse to the axis of the ditch, had been left standing proud from the ditch bottom;

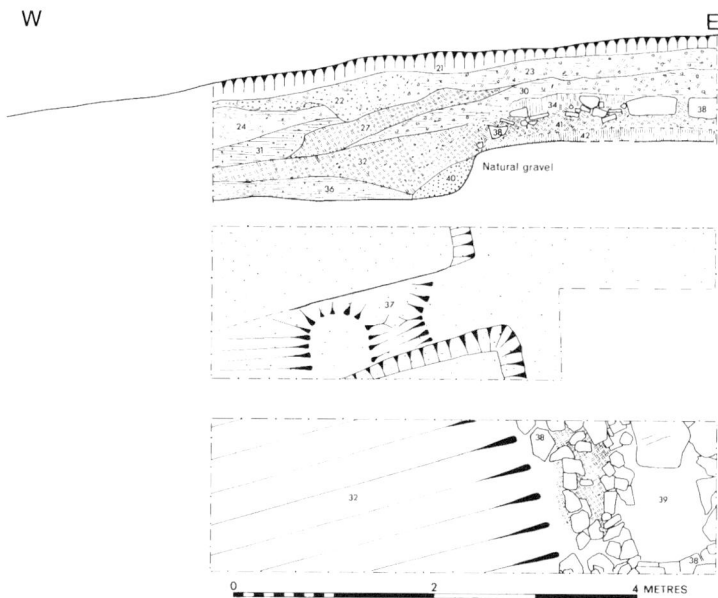

Fig. 7. Thornbury, Trench II, plans and N. section.

this is interpreted as a boundary between two work-gangs. On the E. side of the ditch, a layer of buff clay loam of ashy appearance with many flecks of charcoal and burnt daub (L42) may represent an old ground-surface. The ditch contained three successive fill-layers: redeposited gravel (L40) against the inner slope, perhaps the product of rapid erosion; dark blue-grey silt with $c.6\%$ gravel, flecks of burnt daub and organic material (L36); and sticky yellow-brown clay interspersed with small lenses of gravel and loam (L32), containing flecks of burnt daub and a group of bones (1 human humerus fragment; 11 bones and 3 teeth of horses, from at least two individuals aged 4+ years, all dog-gnawed; 1 cattle bone). The horse bones, which were a homogeneous group, produced a calibrated radiocarbon date of AD 80–530 (Table 1).

A deposit of grey-brown clay with flecks of burnt daub (L41), overlying L42, formed an interface with L32. Bedded in L41 was a footing of corallian ragstone rubble (F38), surviving to a height of between one and three courses (Fig. 8). It was built mainly of small stones bonded with clean blue clay, but included two large blocks. At the core of the footing was a sub-rectangular void, the fill of which (L39) was identical with the underlying L42.

Unfortunately the relationship between the first ditch and the footing could not be established, since the interface between L32 and L41 left the sequence of these layers ambiguous. One possible interpretation is that L41 cut L32 – in other words, that the wall was built after the first ditch had silted up. But the reverse sequence is also possible: the first ditch could have been dug up against the face of an already-existing wall, removing all trace of older ditches associated with it. This is a major difficulty which can only be resolved by further excavation.

Over the footing F38 were a patch of ashy grey loam with burnt daub flecks (L34), a dump of rubble (F35), and then a slump-layer of red-brown silt loam containing gravelly patches and numerous lumps of burnt daub (L30), which also overlay L32. Two layers overlying the downwards slope of L30 are best ascribed to successive ditch phases: blue-grey clay with numerous red daub flecks (L27), and gravelly buff-grey clay silt (L31). A layer of red-brown silt loam containing many large lumps of burnt daub (L23), virtually identical with L30, overlay L30 and L27; cutting its surface was a post-hole (F26) of $c.30$ cm. diameter and $c.20$ cm. deep, with three packing-stones and a light-brown clay fill. L23 was truncated at its lower end by another probable ditch cut, with fills of brown clay silt (L24) and gravelly buff-yellow clay silt (L22); L24 produced a whetstone fragment. The topsoil (L21) contained modern pottery.

INTERPRETATION OF THE EXCAVATED EVIDENCE

The potsherd sealed by the fill of the primary ditch in Tr. I (L11c) is probably 5th- or 6th-century (below, p.71); it is thus not wholly incompatible with the radiocarbon date-range from bones in the fill of the primary ditch in Tr. II (L32): AD 190–390 at 68 per cent confidence, or AD 80–530 at 95 per cent confidence. It is therefore a reasonable hypothesis that the ditch was dug, or was still being kept clean, in the sub-Roman or early Anglo-Saxon period, though the material in L11c provides little more than a *terminus post quem* for the silting-up of the ditch. But whereas the possible footing in Tr. I (F8) definitely post-dated the primary ditch, the relationship between the footing in Tr. II (F38) and the primary ditch there was ambiguous. It remains perfectly possible (assuming no connection between F8 and F38) that the rampart and ditch were both in origin Iron Age, the latter being scoured out in the early Anglo-Saxon period, or that an early Anglo-Saxon ditch was dug against the face of an Iron Age rampart. Alternatively, F8 and F38 could both belong to a rampart post-dating the filling of the primary ditch. The likelihood of an Anglo-Saxon presence on the site is in all cases strong, and is strengthened by the fact that all four potsherds recovered are of that date.

The construction of the footing or revetment has some distinctive features. The portion of F38 within the area of Tr. II comprised a much-damaged outer face towards the ditch, and the four inner faces of the box-like cavity at the core of the wall. The outer face included five small stones in line, which were in-set in relation to the larger blocks surviving at the two sections and should probably therefore be interpreted as a second row from which larger facing-stones had been robbed away. Assuming that the inwards-facing skin

Fig. 8. Thornbury, Trench II: stone footing (F38), looking N.

of walling (mainly outside the trench area) was of similar width to that on the ditch side, the total thickness of the wall at its base would have been some 2.2m. The filling of the cavity (L39) was identical to the underlying layer (L42), and may have originated as turves cut from the ground-surface. Unless the cavity is an abnormality it must be concluded that this massive footing consisted of two parallel faces, linked by transverse walls set at *c.*1.5m. centres, with the voids filled with earth or turves. There is no evidence that the stone facing continued to a significant height above ground-level (indeed, the general lack of rubble in later ditch-fills suggests that it did not); a timber-revetted bank on a stone footing is perhaps more likely. Finally, the burnt daub spread through nearly all layers and features in Tr. II deserves comment. The material might derive from the firing of a timber-laced rampart, though the burning of scrub on an old ground-surface would have similar results.

THE POTTERY BY MAUREEN MELLOR

Four early Saxon sherds were excavated. Two, from L11b and F14, were in predominantly sandy fabrics (fabric III); the other two, from L11c and F8, were grass-tempered (fabric IV) and possibly from one pot, with the same admixture of other detritus and laminated in the same way. The grass-tempered sherd in F8, from the shoulder of a large burnished storage-jar, was decorated with a raised band between two rows of small dots. A similar vessel with the same style of decoration was found in a sunken-feature building at Barrow Hills near Abingdon,[42] though its fabric was predominantly sandy and it was exceptionally well-made, possibly being finished on a slow wheel. The Barrow Hills example came from what is believed to be the early focus of the site, possibly 5th-century; this context produced little or no organic-tempered material, however, and the Binsey sherd may be rather later, perhaps 6th century. Grass-tempered pottery is also reported from the nearby deserted village site of Seacourt.[43]

CONCLUSIONS

The name recorded as *Thornbiri* comprises the elements *þorn* and *burh,* 'thorn' and 'fortified place';[44] it would be perverse to suggest that the 'thorn-grown fortress' was anything other than the oval defensive enclosure identified in 1987–8. It remains to consider what the *burh* actually was, and what its discovery contributes to our understanding of St. Frideswide's legend.

The best local parallels for the shape and location of the enclosure are Iron Age, and while the stratigraphical and radiocarbon evidence does not especially support such a date, it certainly does not exclude it.[45] The long island of gravel within the floodplain immediately E. of Binsey church and adjacent to the present main stream of the river has revealed cropmarks of ring ditches, pit alignments and enclosures of Bronze Age, Iron Age and probably Roman date,[46] and fieldwalking by David Wilson has produced Iron Age and Roman pottery.[47] Small late Bronze Age to Iron Age valley forts, on both the floodplain and the terrace-edge, can almost be described as a feature of the Upper Thames

---

[42] No. 185, Fig. 16 from SFB F3307, Fabric 24; typescript at Oxford Archaeological Unit.

[43] Not published; pers. comm. M. Biddle. (These sherds have not been located among the Seacourt material in the Ashmolean. I am grateful to Arthur Macgregor for his help with this.)

[44] The final element is undoubtedly *burh* (Margaret Gelling, pers. comm. 1987); the etymology 'thorn-tree hill' proposed in *Place-Names Oxon.* i, 26 was based on the 1293 spelling *Thorneberg,* the earliest form then available.

[45] This paragraph is based entirely on material supplied by George Lambrick, who has in preparation a more detailed discussion of valley-forts in the Upper Thames.

[46] P.P. Rhodes, 'New Archaeological Sites at Binsey and Port Meadow, Oxford', *Oxoniensia,* xiv (1949), 81–4.

[47] Pers.comm. D. Wilson esq.

basin, Thornbury being potentially the seventh such site to be identified.[48] The footing of 'box' construction would be appropriate in an Iron Age context: the forts at Cherbury and Bladon had stone revetments, in the case of Bladon with a soil infill.[49] The burnt material found distributed through all layers in Tr. II may be significant in this context: evidence of extensive burning on Iron Age defensive enclosures is common in southern England,[50] and has been identified locally at Bladon, Cherbury and Burroway.[51] Burroway had a timber 'box' rampart with soil infill, fired during the burning episode, and a similar source is possible for the burnt clay at Binsey, where the absence of rubble in the ditch fills suggests that the rampart above foundation level was of timber rather than stone.

Alternatively, the fort could be sub-Roman or early Anglo-Saxon, and so far as it goes the very limited dating evidence supports this conclusion. The 5th- and early 6th-century colonisation of the Upper Thames must have involved the use of fortified places, and there seems a serious possibility that Thornbury was one of them.

Thus any religious occupation of the site may have involved re-using an already ancient fortress. It is worth notice in this context that *burh* has a well-attested secondary meaning of 'monastic enclosure'. Tetbury *(Tettan byrig)* occurs as *Tettan monasterium* in the late 7th century, and Westbury-on-Trym *(Uuestburg)* as *Westmynster* in 804.[52] It seems likely that many *-burh* placenames denote monastic sites, especially those compounded with female names; an example not far afield is Bibury ('Beage's monastery'?), where five hides were leased to the thegn Leppa and his daughter Beage in 718×45.[53] The first element *porn* would be apposite to this meaning if it denoted not a cover of undergrowth but an enclosing hedge, such as the 'great thorn hedge' which surrounded St. Wilfred's monastery at Oundle.[54]

It could be argued that such parallels are made superfluous by the archaeological evidence, which suggests that the earthwork, whether Iron Age, sub-Roman or early Anglo-Saxon, was at all events in existence before St. Frideswide's time. But the 'monastic' usage of the term is important as a reflection of the fact that Iron-Age and Dark-Age forts, like Roman walled enclosures, were places normally and naturally selected for the new monasteries of the 7th and 8th centuries. Many early English minsters were *burga* in the sense of being pre-Anglo-Saxon fortified places, such as the Iron Age hillforts enclosing minster churches at Aylesbury and Hanbury.[55] If Thornbury was still a conspicuous earthwork it would have been a prime candidate for monastic re-use, especially perhaps as a cell or retreat-house dependent on the main monastery at Oxford.[56]

Finally, the possibility remains that the stratified material is residual, and that Thornbury was constructed at the outset as an Anglo-Saxon monastic enclosure. Since this category of site has received little archaeological notice it is hard to find close parallels, but enclosures of a similar general shape and size can be identified surrounding known minster churches.[57]

---

[48] The others are Salmondsbury, Burroway, Cherbury, Cassington, Dyke Hills and ?Goring.
[49] R. Ainslie, 'Bladon Round Castle, 1987', *South Midlands Archaeology (CBA Group 9 Newsletter)*, xviii (1988), 94.
[50] R.J. Bradley, *The Social Foundations of Prehistoric Britain* (1984), 134–6.
[51] G.H. Lambrick, 'Clanfield, Burroway', *South Midlands Archaeology (CBA Group 9 Newsletter)*, xiv (1984), 104–5; Ainslie op. cit. note 49.
[52] For the examples in this sentence and the next, with others, see F.M. Stenton, 'The Place of Women in Anglo-Saxon Society', in *Preparatory to Anglo-Saxon England* (1970), 320–1.
[53] W. de G. Birch, *Cartularium Saxonicum*, i (1885), No. 166.
[54] Eddius Stephanus, *Vita Wilfridi*, ch. 67.
[55] For these and other examples see J. Blair, 'Minster Churches in the Landscape' in D. Hooke (ed.), *Anglo-Saxon Settlements* (1988), 41–7; D. Hooke, *The Anglo-Saxon Landscape: the Kingdom of the Hwicce* (1985), 219, 91.
[56] As argued above, p.22.
[57] Cf. the examples illustrated in Blair, op. cit. note 55, Fig. 2.3. Other cases are Bampton, Oxon. (J. Blair in *South Midlands Archaeology*, xviii (1988),90, Fig. 1) and Tetbury, Glos. (*V.C.H. Glos.* xi, 260).

From the written legends and traditions, centuries later than Frideswide's time, the existence of an early monastic settlement at Binsey can only be inferred as a tenuous possibility. The importance of the newly-discovered earthwork is that its evidence, so independent and so different, points in the same direction: Binsey chapel stands in just the kind of place that mid-Saxon monastic founders did in fact favour. Any further advances must be through archaeology, following the leads suggested by the scraps of pottery in the ditches and the 8th-century *sceat* found somewhere nearby.[58] An extensive excavation within the earthwork might add significantly to our knowledge of the Oxford region in both the Iron Age and the Anglo-Saxon period.

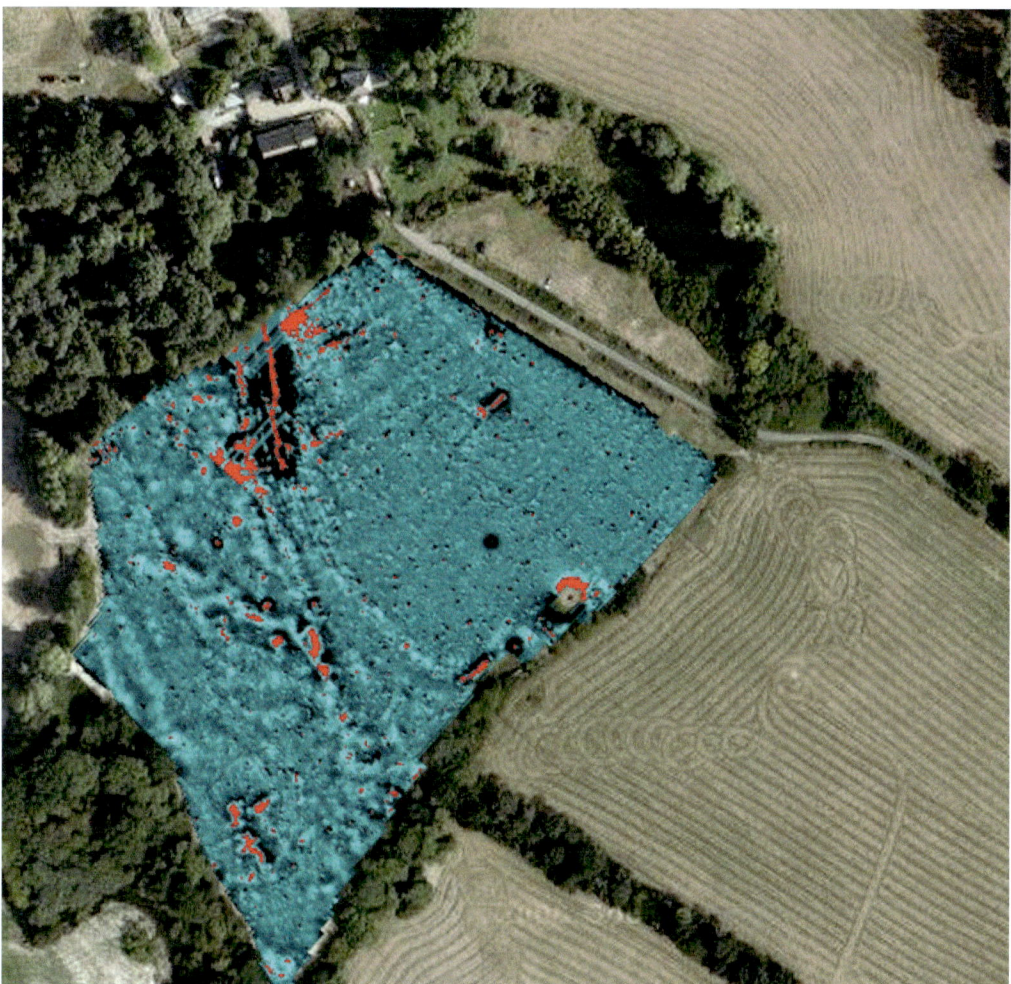

Fig. 9. Thornbury, Binsey: magnetometry survey by Roger Ainslie, 2008, clarifying some details of the 1987 survey. The anomalies in the western area probably indicate extensive earlier burning through which the the earthwork was dug, thus explaining the burnt daub encountered in Trench II.

---

[58] Above, p.22.

Author's Addendum, 2014

During the twenty-eight years since I wrote this study, a great deal of work has appeared on Anglo-Saxon England, including some important publications on Oxford and Oxfordshire. The following brief bibliography supplements the older works cited in the footnotes:

For the general context of seventh- and eighth-century royal nunneries, see: Barbara Yorke, *Nunneries and the Anglo-Saxon Royal Houses* (2003); Sarah Foot, *Veiled Women* (2000); John Blair, *The Church in Anglo-Saxon Society* (Oxford, 2005), especially pp.84-91.

For Oxford and its minster, see: John Blair, *Anglo-Saxon Oxfordshire* (Stroud, 1994), pp.52-68, 87-92; Anne Dodd (ed.), *Oxford Before the University* (2003). William of Malmesbury's brief account now exists in a new edition: *William of Malmesbury, Gesta Pontificum Anglorum*, eds. M. Wintertbottom and R.M. Thomson, (2007), I, pp.478-81, II, pp.230-1. The late 1980s saw intensive study of the site and buildings of Oxford Cathedral, including excavations; these were published in a special issue of *Oxoniensia* (53, 1988), and re-printed as J. Blair (ed.), *St Frideswide's Monastery at Oxford: Archaeological and Architectural Studies* (Gloucester, 1990). Further archaeology has strengthened the hypotheses about the origins of the minster proposed above, both in identifying a late seventh-century female burial near the present cathedral choir, and in confirming that St Aldate's was a significant late Anglo-Saxon church: see A. Boyle, 'Excavations in Christ Church Cathedral Graveyard', *Oxoniensia*, 66 (2001).

For the minsters of Eynsham and Bampton, see: Susan Kelly, 'An Early Minster at Eynsham, Oxfordshire', in O.J. Padel and D.N. Parsons (eds.), *A Commodity of Good Names: Essays in Honour of Margaret Gelling* (2008), pp.79-85; Alan Hardy et al., *Ælfric's Abbey: Excavations at Eynsham Abbey, Oxfordshire, 1989-92* (Oxford, 2003); S. Townley (ed.), *Victoria County History of Oxfordshire XIII: Bampton Hundred Part 1* (Oxford, 1996); John Blair, `Holy Beams: Anglo-Saxon Cult Sites and the Place-Name Element *Bēam*', in M.D.J. Bintley and M.G.Shapland (eds.), *Trees and Timber in the Anglo-Saxon World* (Oxford, 2013), 186-210.

St. Frideswide's Binsey as Sacred Space

MARTIN HENIG

Binsey church stands today half a mile from its village, isolated from the restlessness of modern life and with only its ancient well and a farm-house beside it. A substantial ditch and in places a hedge surrounding the area reminds us of its earliest incarnation as *Thornbiri* (Thornbury), the secluded refuge of the virgin princess Frideswide.[1] Of course not everything is quite what it seems. The church which we now see dates no earlier than the twelfth century in its earliest fabric, and the well, albeit ancient in origin, has been thoroughly Victorianised. The 'humps and bumps' in the field beside the churchyard are probably the platforms of medieval houses dating from a time before the village migrated nearer the main channel of the Thames, in order to command the ferry crossing to Oxford. Throughout the medieval period, when the road from the west ran past the church, it was not nearly as remote as it is now. Indeed, even the modern tranquility of Binsey which sets it as a place apart, is easily shattered when the wind blows in the wrong direction and one becomes all too conscious of the traffic on the nearby Oxford by-pass.

And yet we are not wrong to see this churchyard as 'Sacred Space', one of the out-of-the-way places associated with quiet 'martyrs' of whom St Frideswide is a sterling example: saints who witnessed to the faith by confronting the demons in a desert of their own choosing rather than having been thrown to them by wicked men. In one sense the triumph of the church's patron, St Margaret of Antioch, over the forces of darkness is epitomized quite as much by her victory over the dragon (representing the devil) as it was by her subsequent execution during a Persecution of Christians. Margaret's votary Frideswide's rejection of the wicked advances of her unwelcome suitor the Mercian King Algar demands to be interpreted as her own triumph over evil sealed by her choice of holy virginity rather than that of worldly rule as a queen.[2] Whether Binsey, within its enclosure, was in fact St Frideswide's original monastic abode from whence she set out to found her major religious foundation on the site of present-day Christ Church, or whether it was rather her retreat from the busy world of her major foundation matters little, although in contrast to the Medieval life of St Frideswide and the schema for her history proposed by John Blair in this volume which sees her as Mercian I prefer to see her as a West Saxon princess. Binsey lies south of the Thames in what as historically ancient *Gewissean* (i.e. 'West Saxon') territory, and that might suggest that she originally lived here and that the monastery at St Frideswide's (Christchurch) at present-day Oxford was a West Saxon bridgehead into former Mercian lands. At least St Margaret's healing—i.e. 'treacle'—well, whose waters had such powerful therapeutic properties that they cured the now penitent Algar of his blindness, is at Binsey.

A section across the wide ditch part of which is still an impressive earthwork encircling the church and its associated buildings was excavated by John Blair, and has yielded a sherd of organic-grass-tempered pottery of early Anglo-Saxon date, perhaps as early as the sixth century. It is tempting to interpret it as a monastic *vallum* like that which can still be seen at St Columba's monastic settlement at Iona off the west coast of Scotland. Any remains

---

[1] Blair, *Thornbury, Binsey*, this volume.
[2] For the link between virginity and martyrdom see P. Brown, *The Body and Society. Men, Women, and Sexual Renunciation in Early Christianity* (New York 1988), 73–75, on Vibia Perpetua, martyred in Carthage in 203, after likewise confronting a dragon in a dream.

St Margaret's Church and Church Farm Cottage in 2008. (Russell Dewhurst)

of buildings of this time, very probably of flimsy materials (as it is surmised were those of the early monastery on Iona), would probably have been destroyed in the construction and later expansion of the church or are now inaccessible.[3] Some further excavation might be possible to define the nature of the early foundation here, which might well antedate Frideswide, but as so often with early Christian sites in Britain our conclusions are bound to be speculative.

Frideswide's England was still largely tribal. The break-up of the Roman provinces of *Britannia* in the fifth century into cantonal groupings resulted in a society which more largely mirrored those of the Iron Age centuries than the sophisticated centalised authority which Roman Britain at least purported to be. It was universally agreed until very recently that the major change in society was the result of the invasion or at least the massive infiltration from the Continent of peoples speaking Germanic languages, although recently suggestions have been made that the tribes of Eastern Britain (Caesar's *Belgae*), had been speaking Germanic dialects all along.[4] In that case Oxfordshire would have lain at or near the linguistic dividing line between the Brythonic (Celtic speaking) Dobunni (later the *Hwicce*) and the Atrebates, plausibly Belgic and ancestors of the Saxon *Gewissae*. The affiliations of the Catuvellauni might have been more mixed and, in any case, the political

---

[3] Blair, *Thornbury , Binsey*, this volume.

[4] M. Goormachtigh and A. Durham, 'Kentish place names – were they ever Celtic?', *Archaeologia Cantiana* 129 (2009), 279–93 argues from place-name evidence that Kent was part of the Belgic area speaking a Germanic dialect. Daphne Briggs has advanced the same opinion with regard to Iron Age Icenian coins from Norfolk cf D. Nash Briggs, 'The language of inscriptions on Icenian coinage' pp.83–102 in J.A. Davies, *The Iron Age in North East Anglia. New work in the land of the Iceni* (BAR Brit.ser.549, Oxford 2011).

complexion of myriad small polities in the region would have been very tangled indeed, with minor chieftains often owing allegiance to more powerful over-kings (such as the rulers of Mercia north of the Thames and of the *Gewissae* to the south).[5] All that we can ascertain of Frideswide was that she lived in the eighth century, and that she was the daughter of a minor king called Didan, both of whom were evidently Christians.[6] If I am right (contra Blair) we could see him ruling somewhere in the region of Dorchester on Thames perhaps.

If there were, in fact, no Anglo-Saxon invasions in the fifth century such as we hear about in Bede and the *Chronicle*, most certainly nothing that could have resulted in the extermination of the indigenous population in the East of Britain, we can seriously question and then dismiss the assumption that pre-existing religion, both pagan and Christian, was extirpated. To what extent pagan cults still very evident at the date of the mission of St Augustine of Canterbury mirrored what had existed in Roman times requires much more consideration, together with the possible continuity of Christianity in the region from Roman times. Along one of the branches of the braided river to the east of Binsey, the Bull-Stake Stream perhaps preserves in its name the memory of cultic practice in which bull's heads, *bucrania*, may have marked an ancient boundary. However, careful readers of Bede's *Ecclesiastical History* will see that the main 'problem' encountered by the Roman missionaries at the end of the sixth century was that the island was swarming with British bishops (though we have no way of telling how many of these were ethnically Western British (Brythonic) or Irish Goidelic speakers).

The survival of Christianity is perhaps attested most dramatically in the South-East at the great pilgrimage site of St Alban's (outside Roman *Verulamium*). However, there were other saints venerated in Eastern Britain, amongst them Bishop Augul(i)us in London and a St Sixtus whose cult was suppressed by St Augustine of Canterbury. This last may have been venerated at Winchester, Silchester, or Cirencester, or some lesser place in central southern Britain.[7] Roman villa buildings survived, very probably as centres of Christian worship, into the sixth century at Rawler Manor near Croughton in Northamptonshire, where a sixth-century 'Anglo-Saxon' bead lay directly on top of a mosaic depicting Bellerophon slaying the Chimera. This image is otherwise only found on three sites in Britain, all associated with Romano-British Christianity, and was evidently used as a metaphor of Christ's victory over Satan.[8] Even more striking evidence for continuity has been observed at Bradford-on-Avon in Wiltshire, where a large octagonal font was constructed on top of a geometric fourth-century mosaic, probably in the fifth century.[9] This would seem to imply an intensification of Christianisation in the countryside at that time. Continuity can also be seen in cemeteries, amongst them a large Roman Christian cemetery at Queenford Farm near the ancient Roman town of Dorchester (*Dorcic*), Oxfordshire, which adjoins the fifth- and sixth-century cemetery, which in the archaeological reports is ascribed to the

---

[5] I owe a great deal to the very creative thought and lively discussion with my former pupil Stephen J. Yeates whose books *The Tribe of Witches* (Oxford 2008) and *A Dreaming for the Witches* (Oxford 2009) and especially his masterly *Myth and History. Ethnicity and Politics in the First Millennium British Isles* (Oxford 2012) are massively rewarding in revising our understanding of Britain during this period.

[6] The two 12th-century recensions of the saint's life are printed as (A) and (B) in J.Blair, 'Saint Frideswide reconsidered', *Oxoniensia* 52 (1987), 71–127. They are reprinted in this volume by the kind permission of the author and of the Oxfordshire Architectural and Historical Society.

[7] R. Sharpe,'Martyrs and Local Saints in Late Antique Britain', 75–154 in A.T. Thacker and R. Sharpe, *Local Saints and Local Churches in the Early Medieval West* (Oxford 2002)

[8] M. Dawson, 'Excavation of the Roman villa and mosaic at Rawler Manor, Croughton, Northamptonshire', *Northamptonshire Archaeology* 35 (2008), 45–93, with David Neal's description of the mosaic on pp. 54–58, figs 9 and 11.

[9] K. Bowes, *Private Worship, Public Values, and Religious Change in Late Antiquity* (Cambridge 2008), 176–8 and fig.53.

modern village of Berinsfield but is actually merely a continuation of the old Dorchester burial ground.[10] One possible resident of sixth-century Dorchester was, however, buried further away at Long Wittenham, along with a little wooden beaker sheeted with bronze ornamented *en repousée* with Gospel scenes of the Marriage at Cana, Christ healing the blind man (most probably), and Christ and Zacchaeus. That it has close affinities with similar vessels from Belgium is suggestive of continuing contacts between Christians in Britain and those on the nearer Continent.[11] To the north of the river there was another Roman town at Alchester, just south of Bicester (its probable successor), where similar continuities are suggested.

In Western Britain 'Celtic' Christianity was never urban. It had a great deal in common with the eremitical tradition so familiar from Egypt and the East, and found much to model itself on there. Like the Desert Fathers, the 'saints' of Ireland and Wales sought secluded places, a monastery or even a simple an oratory surrounded by a wall or bank and ditch (*vallum*) that was generally oblong or circular, as already mentioned in the case of Iona.[12] Isolation was essential. Such places abound in Wales, many still designated with the prefix *Llan*, meaning an enclosed space, usually set apart for religious reasons. These survive right up to the Wye Valley, in places such as Lancaut (Llan Cewydd) in Gloucestershire or Llandogo on the Welsh bank of the River Wye.[13] Pre-existing Roman fortifications could be used, as at St Tathan's at Caerwent, and St Fursey's possibly (but by no means certainly) at Burgh Castle, Norfolk.[14] These however, provided too ready a focus for others to settle and many saints including Fursey would often feel the need for more complete withdrawal. They sought remote and often previously uninhabited sites, their main purpose being to exile themselves for Christ. On his or her *peregrinatio* the holy man or woman sought to wrestle with the powers of evil in desert places, like the hermits in the Egyptian desert. Indeed, the impulse towards seeking out such solitary places doubtless came from that region.[15] These witnesses, martyrs in the truest sense, would have been held in high regard by people living in the vicinity, and might even draw disciples, but the main justification for living apart in this way was to dedicate oneself wholly to God. Some were very remote indeed, like the Irish monastic settlement at Skellig Michael in County Kerry, or some of the Columban settlements like the nunnery of Sgor nam Ban Naomh ('The Scree of the Holy Women') on the Isle of Canna in the Hebrides.[16] St Samson's retreat in a cave on the Cornish coast would have been equally inhospitable.[17] St Cuthbert (c.636–87) as Prior of Lindisfarne would retreat from the company of others and on one occasion at least spent the night standing in the sea deep in prayer. We are told two otters ministered to him and tried to dry him; later he sought real seclusion by building a hermitage on the

---

[10] C.M. Hills and T.C. O'Connell, 'New light on the Anglo-Saxon succession : two cemeteries and their dates', *Antiquity* 83 (2009), 1096–1108.

[11] G. Chenet, 'La tombe 319 du cimetière mérovingien de Lavoye (Meuse)', *Préhistoire* IV (1935), 34–118 at pp.87–91.

[12] J. Blair, *The Church in Anglo-Saxon Society* (Oxford 2005), 19–20 fig.4; cf. S. and J. Zaluckyj, *The Celtic Christian sites of the central and southern Marches* (Little Logaston 2006), *passim*. For the nature of welsh spirituality, see O. Davies, 'Celtic Christianity' in *Early Medieval Wales: The Origins of the Welsh Spiritual Tradition* (Cardiff 1996)'.

[13] C. Parry, 'A survey of St James's Church, Lancaut, Gloucestershire', *Trans. Bristol Glouc. Archaeol. Soc.* 108(1990), 53–103; J. Knight,'Society and Religion in the Early Middle Ages', pp.269–86 in M. Aldhouse-Green and R. Howell, *The Gwent County History I. Gwent in Prehistory and Early History* (Cardiff 2004), 273–5.

[14] Ibid 279 for Caerwent; M.P. Brown, The Life of St Fursey. What we know; why it matters (Norwich 2001), 17–18 and O. Rackham, *Transitus Beati Fursei. A translation of the 8th century manuscript Life of Saint Fursey* (Norwich 2007), 54–5 on Cnobheresburgh.

[15] See B. Ward, *The Desert Fathers. Sayings of the Early Christian Monks* (London 2003) for a good introduction.

[16] M.P. Brown, *The Lindisfarne Gospels. Society, Spirituality and the Scribe* (British Library, London 2003),402–6, fig.175 and idem, The Lindisfarne Gospels and the Early Medieval World (London 2011) , 159 fig.78 for Skellig Michael; J.L. Campbell, *Canna. The story of a Hebridean Island* (Oxford 1984),7 and col. pl.15.

[17] J. Blair, *The Church in Anglo-Saxon Society*, 18–19.

Farne islands.[18] Many years later St Frideswide's near contemporary, Cuthbert's successor Bishop Eadfrith (698–721), retired on retreat each Lent to a small island, Thrush Island or Cuddy's Island, a tiny wind-swept islet off Lindisfarne. There, in the last years of his life between 715 and 720, he wrote and illuminated the greatest of all Insular Gospel book, the Lindisfarne gospels, as *Opus Dei*, a work for God, though he did not live to totally complete it.[19] It must often have been cold, often dark, and Eadfrith must frequently have suffered from cramp and from hunger, but as he worked he lived in prayer and made a supreme offering to his God and ours. Thus the book itself became 'sacred space'.

One other unifying aspect of such eremitical sites, apart from their extreme isolation, deserves a mention. However ascetic the hermit, water was a necessity for her or him, and not merely for obvious bodily needs. Running water was required for the administration of the Sacraments, notably Baptism, and also for healing. Very probably this focus was a legacy from both pagan and Christian Roman Britain. Springs had long been considered sacred. In Roman Britain, and most probably earlier, there were spring-based sanctuaries at Bath in Somerset, Buxton in Derbyshire, Springhead in Kent and in many other places. In a Christian context, the Christianisation of a shrine of the nymphs at the Roman villa (?) at Chedworth, Gloucestershire, and above all St Cuthbert's wonderful fountain at Carlisle, are particularly notable .[20] Niamh Whitfield has noted the ubiquity of holy wells in Ireland, as in Wales. Holy wells in Wales include that associated with St Winefride at Holywell in north-east Wales, whose impressive late medieval well-chamber miraculouosly survives. The little well below the beautiful and isolated little church of St Issui at Partrishow in Breckonshire most probably has ancient even prehistoric origins. The small partly Romanesque church building is reminiscent of St Margaret's Binsey in appearance and in the isolation of its site. Wells are almost as common in England and surely for the same reason as in traditionally 'Celtic' lands.[21] John Blair, among others, has freely accepted this hypothesis.[22]

There are two different approaches to the local context of this site. The first of these would see Binsey reflecting a Romano-British Christianity that was becoming established, even in the countryside, from the later fourth century. One could thus envisage Binsey, within its ditched enclosure, as the remains of an Iron Age and Roman village that became the refuge of holy men and/or women or else as a *de novo* settlement of fifth- or sixth-century date in what used to be called 'sub-Roman Britain'. There may even have been unknown predecessors to St Frideswide at Binsey. Frideswide's name is Old English, but as we have seen it is possible that the Iron Age and Roman inhabitants of south Eastern Britain were also ethnically and linguistically Teutonic. In any case it is doubtful that she would have regarded her ethnicity as of much importance. The developed eremitical tradition she represents is very much an Insular one, common throughout Western Britain

---

[18] D.H. Farmer (ed), *Bede: Life of Cuthbert* [in *The Age of Bede*] (London 1983) chs. 10 and 17.
[19] Brown,The Lindisfarne Gospels, Society, Spirituality and the Scribe, 20–22, 397,406 figs 6 and 176; idem, *The Lindisfarne Gospels and the Early Medieval World*, 160 fig.79 and passim; and see also idem, 'The Book as Sacred Space',in P. North and J. North, *Sacred space, House of God, Gate of Heaven* (London and New York 2007), 43–63 especially pp.49–50.
[20] M. Henig, 'murum civitatis, et fontem in ea a Romanis mire olim constructum: The arts of Rome in Carlisle and the Civitas of the Carvetii and their influence', in M. McCarthy and D. Weston (eds),*Carlisle and Cumbria. Roman and Medieval Architecture, Art and Archaeology,* BAA Conference Transactions XXVII (Leeds 2004), 11–28 at pp.13–17.
[21] Holy wells in Wales include that associated with St Winefride at Holywell in north-east Wales, whose impressive late medieval well-chamber miraculously survives. The little well below the little church of St Issui at Partrishow in Breckonshire most probably had more ancient precedents. See also T. J. Hughes, *Wales's best one hundred churches* (Bridgend 2006), pp.102–4 (Holywell);181–3 (Partrishow).
[22] N. Whitfield, 'A suggested function for the Holy Well?', in A. Minnis and J. Roberts, *Text, Image, Interpretation. Studies in Anglo-Saxon Literature and its insular context in honour of Éamonn Ó Carragáin* (Turnhout, Belgium 2007), 495–513. Cf. Blair, *The Church in Anglo-Saxon Society*, 377–9.

if originally derived from an Eastern model. Thus it is not surprising that Binsey has very much the feel of one of those *Llan* or isolated holy sites of the West.

A second approach sees the Christian aspects of this site as later in development, essentially the product of the eighth century, set for ease in an abandoned Iron Age defence or a *de novo* eighth-century banked and ditched enclosure. The 'Celtic' element might here be taken as simply a product of the imported 'Celtic' heritage of the Anglo-Saxon church. From our standpoint it makes little difference. Incidentally, the suffix *–burgh*, found in *Thornbiri*/Thornbury, implies a defended enclosure and was also often used for religious sites. Locally there is another instance of this at Charlbury.[23]

Whether a long-inhabited site or a recent foundation, this place served as a spiritual power-house for Frideswide to pass her time in illuminating or copying texts, or simply in prayer and contemplation. Even if the place were to be fully excavated the archaeological traces would never amount to more than a scatter of potsherds and a few post-holes, and might not tell us a great deal more than we have already surmised. The sort of early 'monastery' we should envisage would never have been more than a few wattle-and-daub huts, possibly with a small wooden chapel attached. It is not of course that buildings of Roman type were at all unknown to the Anglo-Saxon mission. St Peter and St Paul in Canterbury was associated with St Augustine, and the earliest phase of the Old Minster at Winchester with St Birinus; while at Bradwell-on-Sea, Essex there is a further remaining example of a church constructed in the Roman style.[24] It is very likely that such a building would have been found at Dorchester-on-Thames, possibly on the site of the Abbey, and it is also possible that the church at Silchester (*Calleva Atrebatum*), if not of the fifth or early sixth century, belongs to the same period, immediately before Silchester was abandoned.[25] For the most part high quality architecture in stone or brick, which characterized construction under the Roman Empire, does not appear to have survived the economic disruption and the severing of political ties between Britain and the Central Empire. Certainly even though there is literary and epigraphic evidence for continuing Latinity in Britain, the *architectural* knowledge generally needed to be re-imported, the masons in the first instance coming from Gaul or even Italy. It would only have been employed in this period at major centres of royal power. These were all busy places, centres of mission and not of retreat, the purpose to which Binsey seems to have been dedicated from the beginning. We can see St Frideswide's major foundation on the site of present-day Christ Church as a late example of such an important, quasi-royal, Minster Church.

Although the refuge of a lady of evidently high birth, Binsey was by no means purely or even mainly the reflection of royal patronage. Like St Columba's Iona and St Cuthbert's Holy Island of Lindisfarne, it would have been very simple in appearance, a powerhouse of prayer and isolated reflection rather than merely of temporal power.

---

[23] S. Draper, 'The significance of Old English Burgh in Anglo-Saxon England', *Anglo-Saxon Studies in Archaeology and History* 15 (2008), 240–53 at pp.242–3 for early monastic enclosures.
[24] E. Fernie, *The Architecture of the Anglo-Saxons* (London 1982),36–7 fig.15 (Canterbury) 39–40 fig.20 (Winchester) and 38 (Bradwell).
[25] Its plan, as pointed out to me by Canon John Wilkinson, approximates to that of fifth-century Syrian Churches. Cf. Z.T. Fiema, C. Kanellopoulos, T. Waliszewski and R. Schick, *The Petra Church* (American Center of Oriental Research, Amman, Jordan 2001),158–66, figs 17–23.

Pilgrimage to Binsey: Medieval and Modern

LYDIA CARR

Binsey's holy well, with its literary and spiritual overtones, represents a key attraction of the little church for the modern visitor. In this brief essay, the broad history of pilgrimage in England is considered before approaching Binsey's own post-Reformation history. Others have dealt with the history of St Margaret's Well authoritatively in this volume; little of value can be added here to these excellent historical and archaeological syntheses.

PILGRIMAGE IN ENGLAND: SACRED SPRINGS

The attitude of the present English church towards holy wells is a peculiar one. Where other nations attempted to 'reform' away all trace of superstitious water, or else 'Lourdize' springs into a holy business enterprise, England's wells still remain under the radar for many sections of her national church. The suspicious whiff of Popery or rural ignorance that hung about such waters was dealt with in the past by dismissing it as superstition, or by transforming wells into semi-medical spas as at Bath and Harrogate. Traces, where they remained, of a more spiritual aspect to the 'cure' were discouraged. It is typical of the Anglican Church's desire to avoid extremes whenever possible, and of its dry urbanity when faced with enthusiasm. This distaste does not necessarily represent a lack of faith, but a discomfort with its public expression.[1]

Matters were different prior to the Reformation. Pilgrimages were a popular activity in medieval England, whether they took the traveller to Jerusalem or to Canterbury. This activity may be traced back to the Roman and even to the pre-Roman period, and certainly to pre-Christian worship practices. Even small sites dedicated to local saints could become modestly famous for their healing and oracular powers; it is reasonable to assume that many of these were among the places Pope Gregory mentions in his famous seventh-century letter to the missionary Mellitus. Gregory wanted native temples preserved, their idols cast down and replaced with Christian saints' relics, and the premises sprinkled with holy water. He meant, of course, water blessed by a priest, deriving its agency from that of the actions of the person performing the blessing, and not from its own origins. The two types of 'holy' water were still frequently conflated throughout Europe.

It is clear that water, particularly in pure springs, represents a primal object of respect and religious observance. Like fire, seeds, and animals of the chase, clean water is necessary to human survival in a way unimaginable unless it is absent, and a potentially rare resource in a pre-modern landscape. For primitive tribes living at subsistence levels, a source of pure water was something to be treasured and protected. Such protection could of course be physical, but was also psychological: the association of a supernatural spirit with a water source gave it the power to protect itself from harm. Logically, something endowed with the power to harm might also heal; and so the stories of cures spread, and people began to travel specifically with the intent of visiting a well.

However, the number of pre-Christian pilgrims or pilgrimage routes to wells in England is confused by a lack of pre-classical written evidence. True examples are further obscured by poor archaeological and anthropological recording practices. The tendency

---

[1] This may be said to be lessening under the effects of modern cultural practices; see, for example, the revival of the cult of the Virgin at Walsingham in Norfolk.

of modern faiths to unquestioningly adopt the romantic symbols of a perceived pagan past has also caused problems in determining what represents a genuine continuance of a spiritual practice rather than a modern interpolation. Of those wells that are firmly established as dating to at least the pre-Roman period, Bath (*Aquae Sulis*), that is 'the Waters of the goddess Sulis Minerva' is the best known today. Smaller springs more comparable to Binsey may include Coventina's Well, dedicated to the nymph-goddess Coventina in Northumberland, which has a well-established history of Roman deposits though it seems thereafter to have fallen out of use.[2]

These wells were used in a number of rituals, some of which were carried over into the Christian era, and which are roughly divisible into *deposit* and *healing*. The familiar practice of votive deposition, inherited and remade by the Church, may be traced back to this primitive urge to thank or bribe; some ancient wells, when dragged, show objects ranging from pins and needles all the way up to gold, money, and arms. The spring at Bath has provided the largest number of Latin lead curse tablets in England. Some swamps and bogs in Northern Europe (including the famous body from Lindow Moss, Cheshire) even show limited deposition of human bodies.

In the high Middle Ages, the more homicidal rituals apparently ceased. Their place was taken by the veneration of relics, particularly of the body parts of holy individuals. A fragment of a finger could make a site worthy of veneration; the translation of St Winifred's body to Shrewsbury in the twelfth century established the town's new Benedictine abbey as a nayional player in ecclesiastical politics. Some relics became peripatetic, traversing the medieval landscape. With the development of a standardized Church, travelling to confess sins in a particularly auspicious place became popular; Binsey may have been a popular location for this, as it was located near a good medieval ford.[3]

To modern eyes, the medical uses of pilgrimages and wells looms most practically. At a time when many people never travelled more than a few miles from home, and in which diets could therefore become nutritionally deficient, mineral waters could genuinely alleviate some forms of illness. Lydney Park in Gloucestershire displays Roman and prehistoric iron workings beside a combination temple and hydro-spa. The red, rusty water of the hillside is still an excellent source of potable iron. Anemic patients, or the pregnant women who are thought to have particularly used Lydney, would have found real relief in a course of treatment there.[4] The waters at Bath show a high level of calcium, bicarbonate, and magnesium, and are naturally effervescent; hence their association with skin disease and gastric problems. In short, some 'miracle cures' really were effective on a purely physical level.[5]

There is no evidence of any chemical content of this type in the water at Binsey, or in many other wells. But even the act of going on a pilgrimage could potentially relieve some medical issues, such as chronic vitamin deficiency. Travelling in the sunlight would cause exposure to fresher air and better sun than that available in close housing, and a long enough journey would thus at least relieve respiratory problems and Vitamin D deficiency. Psychologically, removing a patient from the causes of mental problems such as stress might lessen their effects.[6]

---

[2] L. Allason-Jones and B. McKay, *Coventina's Well* (Oxford 1985); B. Cunliffe (ed), *The Temple of Sulis Minerva at Bath.2 The Finds from the Sacred Spring* (Oxford 1988).
[3] Blair, *Thornbury, Binsey,* this volume.
[4] M. Wheeler and T. V. Wheeler, *Report on the excavation of the prehistoric, Roman and post-Roman site in Lydney Park, Gloucestershire* (Oxford, 1932).
[5] A. Cruse, *Roman Medicine* (Stroud 2004),136–7 fig. 66.
[6] R. Scott *Miracle Cures* (Berkeley and Los Angeles, 2010), 13, ch.6.

Modern medicine has accustomed its victims to pills, shots, and other internal, largely unseen cures. Tolerance for pain has decreased in tandem with the ability to relieve it with ease via chemical therapies. For the medieval traveller, unused to the ease of taking paracetemol for joint aches or antacids for a stomachache, a gradual cessation of pain as the result of pilgrimage would have seemed all the more marked—and miraculous. The very shock of immersion in cold water might on occasion be of aid, particularly in the case of hysteria. Again, the benefits seen might be temporary, but the relief for the sufferer was genuine while it lasted. It is important to recall this when considering the other medical basis for the real efficacy of pilgrimages for some travelers. That is psychosomatic; in other words, by believing so strongly that a saint could cure them on the performance of a specific task, patients might experience a cure. The religious and the medical were thus inextricably linked from their earliest development, and not disentangled until relatively recently. Bath's changing dedications provide a timeline for the process; it was dedicated first to the Celtic Sulis, then to the Roman Sulis Minerva, then to the medieval Christian king Bladud. Subsequently it became the preserve of Protestant doctors and the gout, and today belongs to beauty treatments and spa breaks.[7]

The old style of pilgrim travel faltered during the Reformation. Early Protestants made pilgrimages a major target for Catholic criticism, alleging that the encouragement of pilgrims by the Church was the encouragement of idol-worship for its own financial gain. Such distrust of miraculous objects was not a new feature of Christian life, and Chaucer's fourteenth century pilgrim-Palmer remains the best and funniest exponent of it. While various aspects of old church dogmas such as transubstantiation were allowed to survive or to creep back in to Anglicanism over time, traditional pilgrimages continued to be discouraged by the English authorities.[8] The purer concept of Christian pilgrimage was not abandoned, however, but expanded exponentially. John Bunyan and others encouraged good men and women to see their entire lives as an allegorical pilgrim's progress. The act of walking became a powerful metaphor for the spiritual journey of the Christian, and Chaucer's rowdy, amiable band of holidaymakers from all walks of life was replaced in the popular imagination with Christian and his partially solitary journey.[9] The landscape of Bunyan's 1678 allegory *The Pilgrim's Progress* is a blasted one of empty heaths and morally bankrupt towns, populated mostly by the wicked, the careless, and a very few helpful guides. The Protestant vision of pilgrimage is of an internal struggle against one's own worse nature, a perpetual fight carried out, like prayer, in private.

Other factors also diminished the need for pilgrimages. Medicine and lifestyle were both improving, lessening the chance that a simple cold-water douche might help a problem. Springs with some genuine therapeutic content secularized and became the resort spas of the seventeenth and eighteenth centuries. Medical tourism emerged out of the old pilgrim networks.

PILGRIMS TO BINSEY: POST-REFORMATION TRADITIONS

The Oxford area was once full of holy and semi-sacred springs, hardly surprising in a region of water-meadows. Binsey's chapel and well are dedicated to St Margaret of Antioch, but have been persistently associated closely with the Saxon St Frideswide since the building's inception. The pairing of these two saints, the early Eastern martyr and the regional princess-nun, reveals the deep desire of the Roman and the British churches to *localize* their

---

[7] Peter Davenport, *Medieval Bath Uncovered* (Stroud 2002).
[8] N.H. Keeble, *The Restoration: England in the 1660s* (Oxford 2002), 238–240.
[9] Ibid, 243–244.

St Frideswide depicted in stained glass at St Frideswide's Church, Osney, in Oxford. (Russell Dewhurst)

faith. The same desire rebuilt the Bethlehem stable at Walsingham and established Joseph of Arimathea in Cornwall.

Binsey was drawn into the Frideswide narrative as a perceived location on the saint's flight from marriage, 'Thornbury'. The church began its existence as a chapel attached to a larger manor house or court, part of a larger complex that most probably incorporated the large earthworks to the south of the present church (see Blair and Munby in this volume for further details). The entire group belonged to St Frideswide's Priory in Oxford proper; Anglo-Saxon pottery finds and historical references suggest that it was owned by the priory from its Christian foundation. This ownership continued through the medieval period, and indeed to the present day via the Priory's direct successor Christ Church.

Binsey is traditionally supposed to have been used as a retiring house for members of the Priory, most famously the religious visionary Edith Lancelin in the early twelfth century. While the chapel is isolated today, in the medieval period it was close to a popular road and ford linking Eynsham and Oxford, and would have been much more convenient to traffic.[10] The seventeenth century antiquary Anthony à Wood reconstructed its history in his gossipy but vivid style as it moved through the past to his own time. He is given here in the vivid original, without criticism. Blair, in this volume, provides a more measured view of Wood's value as a historian, but his interest in this context is as an imaginative recorder of the traditions and practices of his own time, not others.

> Leaving *Binsey* Town, and going about a Quarter of a Mile N. W. from it, we come to the forlorn Church or Chapel belonging to it.

---

[10] Blair, *Thornbury, Binsey,* this volume.

BINSEY CHURCH

    For I shall call it a Church, having been always decimated and taxed as a Parish Church. Was first built with Watlyn and rough hewn Timber, to the Honour of St *Margaret,* by St *Fridiswide,* about the Year 730, which *Fridiswide* being the Owner of this Soil, and taking great Delight in its solitary Shades and Privacy, being then environed with Woods, not only built this Church, but also several other Edifices adjoining, purposely, that she and her Sisters the Nuns, who lived with her in *Oxford,* at the Priory of St *Fridiswide,* might retire in Times of Distraction in the City. The famous Lady re-edifying this Church, and enlarging the Buildings adjacent, instituted it to be a Cell or a Place of Retirement, as it had been for herself, for her Nuns; and here, not only at some Times they enjoyed themselves in great Repose and Devotion, but also were hither sent their more stubborn Sort, to be punished for Crimes committed against the Prior or his Brethren; which was commonly, either by inflicting on them Confinement in a dark Room, or by withdrawing from them their usual Repast, or the like.

    In the Repository in the South Wall of the Chancel, was long standing her costly Statue, bedecked with Ornaments. To which the superstitious People, that came frequently to this Place, using Adorations on their Knees, have, to People's Amazement, worn the very Pavement about it hollow, as is now to be seen.

    This Church continuing to St *frid.* Priory till its Dissolution, was annexed by the Cardinal to his College; afterwards, by King H. VIII. to *Christ-Church,* in whose Possession it still remains.

    —Is old, of Brick, without a Spire or Tower,—about 16 Yards long and *6* broad, — having but one Isle. — The Altar measures not 3 Yards in Breadth. — Two Bells.—In the East Window is painted *Jesus* with his Cross, and a Virgin, supposed *Margaret* or St *Fridefwide,* bearing a Cross.

    At the general Taxation this stands thus: *Capella de Binsey Pertinens ad Priorem de St Frid. vis.* and *vmd.**—It is now a Donative, worth about 50/. *per Ann.*—Curate, Mr. *Cutherode,* A. M. of *Christ-Church.*

    At the West End, about three Yards distant from this Chapel was the noted Well of St *Margaret,* which, as the Story goes, St *Fridifaide,* by her Prayers at the Building of the Chapel, caused to be opened…Over this Well was a Covering of Stone : On the Front the Picture of St *Frid.* pulled down by Alderman *Sayre,* of *Oxon,* Anno 1639.

    To this Well and her Image, and Reliques in the Chapel, did the People come on Pilgrimage with as great Devotion to ease their burthened Souls, and obtain an Answer of their Doubts as they would to an Oracle. And here also, when the maimed or unsound had been cured by bathing in, or drinking of this Water, they hung up their Crutches as a special Memorandum of their Cure, for which Reason several Priests inhabited here, appointed by the Prior of St *Frid.* to confess and absolve them, and *Sackworth,* on the other Side the River, distant about Half a Mile South-West, which has not a Stone in it, by the continual and numerous Resort to this Place, became a large Town, had in it 24 Inns, and was a thoroughfare Town from *Eynsham* and the Western Parts, to *Oxon,* long before the other by *Body* was thought of, having a Bridge formerly over the River running by it, of which, and the Ruins of *Sackworth,* are the Stones ploughed up, and those lying in great Abundance in the River.

    A House, by some a Court, with arched Windows and arched Door, joining to the North Side of *Binsay* Chapel, was pulled down in *July* 1678, by the Widow *Fifield,* to sell and save Reparation.

    This Well continued to the last to be so frequented, and especially about a hundred Years before the Dissolution so much, that they were forced to add a Door and Lock to it; besides enclosing it, as before, with a little House of Stone over it. This House about 25 Years ago…was pulled down and taken away and Nettles, Frogs, &c. possess it, now scarce deserving the Name of a Well.[11]

After the dissolution of the pre-Reformation Catholic Church in England, Binsey's chapel-church was small enough to avoid major damage. A few miles away, St Frideswide's bones were less fortunate. Her body was disinterred and famously reburied with that of an apostate nun, and her shrine destroyed. Binsey, while part of the priory and network of college lands running from Christ Church to Godstow, was never under the same kind of scrutiny. It did lose its locked and decorated stone well-house in 1639, the second such

---

[11] A. Wood and J. Peshall, *The Ancient and Present State of the City of Oxford* (London 1773), 320–322.

St Margaret's Well. (Robert Mealing)

St Margaret's Well – detail. (Julian Munby)

> St. Margaret's Well
> S. Margaretae Fontem
> Precibys S. Frideswidae ut fertur concessum
> inquinatum diu obrutumque
> in usum revocavit
> T.J. Prout Aed. Xti alumnus vicarius
> A.S. MDCCCLXXIV

T J Prout of Christ Church, Vicar, brought back into use St Frideswide's well, made to produce [flow] by the prayers of St Frideswide, and for long collapsed and [fouled] polluted, A.D. 1874 structure erected to protect the small spring from its devotees.[12] The chapel of the former retiring-house was re-imagined as a parish church, a function it had probably been fulfilling for many years anyway, and the canon's manor fell into disuse and disrepair.

Traffic patterns shifted, a bridge was built, and St Margaret's and Binsey began slowly to take on the form they have today: a string of less than a dozen houses, a small pub, and a remote churchyard at the end of a one-way road. The well fell into disrepair between the seventeenth and early nineteenth centuries. Doctors discouraged the idea of a holy cure, and ecclesiastical fashions prohibited the popish practices of pilgrimage and confession. It is very possible that the spring continued to be used locally by poorer residents as a cure-all, but only because other, similar sites continued in that way during this period. By the 1660s, Wood could still describe a number of small wells and springs, holy and secular, within the city's purview.[13] Binsey's spring is described 'three yards distant' from the church in the vivid, almost zoological terms quoted above. It had lost both its religious and therapeutic value, and was in a perceptible decline.

That began to change in the nineteenth century, as England's Gothic past became romanticized. Pilgrimages and the Middle Ages were fashionable. By the time the FSA Robert Hope visited in October 1887, as part of a survey of English wells, the church was looking cared for again.

> …the churchyard was tidily fenced and very neatly kept. At the well a descent of some five steps brought one to an arched vault, beneath which, in the centre of the flooring, was a round basin containing the water of the well, the surface of the water being about six feet below the level of the ground.[14]

St Margaret's took on its modern form with the erection of a Victorian well-head in 1874 by the vicar of the day, T.J. Prout. He repaired the church's fabric and restored the primacy of the well to the site. He was also indirectly responsible for Charles Dodgson's 1862 picnic by the well—the treacle well of *Alice*. The word treacle was used in the medieval period to denote a healing substance; it is a very donnish pun.

With the increased romanticism of the Victorian period, the idea of holy wells and pilgrimages began to be attractive once again. At the same time, a movement towards a 'rediscovery' of a perceived Celtic or pagan past began to gather steam. It is not surprising that as Prout rebuilt the well-head, the first modern Eistedfodds were taking place, and the first modern Druids enjoying the first of many disputations about which ancient tradition they were going to represent. These neo-Druids would provide the spiritual ancestors of some modern pilgrims to Binsey, in the neo-pagans who have claimed (they would perhaps say re-claimed) its well as their own. A visitor to Binsey today will see faceted crystals left by the well's edge, a twentieth-century New Age custom re-used by an ancient spring. The yew tree over the well also shows a recent growth of fabric strips and ribbons, representing the resurgence of a genuinely ancient custom used across England at spring sites. What is signifies is hotly disputed, but it cannot be denied that the practice dates back centuries. The practice of dressing the well with flowers has also made a return.

Christian usage of the shrine has also increased, with the Anglican church's wholesale and in some cases indiscriminate adoption of romantic symbols of the past. It is entertaining to consider what some of the Protestant leaders of the Elizabethan era would have to say about the modern church's use of labyrinths, saint's shrines, beatifications,

---

[12] R.C. Hope, *The Legendary Lore of the Holy Wells of England* (London 1893), 126.
[13] For example, the Ho;ywell Green well enclosed in 1651 by Cowdrey the 'precise shoemaker of St Peter's in the East'. Ibid, 119, 12.
[14] Ibid, 126.

Binsey churchyard. (Sue Dewhurst)

rosaries, pilgrim's medals, holy water, and other attractive medievalisms. The well is once more brought into regular use by the vicars of St Margaret's church, and its waters used in baptisms and blessings. There is an inevitability about this. Throughout its history, in the spontaneity of response to this little spring, the earliest moments of human religion—and the most recent—can still be read.[15]

---

[15] In 2011 St Margaret's was one of fifteen churches specially selected by Bishop John Pritchard as part of the Oxford Diocese's Pilgrim Project. A full explanation of this interesting and popular program can be found at http://www.oxford.anglican.org/the-door/features/thinking-about-pilgrimage-in-2011.htm.

The Clergy of Binsey

RUSSELL DEWHURST

In 1293, the chaplain sent from St Frideswide's Priory to serve 'Thornbury'—that is, St Margaret's chapel, Binsey—was a priest named Simon. History does not record the reason for Simon's visit, one day, to Deddington, but his trip was to end in his imprisonment on a charge of murder. While he was in the parish church, a fight broke out between two men called William Morel and Robert de Luceles. Looking around for a weapon, Robert seized an iron candlestick, sharpened at both ends, and began to swing it at William. Seeing all this, Simon intervened, intending to break up the fight. He grabbed hold of the candlestick and tried to hold it out of the reach of the brawlers. But in his rage, Robert managed to tear the candlestick from the priest's hands and, in doing so, impaled himself in the stomach. Medieval medical care being what it was, Robert subsequently died from his wounds, and Simon was arrested on suspicion of murder. He was taken to Oxford and imprisoned in the gaol there. A guilty verdict from a murder trial would have led to his execution. Fortunately, the true story reached the ears of the necessary authorities, and Simon received a royal pardon.[1]

It is only because of this event in Simon's life—his coming to the attention of the king and gaining a pardon—that he is the first of Binsey's priests we know by name. He served St Margaret's chapel on behalf of St Frideswide's priory, a house of Augustinian canons in the centre of Oxford where Christ Church now stands. Henry I had granted the chapel to the priory as part of its foundation charter in 1122.[2]

At that earlier time of the priory's foundation—170 years before Simon's arrest—there lived Nicholas Breakspear, who was to become Adrian IV, the only English pope. Several guidebooks to Oxford claim that Breakspear was 'rector' of Binsey. There is, however, little evidence of this connection dating from before 1879[3]. It's true that there is a certain amount of confusion about Nicholas Breakspear's early life, and it is just possible that, in his twenties, he could have served Binsey chapel before it became associated with the priory. But no contemporary sources even hint at this possibility and unless more evidence comes to light, we must consider Binsey's papal connection as a pious legend, and Simon as its first known priest.

In being sent by the priory to serve a local church, Simon was not atypical. St Frideswide's priory was involved in the running of several of Oxford's churches, providing priests to say mass and hear confession. Perhaps the most influential figure in the priory's history was the second prior, Robert of Cricklade, who wrote lives of St Thomas Becket and of St Frideswide herself. He oversaw the construction of the priory chapel: still standing and now the chancel of Christ Church cathedral. Robert's successor, Philip, recorded over one hundred miracles taking place at the shrine of St Frideswide before 1180, attracting many pilgrims and visitors.

For most of the four centuries that Binsey was associated with the priory, chaplains were appointed and removed at the pleasure of the prior. Richard Montagu was the first recorded Canon of St Frideswide's to be appointed for life to the chaplaincy of Binsey, 'in

---

[1] Calendar of Close Rolls, 1288–96, 300
[2] The Cartulary of the Monastery of St. Frideswide at Oxford, Foundation Charter of Henry I.
[3] Notes and Queries, 1879

The porch of St Margaret's Church. (Sue Dewhurst)

The chancel of St Margaret's Church. (Russell Dewhurst)

consideration of his many labours on behalf of the priory.'[4] His appointment for life was confirmed by the Pope, St Boniface IX, in 1397.[5] But this gift doesn't seem to have been a very valuable one. There was no set income for the chaplain, who probably had to rely on gifts and fees from pilgrims. When pilgrims were few, such as during times of plague, he might be near starvation. In a 1423 visitation, the Bishop of Lincoln found excessive and 'voluptuous' expenses under prior John Dodforde, yet little of this got as far as Binsey. The bishop ordered that the chaplain of Binsey should be properly supported, with food and clothing for himself and one servant.

The Reformation which brought so much upheaval to the religious life of England worked out in an unusual way for St Frideswide's priory. Sooner or later, all communities of monks and nuns were dissolved at the greedy hands of Henry VIII, and the priory was no exception. St Frideswide's priory, though, rose from its ashes in the form of Christ Church, a new foundation of Henry VIII which was to be cathedral of the new diocese of Oxford and a college of the university there. Christ Church, founded in 1546, took over the priory's site along with very many of its rights and properties. In particular, Christ Church was granted the manor and rectory of Binsey and the chapel of St Margaret's, Binsey.

For the residents of Binsey, it surely seemed that relatively little had changed. The great ecclesiastical institution on St Aldate's may have changed its name, but it still owned the land, collected the rent and the tithes, held courts, appointed the priest to St Margaret's, and so on. The links with Christ Church brought benefits too. As rector, Christ Church was responsible for repairing the church's chancel. When necessary they supported Binsey residents in court, as in 1598, when the Dean and Chapter sued for Binsey freemen to enjoy rights of common on Port Meadow.[6] Binsey was by now considered a full parish, and residents of Binsey began to be buried in the churchyard rather than having to be taken into Oxford.

The founding charter of St Frideswide's Priory had freed Binsey chapel from the jurisdiction of any bishop or archdeacon, and this exemption continued after the reformation. Binsey, to use the technical terminology of ecclesiastical law, was a 'donative peculiar'. So, for example, Christ Church could appoint clergy to serve Binsey without any need to consult or inform the Bishop of Oxford, and some matters involving wills and probate, which would otherwise have been handled by Oxford's consistory court, were dealt with directly the Dean and Chapter of Christ Church. Binsey's peculiar status in church law made a real difference to the lives of its residents, both inside and outside their church building.

Peculiar status was of interest to non-residents too. Before Lord Hardwicke's Marriage Act of 1753, it was possible to marry secretly, and more or less legally, in certain clandestine marriage venues. The marriage registers for the first part of the 18th century suggest that Binsey was just such a venue. In this quiet little village, dozens of marriages took place out of the public eye. Often, one of the many clergy attached to the university would officiate: whereas parish clergy could be punished for conducting clandestine marriages, fellows and chaplains in the university were more or less immune.[7]

Some of Binsey's unusual status was ended in 1746 for financial reasons. The chaplain who served St Margaret's received only a tiny stipend from Christ Church. The incomes of poor parishes across the country were being augmented from a fund called 'Queen

---

[4] 'Houses of Augustinian canons: The priory of St Frideswide, Oxford', *A History of the County of Oxford: Volume 2* (1907), 97–101
[5] *Calendar of Papal Letters*, i, 163 (Jan 1397).
[6] Binsey Estates: Ms 47 in Christ Church Archives.
[7] On clandestine marriages, see R.B. Outhwiate, *Clandestine Marriage in England, 1500–1850*. (1995)

Anne's bounty', established, as the name suggests, by the generosity of Queen Anne. In total £600 of capital was offered to improve the income of the chaplain of Binsey. One of the conditions of accepting the money was that Christ Church lost a little of their control, and the priest—now technically termed the 'Perpetual Curate' of Binsey—gained a little security.

Even after the augmentation from Queen Anne's bounty, Binsey was not a rich living. Christ Church offered the chapel at Binsey to the ordained students of its college, i.e. its fellows. The work was not well-paid, but it was very local and, given the size of the population, not arduous. Students could continue with their university interests while gaining experience in a parish context. One example is the bookish Clayton Mordaunt Cracherode, nominated to Binsey in 1762, whose experience there taught him that he was not cut out for a career in the church.[8] Most of the perpetual curates of Binsey stayed for a relatively short period of time.

Nevertheless, the nineteenth century brought some interesting characters to the village as its priest. William Corne (minister at Binsey 1806–1818) left £100 for the purpose of establishing a Sunday school in the village,[9] and the school was still going strong as late as 1854. The scholarly Charles Lloyd was at Binsey for just two years, between 1818 and 1820 but was a significant figure in the University and in the Church. He lectured on the catholic and primitive nature of the Book of Common Prayer, and was a significant influence on the young John Henry Newman and Edward Pusey, who were to lead the Oxford Movement.[10] Lloyd became Regius Professor of divinity in 1822, and Bishop of Oxford in 1827.[11] J.A. Cramer (minister at Binsey 1822–45) was Regius Professor of modern history, and stayed for longer than the traditional two or three years, as did Robert Hussey (minister 1845–56), who was Regius Professor of ecclesiastical history. Hussey was known as a careful and committed pastor who regularly visited his people but he complained that there was in the village 'a state of ignorance' and 'much godless apathy, which no human means seem able to touch.'[12] Hussey was able to combine his parochial and university work with the roles of rural dean of Oxford and proctor in convocation for the diocese, and died in post at Binsey.

T.J. Prout (minister 1856–1891) was a friend of Lewis Carroll, as described elsewhere in these essays, but his name is best known to visitors to St Margaret's from the inscription over the church's well. Prout restored both the well and the church interior, considering but finally rejecting the idea of an octagonal altar. We find the church today little changed from how Prout left it. Eventually, Christ Church tried to persuade Prout to give up the parish, but he refused, arguing that 'Binsey has been held for generations by men who have done their full share of work in college and have become to a certain extent "emeriti"'.[13] Prout was remembered well into the late twentieth century for his frequent use of an ear-trumpet.[14]

During the mid-nineteenth century, there was usually just one service a Sunday at St Margaret's, alternating between Morning Service at 11.00 A.M., and Evening Service at 2.30 P.M. or 3.00 P.M. The congregation was about twenty, from a total village population

---

[8] A. Griffiths, *Landmarks in Print Collecting* (British Museum Press, 1996)
[9] *Commissions of Inquiry into Charities in England and Wales: Sixth Report, Appendix*, 453. 1822.
[10] J.H. Newman writing to his sister Harriet on June 4, 1829, said of Lloyd that he 'brought me forward, made me known, spoke well of me, and gave me confidence in myself'.
[11] W.J. Baker, *Beyond Port and Prejudice: Charles Lloyd of Oxford*. (Maine, 1981)
[12] Visitation Return, 1854, at Oxfordshire Records Office.
[13] Christ Church MS Estates 61, 413.
[14] T.H. Aston & M. Brock, *The History of the University of Oxford: Nineteenth-century Oxford, part 2*, (2000, 224)

The font at St Margaret's. (Karl Wallendszus)

of around eighty. In addition, there was a monthly service of Holy Communion, which attracted about five communicants.[15]

Most parishes in the Church of England elect two churchwardens, but Binsey coped for most of its history with only one churchwarden. From 1921 almost all parish churches had a Parochial Church Council (or 'PCC'), but Binsey never did, no doubt because of its small size. By 1963 the Vicar and churchwarden were calling themselves the 'custodians' of St Margaret's, and acting instead of a PCC.

From 1919 Binsey was held 'in plurality' with the small neighbouring village of Wytham, that is, the same priest served both village churches. For some years, Wytham and Binsey shared a small choir who sang evensong in Binsey and then walked across to Wytham to sing evensong over again.

With the building of the A34, the link between the two parishes was no longer practical, but Binsey was still too small to warrant a Vicar of its own. In 1950 Arnold Mallinson was given permission to hold the living of Binsey in plurality with that of St Frideswide's Church on Botley Road in Oxford, where he had been Vicar since 1933. Mallinson was a numismatist of some renown, and in the words of the *Oxford Mail*, 'perhaps his most enduring characteristic [was] his amazing picaresque style'. He is also fondly remembered for the stuffed owls he placed in the roof of Binsey church to discourage the bats.

With Mallinson's retirement in 1976 the future of the two parishes was in some doubt. After some delay, it was decided that St Frideswide's and Binsey would be permanently merged into one parish; this has meant, for example, that the two churches now share one set of marriage registers.

In 1979, Robert Sweeney was presented as Vicar of this new, larger parish in a united benefice with St Thomas's, Becket Street. He served until his retirement in 2003. For most of the next two years, the temporary priest-in-charge was Tom Meyrick, great-grandson of Cyril Meyrick who had been minister at Binsey between 1919 and 1924.

St Frideswide with Binsey parish was briefly again a separate parish in 2005–2009 when the current writer was priest-in-charge, and one of the few ministers of Binsey not to have been a graduate of Christ Church. In this period, the pattern of services was very similar to that of the nineteenth century, but Prayer Book Evensong, now at 3.30 P.M., was only held during the months of British Summer Time because of the lack of heating. The monthly morning Celebration of Holy Communion, on the other hand, continued throughout the

---

[15] Visitation Return, 1854, at Oxfordshire Records Office.

year. Most weeks, the congregation was relatively few in number, but the church filled to bursting for St Margaret's Day, harvest thanksgiving, and Christmas carols.

From 2009 to 2011 St Frideswide with Binsey was held in plurality with North Hinksey (and also with Wytham until 2010) by the Revd Dr Anthony Rustell. Dr Rustell presided over the creation of the Osney Benefice, formed as a union of the two parishes, which nevertheless retain their own identities. After a year's interregnum, the Revd Clare Sykes was inducted as Rector of the new benefice in 2012.

Despite the many changes of recent years, Binsey's link with Christ Church is still strong. Christ Church is still landlord of most of the houses in Binsey, and the college is still the patron of the parish and so continues to be involved in the appointment of the parish's clergy. The historic relationship continues to be expressed in many other ways, as when the Dean of Christ Church opened the first village fete in living memory in 2008.

In 2002, Christ Church restored the shrine of St Frideswide in the Latin chapel of the cathedral. The shrine we now see is almost identical to that which would have been known to Simon, the thirteenth century chaplain of Binsey whom we met at the beginning of this essay. The original construction of the shrine (in what was then St Frideswide's Priory) finished in 1289, just four years before Simon's arrest and pardon. Thus the shrine points to the link, stretching across the centuries, between the village of Binsey and the medieval Priory that became Christ Church.

The Binsey communion cup. Inscribed 'To the Service of ALMIGHTY GOD / The Gift of Daniel Porter for the use / of the Parish Church of Binsey 1690.' (Karl Wallendszus)

Life in Binsey as Recorded in the Church Registers

CARL BOARDMAN

Within easy walking distance of the centre of Oxford, Binsey has nevertheless always seemed a world apart. Unable to expand, since rivers hem it in all around, it remains a tiny hamlet, much of it dating from the eighteenth century—though parts of The Perch go back a century earlier and the church dates from the 1100s. And it exercises a strange attraction for writers; Gerard Manley Hopkins, Lewis Carroll, and P. D. James have all used the church, village and environs in their work.

Yet its history in surviving documentary sources is surprisingly patchy. It belonged to the priory of St Frideswide through the medieval period, and when that was dissolved passed to Christ Church in 1546; the college was lord of the manor and even held courts there until 1835. The church probably existed because of St Margaret's Well, but had its own problems—not until the 1550s did it get the right to bury its own parishioners, and Christ Church regarded it as a peculiar, refusing to let the churchwardens attend the Archdeacon of Oxford's visitations until the nineteenth century.

Fortunately all parishes have one important source through which their history can be traced—the parish registers of baptism, marriage and burial, which every clergyman in England was ordered to keep from 1538, creating a record of all the local inhabitants and their interrelationships. Even here Binsey found a difficulty: the earliest known parish register, from 1591 to 1766, vanished without trace many years ago. Only in the early twenty-first century did it re-emerge, turning up in a brown paper parcel on the rectory doorstep, and for the first time in decades it has been possible to investigate the people of the village and how they lived.

Looking through that register and its successors, the first thing that strikes one should come as no surprise. In a village which was so well defined and cut off from other communities, dynasties emerged; families which dominate the register entries for centuries. The Hearne family are there from the very beginning and continue well into the eighteenth century; so too the Major family. The Crutch family are found regularly until 1719 when the last member, the widow Anne Crutch, died. Other families arrive later but are even longer-lived; the Prickett family are first heard of in 1654 but continue into the present day.

Yet sometimes there are single entries, people who seem to have come from nowhere. Often they were literally passing through. In 1635 'the son of Robert Winkells, a tinker and a stranger' was baptized, Binsey obviously being the village Robert and his wife had reached when she came to term. Sometimes they stayed for ever without wishing or expecting to; in 1723 'Susannah Brown, a traveling woman, buried, being killed by a horse at Port Meadow Race, 30 August'.

Several of the single entries were coming home. 'J Major, shoemaker, who lived near St Martin's Church Carfax, born in Binsey' was buried in 1702, while in 1946 Cleopatra Weston from Ryde, Isle of Wight, returned to her home parish for the last time. Yet some are distinctly odd. John Cable of Bulford, Wiltshire, has his son baptized at Binsey in 1610 for no very obvious reason. Others one can make a guess at. On 29 September 1706 'baptized with private baptism, Sarah, bastard daughter of Thomas Smith living in King Street Westminster, corncutter, and Sarah Bridges, spinster, his maid, born at Churchill near Chipping Norton'; Binsey was an out-of-the-way place, and this was one baptism Thomas would not wish to advertise. Sarah soon found her place in the parish churchyard, one hopes through natural infant mortality rather than anything more sinister.

A page from the Binsey burial register, showing burials in the 1850s, while Robert Hussey was minister. (Karl Wallendszus)

A page from the Binsey baptism register, showing baptisms in the 1860s while T. J. Prout was minister. (Karl Wallendszus)

Binsey was and is an attractive church; people might have more mundane reasons for being baptized or buried there, but from the end of the seventeenth century couples started to find it a pretty, romantic place to be married. A couple from St Thomas' Oxford started the trend in 1672, followed by one from St Peter in the East in 1701; the trend then spread outside the county to Winchester, and in the twentieth century beyond marriage to baptisms. Kent is recorded in 1918, Guildford in 1938, and Rhodesia in 1957; by the 1990s couples were coming to Binsey from Kenya, New York, and Gothenberg.

The number of people who felt themselves to be inhabitants of Binsey rose gradually to peak in the nineteenth century. Between 1593 and 1642 there are 80 baptisms and 46 burials in the registers; 220 years later, between 1813 and 1862, there are 118 baptisms and 73 burials – more people but the same proportions. A tiny village could not maintain a large population, and the discrepancy between baptisms and burials indicates the size of the drain out of the parish to find work elsewhere. Yet Binsey had its advantages in the matter of a healthy environment; Anne Bridgewater was 101 when she died in 1844, and the registers show that the cholera which struck Oxford in 1849 and 1853 entirely missed the village—just far enough separated for the contagion not to spread.

Believing yourself to be an inhabitant of Binsey and actually living there were two different things. Although forty percent of those born in Binsey had left the village before they died, Binsey in this context was more a state of mind than a geographical location. For the first decade of the eighteenth century, there exists the first record of occupations in the register: two bakers, butcher, mason, upholsterer, servant to the Schools, chandler, saddler, barber, miller, apothecary, coffee man, boatman, clergyman, shoemaker, bookbinder, labourer. How could a tiny village support these people? The answer of course is that it didn't; of the whole list, only the labourer actually lived in the village itself. Most of them lived in the parish of St Thomas. Binsey was too small to support more than a minor farming community and the odd boatman, so the surplus population had moved to the city and learned city occupations—yet their descendants continued to consider themselves Binsey inhabitants and turned to the church in the village for their key celebrations.

A century later, the occupations of those with addresses in the village gives a far more accurate depiction of its character: four farmers, thirteen labourers, a grazier, two carpenters, a gardener, a fisherman, a carter, a tailor—and a lodger with two London servants. A century after that, the list has reduced further to seven labourers, a carpenter, a cowman, and a boatbuilder—but a new trend is beginning. By now they are sharing the village with a motor mechanic, an electrical engineer, a college porter, a stonemason, a chemist, an architect, a motor driver, a fruiterer, a builder, a member of the school of forestry, and a civil servant and clerk of works. These are not entirely incomers; the last two bear the classic Binsey names of Prickett and Goatley. Today, inhabitants for whom there is no work in the village now take advantage of improved transport to live there while working in Oxford, and others who have no birth connection with the place nevertheless choose to live there.

Yet the actual number of inhabitants living in Binsey itself continues to fall, and after World War Two the trend shifts again; the registers continue to be full of non-village occupations—various dons, a journalist, another architect, a solicitor, an engineer, a stockbroker, a chef, etc.—but those pursuing them have once again moved outside the village boundaries, to Osney, Wolvercote, and Little Clarendon Street. There has been a return to the early eighteenth century, with those working outside the village looking to it as their community, only this time practically no names reflect the old inhabitants; these are outsiders who have chosen to turn their back on the anonymity of the city and find an identity in the nearby village.

The village green and its cottages. (Robert Mealing)

And ultimately this is what the registers reflect; Binsey not as a huddle of buildings but as a community. In a fast-changing world, we define ourselves by trying to ground ourselves in something with stability, with a past. Hence the enormous popularity of family history as people seek their personal past, but hence too the search for a community in which they can belong, a community with roots stretching back into mediaeval England. The parish registers are vital because they tell us who we are and who we wish to become. The return of the Binsey register was perhaps more important than its sender knew.

Mr Boardman and the Editors encourage all interested readers to contact the Oxfordshire History Centre for further information regarding local and genealogical research.

BINSEY: A CHURCH IN ITS LANDSCAPE

JULIAN MUNBY

Binsey has a strong sense of remoteness today. It is here that the county and city boundary swings away from the main stream of the Thames to run down the Swift Ditch into the Seacourt Stream. This is a peculiarity to Oxford dating to before modern boundary changes: the county boundary originally followed the outer stream on the west of Oxford, then crossed over by Folly Bridge on St Aldate's to follow the innermost stream along the 'Shire Lake' in Christ Church Meadow, and only regained the main stream at Iffley). Until 1974 this boundary marked the division between Oxfordshire and Berkshire, as it had for almost a thousand years, before which it was the boundary between the Anglo-Saxon Kingdoms of Wessex on the Berkshire side and Mercia on the Oxfordshire side. Across in Berkshire lay Wytham and Seacourt, the deserted village beneath the western bypass, and the small hamlet of Botley, all part of the ancient parish of Cumnor, now in Oxfordshire's Vale of the White Horse district.

Binsey was always a rural parish within the City and County of Oxford, and an ancient property of St Frideswide's Priory, believed by the Augustinian Canons of that place to have been with them since the time of St Frideswide herself in the eighth century and later passing to Wolsey's Cardinal College and so to Henry VIII's Christ Church.[1] The continued ownership of the saint's rural retreat by the church at the place of her burial for over 1,250 years is a remarkable feat of continuity and perhaps unique in England. Binsey is not mentioned in the Domesday Book, but the canons of St Frideswide told the commissioners of 1086 that they held four hides near Oxford, and proudly claimed that it had 'never paid tax and was not in any Hundred'.[2] If this included Binsey, it is interesting that both nearby Godstow and the priory's land at Cutteslowe were later thought to be extra-parochial (that is, outside any parish). For secular jurisdiction Binsey should have been in Oxford, or the 'Hundred outside the Northgate', which belonged by ancient tradition to the royal manor of Headington. The place was mentioned by name 'Beneseye' in royal and papal charters to the re-founded Priory from 1122 onwards, and called an 'estate' (*praedium*).[3] Little is known of St Frideswide's lands, on account of the loss of the bulk of their medieval business records, and it is only in the seventeenth and eighteenth centuries that the story can be taken up with the surviving estate records of Christ Church.

This chapter does not attempt to be a history of the village and its people, or the events that have taken place there, but looks at the landscape context of the church and village, to see how the fields, streams and hedges have formed the environs of this surprisingly remote place. This does involve some detailed exploration of the early history of such places as Medley, Langney, and Wyke, but these are perhaps less well-known parts of the history of West Oxford. The evidence under consideration must also include the landscape itself, and the later maps and estate records in the archives of Christ Church.

ISLANDS, PLACES, AND NAMES

Binsey was an island between the Seacourt Stream and the Swift Ditch, the natural flood-relief channels that no longer perform this task. Legend suggests that the church was at

---
[1] See Alan Crossley (ed.), *Victoria County History Oxon* IV (1979), 268–71 for a general account of Binsey.
[2] *Domesday Book*, Oxfordshire, Chapter 14 (14,1), f.157.
[3] S.R. Wigram, Cartulary of the Monastery of St Frideswide [*Cart. S.F.*] I, Oxford Historical Soc. [O.H.S.] 28 (1894), 10–21.

Binsey flooded, 1924. (Oxfordshire County Council - Oxfordshire History Centre)

a place called Thornbury, with Binsey as the small island on which the present village sits (and barely rises above the floods which sometimes cover the green). Medley is the next island on the south of the village green, and Langney was name of the southern end of the parish, with a lost village at Wyke (near Wyke Bridge at the south end of Binsey Lane). The place-names in -ey are from the Old English eg 'island', or Middle English eyt 'small island', frequently used as name elements on the marshy sides of the Thames. Binsey was 'Byni's island', and Thornbury 'thorn -burh' 'defended place', Langney 'long island', and Medley 'middle island' (between Oseney and Binsey, or perhaps between Cripley and Langney). Godstow, 'the place of God' was an extra-parochial area, perhaps once in Binsey, that had also been selected as a remote place of religious retreat with the foundation of its Benedictine nunnery in 1139.[4]

The landscape of this west Oxford fringe is one of low gravel islands rising above the alluvial floodplain. The annual cycle of the Thames, now embanked and controlled with locks and weirs, may be somewhat different from its historic pattern, but periodic inundation must always have been a factor, and in part essential for the hay meadows. Habitation was sought on the highest points that did not flood, and arable land was also to be found on the higher and dryer areas, with pasture and meadow on the lower ground. An unusual feature of the locality are the small floodplain woodlands at Godstow Holt, Church Grove, and Medley Grove.[5]

---

[4] M. Gelling, *Place-names of Oxfordshire* I, EPNS 23 (1953), 26.
[5] These have been studied by Delia Ayres in an unpublished report on their ecological history.

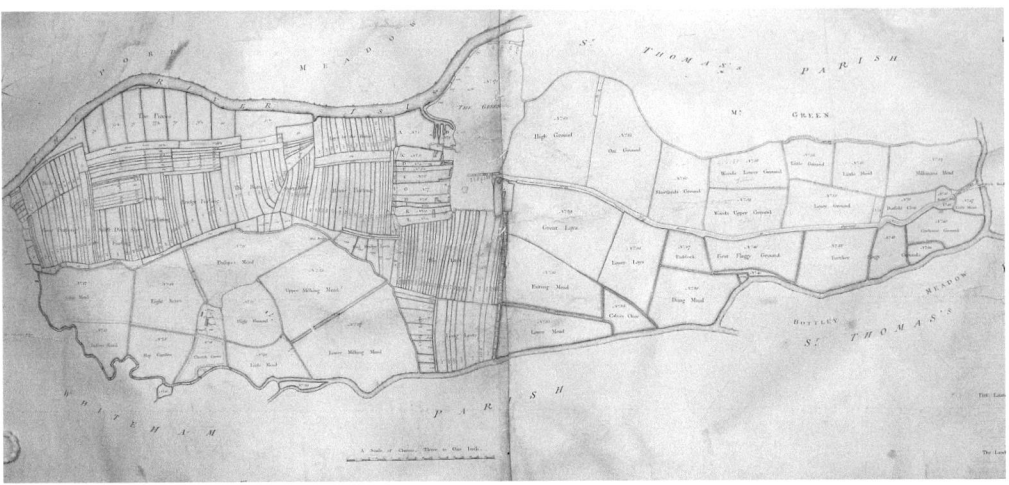

Field map of Binsey by Richard Davis of Lewknor, 1792
Courtesy of the Archivist and Governing Body of Christ Church (MS maps Binsey 2)

FIELDS AND FURROWS

The present field divisions of Binsey belong to the age of enclosure, when the medieval open fields were sub-divided by hedges. The fields themselves are otherwise unchanged, and the ridge and furrow of medieval agriculture remains visible in many places. The arable land was held by the village farmers in scattered strips of an acre more or less spread around in open fields. These were ploughed in such a manner that the centre of the strip was raised as a ridge and the sides sloped down to furrows marking the division between each strip. Groups of strips were arranged in separate furlongs. These had a name, may have been surrounded by a hedge, and were planted and harvested together. The essence of the open field system, apart from the scattered holding of strips, was the shared grazing of the fields after harvest, when the villagers' animals could roam across the strips and consume what remained or what grew up again. At other times the separation of pasture and arable was definite, and usually marked by well-formed hedges to prevent the cattle straying. Access to pastures mighty be controlled according to the time of year, while common pasture on Binsey Green (and sometimes on Port Meadow) was more freely available. The most specialised (and valuable) land-use was hay meadow, again arranged in strips, and sometimes allotted each year to different farmers. The meads lay next the river, and not surprisingly were also moulded into ridges and furrows, at right angles to the river to allow winter flood water to run off into the river. This crop was jealously guarded until hay harvest and might be more accessible later for general grazing in the 'aftermath'.

The land of Binsey is delineated by the main course of the Thames on the east and the outer, Seacourt Stream, on the west. The arrangement of land in Binsey is clearly shown on an estate map by Davis of Lewknor in 1792 in the Christ Church archives, which indicates the arable furlongs and meadow strips along streams.[6] At the north end are to be found the Butts and Great Furlong (running east-west), and then running southwards down the centre of fields are a series of east-west furlongs: Long and Short Swift Ditch

---

[6] Christ Church Archives, MS maps, Binsey 2.

Furlongs, Bridge Furlong, the Butts, Sheep Lake, and just behind the village plots the Home Furlong and Lays by the Hams. To the east of these were a run of long furlongs with strips running north-south: Dry Furlong, Long and Short Ashenden, and between these and the river were a series of meadows collectively known as The Pieces. Most of these are simply descriptive names, with occasional other elements named after people or locations. The Swift Ditch formed the western bound of the arable fields, and was no doubt maintained as the flood-relief channel through Binsey. To its west was a series of large irregular-shaped meadows: Great and Sadler's Mead at the north end, Eight Acres and Hop Garden just north of the churchyard, Philip's Mead, High Ground and Little Mead just to the south, and Upper and Lower Milking Mead further down.

West of the village green were fields with east-west strips: The Lays and the Long Leets. The later lay next to Cross Leets, small strips next to the Swift Ditch, and next to Pool Bridge Leets, both perhaps named after the artificial stream channel. These are all shown striped as if they were arable. South of the village green were two more 'Lay' names, Great Lays and Lower Lays, shown as undivided fields though today they retain traces of ridge and furrow. Perhaps, as in Northamptonshire, these 'leys' were arable or former arable given over to grass, and so still available for post-harvest pasture.[7] These last were next to Fatting Mead, Lower Mead and Calves Close, Dung Mead and Paddock. All of these meadows lay west of the road, and continue down southwards with First Flaggy Ground, Further Flaggy Ground, Cowhouse Ground (in which was a building, presumably the cow house), and Little Mead; the names at the south end of Binsey all suggest dairy farming and cattle breeding. Also south of the village green and east of the road, reaching as far the stream around Medley was a further line of meadows or possibly arable: High Ground, Oat Ground and Shortlands Ground, Woods Upper and Lower Ground, then Little Ground, Little Mead, and Leyey Ground. On approaching Wick Bridge at the south end of the parish and opposite Cowhouse Ground the meadows (Dutfield Close and Milkman's Mead) turn around Noddy Hill which bestrides the road.

In sum, the main village arable was on a ridge of land extending northwards from the centre, with a wide belt of pasture on the west, and a narrower belt on the east; south of the village some of the Leys and Grounds were very likely arable. This arrangement closely follows the geology and landform of the gravel islands rising above the alluvial plain.

BINSEY GREEN AND VILLAGE

The fields were farmed by individual peasant farmers living in the village, whose houses were ranged along the north side of the village green as they are today, with one house on the south side of the green. All the plots have or had long back gardens or crofts behind them, which the villagers could plant or use for grazing (and more recently orchards). There were eight plots in 1792, perhaps formed by sub-division of six primary plots, and in addition what is now Manor Farm at the east end, and the Perch beyond that.

In 1279, the description of Binsey in the 'Hundred Rolls' gives as many as twenty-one peasant farmer tenants of St Frideswide's Priory, so there may have been several more houses. Perhaps the plots were smaller, or there were some more houses on the green; there need have been no 'manor house', though on one of the plots may have been a grange from which a servant of the priory could oversee their interest in the village.

There are now at least five cottages, stone built in the vernacular tradition of the Oxford country fringe, and quite impossible to date from their external appearance, though perhaps

---

[7] David Hall, *The Open Fields of Northamptonshire*, Northants Record Soc. 38 (1995), 22.

containing medieval masonry and structural carpentry of the sixteenth to eighteenth centuries; the same can be said of the small barn by the farm. One cottage is thatched, and another has a steep roof that probably was thatched. The Perch Inn has a thatched cruck roof (in which the roof timbers rise from floor level) that has miraculously survived a series of fires. The 'farmhouse' has been partly rebuilt in brick, and there are two ninteenth-century brick houses at the west end of the row. Apart from the enclosure of the common or green, the village has not greatly changed in a century or so, and remains fairly unspoiled.

LANGNEY AND WYKE

The southern end of Binsey seems to have been regarded as a separate island called Langney. The island was one of the meadows 'behind Oseney' that were linked to the ancient and royal manor of Headington. Headington's ownership of land in north and west Oxford is one of the keys to the history of the City, if the origins of the place are partly to be seen as arising in a mere suburb of Headington.[8] The traveller approaching Oxford from the west entered the royal manor almost as soon as the county boundary was crossed at Ferry Hinksey (this is one of the candidates for the original 'ox-ford'). Here were extensive meadows in Oseney and Botley Meads, extending from St Thomas' and Oseney out to Botley (a hamlet in North Hinksey, in Berkshire), and which remained open and unenclosed until the nineteenth century. The meadows and their valuable hay crop were worth looking after—Hugh Plescy used the Headington crop to keep his nephew at Oxford in 1279.[9] It is because of the value of these hay meadows (in an age that relied on horses) that there are a surprising number of early charters recording their ownership and disputes over their possession.

Langney had been granted to Oseney Abbey by Geoffrey de Clinton (probably as lord of Headington) in the presence of the Empress Matilda, who confirmed the grant when she was at Oxford in July 1141; her charter is the oldest original document referring to a place in the parish.[10] The meadow was later rented by Oseney to St Frideswide's Priory around 1200, though it was recognised that there was still a link to the lord of Headington, and the grant was not absolute.[11] Then in the early thirteenth century St Frideswide's Priory acquired it from Hugh Pluggenait, the Breton Lord of the Manor of Headington, for 25s a year.[12] The Prior, after agreeing with Oseney Abbey that they would no longer claim parochial rights over Langney and Wyke, gave Langney to the men of Binsey. In 1279 St Frideswide was recorded as holding Langney as one of the meadows 'behind Oseney' from Hugh Plescy of Headington for 25s, and the rent was being paid by the Binsey tenants.[13]

As to its location, Langney seems to have been near Wyke, and the Oseney charter renouncing tithes refers to 'Langney and Wyke of the same Langney'. The memory of Wyke survived long enough to give its name to the first bridge of Binsey Lane, called 'Wick Bridge' in 1792, and in 1543 Christ Church leased the manor of Binsey 'with the Wyke and St Margarate's Well'.[14] Wyke (whose name should mean village or dairy farm)

---

[8] Helen Cam, 'The Hundred outside the Northgate of Oxford', *Oxoniensia* I (1936), 113–28, repr. in *Liberties and Communities in Medieval England* (1944), 107–23.
[9] R. Graham, 'Description of Oxford in the Hundred Rolls', *Collectanea* IV O.H.S. 47 (1905), 65; *VCH Oxon* v, 160.
[10] H.E. Salter, *Cartulary of Oseney Abbey* [*Cart. Osen.*], O.H.S. 6 vols, nos. 89–91, 97–8, 101 (1928–36), vol. iv, 60, 84; reproduced in Salter, *Facsimiles of Early Charters in Oxford Muniment Rooms* (1929), No. 96.
[11] *Cart. Osen.* iv, 61 = *Cart. S.F.* ii, 19.
[12] *Cart. Osen.* ii 20.
[13] J. Cooper, 'The Hundred Rolls for the Parish of St Thomas, Oxford', *Oxoniensia* 37 (1972), 108, Record Commission *Rotuli Hundredorum* (1818), ii, 811.
[14] W.H. Turner and H.O. Coxe, *Calendar of Charters and Rolls in the Bodleian Library* (1878), 662 [App.] Ch. 166.

was enough of a settled place to produce people called 'de la Wyke', (including the Oseney Chronicler) and appears fleetingly in a charter of 1313/14 when Reynilda daughter of Walter de la Wyck returned to Oseney Abbey the tenements that she helds in 'la Wick near Buneseye'.[15] The competing interests of the two monasteries continued to cause friction, and as late as 1386 the lengthy settlement of a dispute between Oseney and St Frideswide includes mention of the tithes of 'Reynalds Wyke', ownership of Langney and Medley, and obstruction of a highway called 'Kyngesgate' between le Wyke and Port Meadow.[16] This last must have been an access route leading to the ford across the river, and is a valuable reference to the fact that it existed at that date. The ford above Medley was dredged out in the course of Thames improvements in the nineteenth century, but the river is still not very deep. Intrepid drinkers from Wolvercote claim to have walked across the river from the Perch to Port Meadow but this may have involved a degree of aquatic levitation, and is perhaps not lightly or wantonly to be attempted. On the other hand, cattle are known to swim from Binsey to Port Meadow when they deem the grass there to be greener.

MEDLEY

Medley lies next to Langney at the south end of Binsey, separated from it by a ditch. Next to it was Feneit or Sidelings, which was part of Cripley on the east side of the Thames, and adjacent to Port Meadow. These were ancient properties of the borough of Oxford, but the complicated history of Medley in the twelfth century shows that, like Langney, it was valuable and worth having. It was granted away twice by the townsmen: once to St Frideswide's Priory in the 1130s, and then again to Oseney Abbey in the 1140s; the resulting dispute involved the Sheriff and King Stephen, who confirmed that it was indeed the property of St Frideswide in 1150/52.[17] The matter was unresolved until the reign of King Richard, when in a series of agreements with both St Frideswide's and Oseney the 'citizens of Oxford of the Commune of the City and the Gild Merchant' were finally able to confirm their grant of Medley to Oseney, in a splendid charter that carried not only the town seal (the earliest in England) but for the avoidance of all doubt listed the names of all the citizens.[18]

As well as being as being a separate 'island' with fields and meadows, Medley was always a distinct farm or hamlet, and in the 1279 Hundred Rolls it boasted two cottages.[19] In 1356 it was described as a 'manor', when Richard of Cumnor, a canon of Oseney, was reprimanded by the Bishop of Lincoln for celebrating mass there in an unlicensed oratory, which suggests that it may have been used as a place of retreat for the canons from Oseney Abbey.[20]

Certainly by the seventeenth century Medley was a place of resort, mentioned by George Wither (1588–1667) in his poem of lost love, 'I Loved a Lass'.

> In summer-time to Medley
> My love and I would goe,
> The boatmen there stood ready
> My love and I to rowe;
> For cream there would we call,

---

[15] Turner & Coxe, 359 [Os] Ch. 467 = *Cart Osen* vi 181 (1124)]; Gelling, *Oxon Place-names*, 471.
[16] *Cart. Osen.* ii 565–71 (1116).
[17] *Cart. Osen.* iv, 86–90.; Wigram, *Cart. S.F.* i, 26 (21), 33 (30), 36 (34).
[18] R.H.C. Davis, 'An Oxford Charter of 1191', *Oxoniensia* 33 (1968), 53–65.
[19] Cooper, 'Hundred Rolls', 173.
[20] *Cart. Osen.* vi, 306.

For cake, for pruines too;
But now, alas! She 'as left me,
Falero, lero, loo.

By then it had been sold off, passing to the new Bishopric of Oxford in 1546, sold by the Crown in 1575, and coming to the Spencer lords of Yarnton manor.[21] The Jacobite antiquary Thomas Hearne walked past in 1718 on June 10th (the birthday of James III), remarking that 'the House is much frequented in summer time by Scholars and others, there being good Accommodations there, and it being wonderfully pleasant'; (he also noted that it was 'drown'd often in winter', and best approached by boat in the summer season).[22] Not long after Hearne's visit Medley was acquired by Benjamin Sweet (or Swete), sometime paymaster under Chandos in the Duke of Marlborough's army, and a man who evidently found his position not unprofitable; he also bought the quarter part of Yarnton Manor in 1718.[23] Vast sums were made by Marlborough and by Chandos (James Brydges), who wrote to Sweet in 1709 telling him to 'take care to whom you entrust with your books' and to tell noone of any of his financial business.[24] Sweet took the (customary) one % on all moneys he handled, and was like Marlborough (who had the customary two and a half %) brought before Parliament in 1712 on groundless peculation charges.[25]

Sweet became a Freeman of Oxford in 1721, County Sheriff in 1722, and proceeded to build a gentry mansion at Medley, a decent pile with a central block and side wings, commemorated on Benjamin Cole's map of Port Meadow of c.1720, while according to Hearne the old public house remained in use.[26] However, Sweet was (rightly) refused permission by the Freemen of Oxford to drive across the Port Meadow, and the attempt by Christ Church to widen the gate at Walton Well in 1731 was unsuccessful, while Hearne tells us that he actually lived in a suite in the Cross Inn in Cornmarket.[27] Sweet died in 1744, and his son Adrien (who died in 1755) inherited it; it is said that Sweet's will was overturned on ground of insanity because he left 40s per annum to be spent on feeding sparrows.[28] His heir seems to have kept it going as 'a publick house of refreshment', but sold Medley in 1772. The new owner pulled it down in 1773, and replaced it with the present farmhouse.[29] Only the walled garden of Sweet's house still remains. Apart from a century in the ownership of Christ Church (1861–1954) it has remained a privately owned farm, and is today run as a mixed farm by its current owners, the Gee family, including a popular pick-your-own system for fruit and vegetables.

---

[21] *VCH Oxon* IV, 270.
[22] Buchanan Brown, *Remains of Thomas Hearne* (1966), 197; M.G. Hobson, *Oxford Council Acts 1701–1752*, O.H.S. new ser. 10 (1954), xxxix.
[23] *V.C.H. Oxon.* XII, 476.
[24] Susan Jenkins, *Portrait of a Patron* (2007), 93; G. Davis, 'The Seamier Side of Marlborough's War', *Huntington Library Quarterly* 15.1 (1951), 21–44. For Sweet's papers and correspondence with Marlborough, see the Blenheim Papers in the British Library, Add. MSS. 61135, 61326, 61330, 61406–7, and 62526.
[25] W.S. Churchill, *Marlborough his Life and Times* (US edition Scribner, 1968), iv, 837; see chapter on 'The Peculation Charge', which Churchill roundly refutes.
[26] *Oxford Council Acts 1701–1752*, xxxix; Cole's map is reproduced in M.G. Hobson, *Oxford Council Acts 1752–1801*, O.H.S. new ser. 15 (1962), frontispiece.
[27] *Oxford Council Acts 1701–1752*, xxxix, 178.
[28] T.M. Davenport, *Oxfordshire Lords-Lieutenant, High Sheriffs and MPs* (1888), 79; and see the National Archives, PRO Prob 18/56/34.
[29] Peshall's additions to Wood's *City of Oxford* (1773), in A. Clark, *Wood's History of the City of Oxford* I, O.H.S. 15, (1889), 630; B. Stapleton, *Three Oxfordshire Parishes*, O.H.S. 24 (1893), 230; OCA xxxix.

BINSEY FARMS AND FAMILIES

We hear little of events in Binsey, apart from occasional appearances in the records. The earliest named inhabitant, if a temporary one, was Edyva Launcelene of Winchester, the foundress of Godstow Nunnery, who according to the foundation legend was sent to Oxford in about 1138, and then to Binsey, where she lived awaiting heavenly instruction and was accordingly awoken with a voice telling her to seek the place where a light should come to earth, and so found Godstow.[30] The 1279 entry in the Hundred Rolls sadly does not give the usual list of villagers' names, so we have to be content with scattered references. For example, the Coroner's Roll for 24 August 1299 records that Adam de la Wyke was found dead at Wyke, and that the jury found he had spent the day before in an Oxford tavern and on returning home he had fallen into a wet ditch and drowned. The jury was formed from the hamlets of Binsey and Wyke, and the parishes of St Thomas and St Ebbe.[31] Then on 12 August 1302 John son of John Godfrey of Binsey was found on the riverbank next to 'la Wyke'; the jury found that he had been haymaking until sunset in Botley Mead and drunk so much on account of the heat that he was inebriated when he returned to his house at Wyke, and fell into the water and drowned when he got into his boat. Interestingly this court had jurors from Binsey, St Thomas, St Giles, and St Michael at the Northgate, suggesting that the body was found near a common boundary. The jurors from Binsey were named as John le Schote, William Jones, Thomas Reynald, Walter Jones, Hugh Nichol, and Adam Bonevait.[32] There was little doubt that it was the responsibility of the City Coroner to hear the cases, but the Priory of St. Frideswide liked to maintain their notion of Binsey as a Liberty, and in about 1371 petitioned the King complaining that the town was entering their franchise 'en le ysle de Benseye' in order to hang felons from Binsey there rather than in Oxford.[33] One cannot imagine that there were ever sufficient felons to have made this more than a notional franchise.

The history of the farming community of Binsey remains to be written, and this will largely depend on the recently re-discovered parish registers covering the sixteenth to the eighteenth centuries. The more prominent families are readily apparent from their memorial inscriptions and occurrence in records. The antiquary Thomas Hearne visited the graveyard in December 1718 and inspected the memorials, noting that 'in the foresaid little Church or Chapell of Binsey there is not so much as one old monument,' and he supposed that 'Persons of Note' would have been buried at St Frideswide's Church (i.e. the Cathedral).[34] Be that as it may, there had perhaps not been so many 'persons of note' living in Binsey. He did make notes of three graves, which are of value since the stones are now lost. One was the memorial of one Henry Hearne, buried in 1658, though not, he thought, a relative of his. One curious burial actually had no memorial:

'Just on the West Side of Binsey Church Yard, West of the Church, By St. Margaret's Well, lyes one Jeffery Ammon, without any Grave Stone. He lived in St. Thomas's Parish, Oxon, but desired to be buried here, because he used often to shoot hereabouts Snipes (there being Great Plenty of them here) and other Things. He was an Atheistical Fellow. He desired a certain Friend (viz. Will. Gardner, a Boatman of Oxford, who used to rowe him) to put now and then a Bottle of Ale by his Grave when he came that way, which

---

[30] A. Clark, *The English Register of Godstow Nunnery*, Early English Text Society 129 (1905), 26.
[31] H.E. Salter, *Snappe's Formulary and Other Records*, O.H.S. 80, (1924), 265 (9).
[32] J.E. Thorold Rogers, *Oxford City Documents*, O.H.S. 18 (1891), 163 (xvi).
[33] H.E. Salter, *Munimenta Civitatis Oxonie*, O.H.S. 71 (1917), 148 (154).
[34] Bodleian, MS Hearne's Diaries 100, f. 91.

accordingly he has done, as he desired. This Jeffery was an ingenious man, & a merry Companion.'

The only inscription of note, was (for Hearne) a modern one, to Thomas Crutch of Medley, which deserves to be quoted in full.

> To the Pious Memory
> Of THOMAS CRVTCH
> Who died July the 15.
> 1711 aged 84 Years.
> All that was good and truly just
> Was found in this deceased friend
> Before you moulder then to dust
> With carefulness your life amend
> He laid him down to sweet repose
> Not dreading of approaching death
> For e'er the morning sun arose
> Was forced to resign his breath
> Reader, be true in thy ways
> And constantly provide for Blisse
> So God shall lengthen out thy days
> As he did truly lengthen his.

Ten years later Hearne had a long talk with Thomas Prickett, aged seventy-one, who had been a soldier in the militia and lived with his family at Binsey.[35] The Prickett family are noted from 1615 when Henry Prickett had a 'licence to victual' at Binsey where he lived, no doubt as landlord of the Perch.[36] Families like the Hearnes, Smiths, Crouches and Pricketts occur down to the twentieth century. Mary Prickett (1832–1920), the governess of Alice Liddell, was of this family, if not its Binsey branch, and the Revd T.J. Prout, Vicar 1857–91, and contemporary of Charles Dodgson, is thought to be the model for the Dormouse. The main lessees in 1792 (apart from the three clergymen Barton, Bentham, and Randolph) were Sarah and John Prickett, John Cauzier, and Vincent Shortland.[37] By the twentieth century the land was mostly in Binsey Manor farm, or let to nearby landowners (as Medley Manor Farm and the University Farm at Wytham).

WOODS AND HEDGES

The woodland cover has probably not greatly changed over recent centuries, but the appearance of fields and hedges has certainly done so. The medieval open fields were not divided internally between furlongs, because they were open to common grazing after harvest, but there were likely to be hedges round each large field, and hedges separating areas of arable from commons and permanent pastures. The fields of Binsey suffered from flooding, and it was reported in 1818 that farming had become impractical with land being dispersed in small strips, liable to flooding, and left open until 15 November, after the time for sowing wheat.[38] The medieval peasant holdings were now 'copyholds', held hereditarily and by custom from Christ Church, without deeds of title but 'by copy of court roll', that is a copy of the record by which land was inherited or taken on. By 1821 Christ Church

---

[35] D.W. Rannie, (ed.), *Remarks and Collections of Thomas Hearne* VI, O.H.S. 43, (1902), 264 [Hearne]; *R&C Thomas Hearne* IX, O.H.S. 65, (1914), 399 [Prickett].
[36] R. Blades (ed.), *Oxford Quarter Sessions Order Book* 1614–1637, O.H.S. n.s. 29, (2009), 5.
[37] Christ Church MS Maps, Binsey 2 (1792).
[38] VCH Oxon IV, 270 quoting Christ Church MS Estates 62.

had obtained the surrender of the remaining copyholds (thus extinguishing all rights of common in the fields) and proceeded to enclose the land by sub-dividing the medieval open fields and creating self-contained farms. The college archives contain records of the purchase and planting of thousands of 'quicksetts', the hawthorn trees (and hollies) that now form the hedged boundaries of the fields. They are today interspersed with oak and ash trees, which provide shelter and additional supplies of timber and firewood.[39]

CHURCH LAND

The site of Binsey church is on a separate island raised slightly above the surrounding meadows and outlined by a bank and ditch. The ditch is most marked at the south-east corner at the start of the avenue approaching the church, where it still holds water, and there was a bridge (now filled in) over the ditch. The field is overlain with ridge and furrow (and this is continuous on both sides of the avenue). The bank and ditch form a large circle that includes the church, churchyard and nearby houses, and is mostly shown on the 1792 map where it bounds the field called High Ground. Large enclosures of this kind round ecclesiastical sites are typical of early Christian monastic sites (e.g. in Ireland) and may suggest that this is of some antiquity. Recent exploration with geophysics has shown areas of activity that may suggest structures, while a section dug in 1987 on the south side revealed remains of a ditch and bank. Whether this is an Iron Age defended enclosure reused in the Anglo-Saxon period, or a 'monastic' earthwork is uncertain, but the defended enclosure or 'burh' seems to lie behind the name 'Thornbury' (thornbiri) recorded as the alternative name for Binsey in the Frideswide legend.[40]

THE CHURCH

The church stands in a small churchyard, bounded by a ditch on the south side that closes off the north end of the larger enclosure. A stone wall round the churchyard was built in the nineteenth century and is not shown on the 1790 estate map, when there was only one building north of the church and the churchyard was much larger. The earliest serious account of Binsey and its church comes from the pen of the Oxford antiquary Anthony Wood (1632–1695). He wrote his account of the City of Oxford in the 1660s, and having been brought up in Oxford had access to oral traditions of pre-reformation Oxford. He describes the church as a 'forlone and naked' chapel, and states that the well house, which had a 'picture' of St Margaret (or St Frideswide), and was pulled down in 1639, while another building adjoining the chapel, a 'house with arched windows and arched doore', was pulled down in 1678. His statement about pilgrimage to the well must have some substance in memory, if amplified by speculation:

> To this well also and her image and certaine reliques in the chapple did the people come on pilgrimage with as great devotion to ease their burdened soules and obtaine resolutions of their doubts, as they would to an oracle. And here also, when those maimed and unsound folke had bin cured either by bathing in, or drinking of, this water, hang up their crutches as a speciall memorandum of their cured greifs.

He also believed that there were 'several priests' appointed by St Frideswide to live there 'purposely to confess and absolve those pilgrims.'[41] There is not a great amount of

---

[39] Christ Church Archives, MS Estates 62 [enclosure accounts]
[40] John Blair, 'Thornbury, Binsey: A probable Defensive Enclosure associated with St. Frideswide', *Oxoniensia* 53 (1988), 3–20; this volume, reprinted pp. 55-73.
[41] Clark, *Wood's City* I, 324.

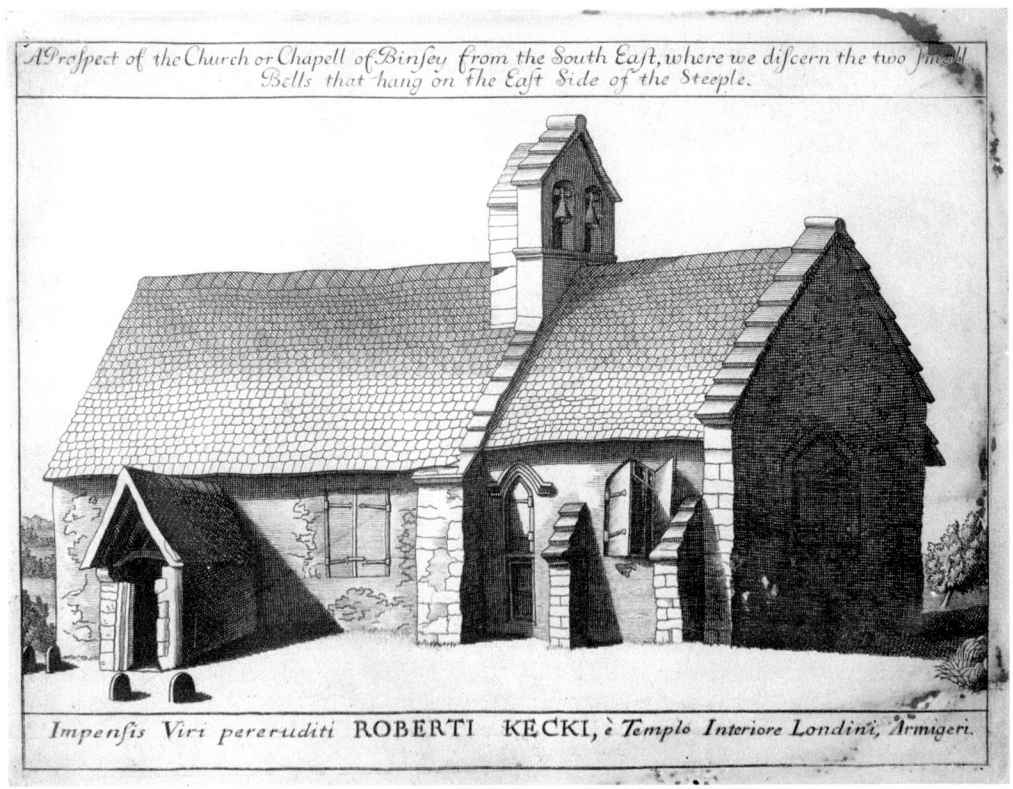

A view of St Margaret's engraved by Michael Burghers, 1710. (English Heritage Archive)

evidence to corroborate this account, though we may assume that some of it was a matter of oral tradition preserved in Binsey. There is in the twelfth-century 'Life and Miracles of St Frideswide' at least one cure (of a partially deaf woman) at the well.[42]

In his account of the church Wood has little history to add, though he makes a couple of important observations, in reporting the surviving 'part of St Frideswide's picture' in the window (perhaps that still to be seen in the east window) and 'the repository or tabernacle in the south wall of the chancell whereon her costly statue bedekt with ornaments was sometime standing.'[43] This is the recess in the south wall of the chancel between the stone basin (piscina) to the east and priest's low window to the west. It may have been a clergy seat (sedilia), though it could have been a canopied niche for a statue, like that of St Beornwald at Bampton;[44] another niche is still to be seen behind the pulpit, which may have contained an image, and perhaps marks the site of a second altar. Wood goes on to remark that the pavement here had been worn hollow by the adoration of pilgrims.

Thomas Hearne was the next learned visitor. In 1716 he passed by returning from Wytham and read the memorial inscriptions, including that of Thomas Crutch 'written in rime in the Country Dialect', as noted above.[45] Two years later in November 1718

---

[42] *Acta Sanctorum* 19 October, see Henry Mayr-Harting, 'Functions of a Twelfth-Century Shrine: The Miracles of St Frideswide', in H. Mayr-Harting and R.I. Moore (eds), *Studies in Medieval History Presented to R.H.C. Davis* (1985), 193–206.
[43] Clark, *Wood's City* II, O.H.S. 17 (1890), 43.
[44] John Blair, 'St Beornwald of Bampton', *Oxoniensia* 49 (1984), 47–54, esp. pls. 2–3.
[45] *R & C Thomas Hearne* V, O.H.S. 42, (1901), 189.

Late twelfth-century south doorway of St Margaret's church. The arch has a single order of roll-moulding, which is overlapped by a band of zigzag and a hood with two rolls flanking a band of dogtooth terminating in each side with a dragon head, The shafts have foliate capitals. The doorway is the earliest feature now extant in the church and can be compared with the contemporary south doorway of St Lawrence's church, North Hinksey, likewise with dragon stops. (Julian Munby)

he returned to copy the inscription and noted the church 'is now roofing, having never been roofed before. The Man told me he had agreed to do it for an hundred pounds.'[46] I think we must read this as being re-roofed, rather than having previously been a ruin. On another visit Hearne tells us that the 'present Church or Chappel of Binsey stands on the right hand side of the old Oratory, of which Oratory there is nothing now remaining.'[47] He was perhaps referring to the site of the well, which he doesn't otherwise mention. On a further visit in December 1718, Hearne took with him Michael Burghers, the Dutch University engraver (successor to David Loggan), 'on purpose to take a Draught of the Church', and this engraving was published the following year in Hearne's edition of the Chronicle of William of Newburgh (above). It was one of a series of views of Oxford antiquities drawn for him by Michael Burghers, and was paid for by Robert Keck (?1686–1719), FRS, a lawyer of the Inner Temple with historical and antiquarian interests (chiefly

---

[46] *R & C Thomas Hearne* VI, 252.
[47] Brown, *Remains of Thomas Hearne*, 196.

Medieval glass in the east window of St Margaret's. (Robert Mealing)

remembered today as the former owner of the Chandos portrait of Shakespeare). Hearne had first come across him as an executor of Dr Radcliffe's will, and corresponded with him until his death in 1719. This was the year of the publication of the Chronicle of William of Newburgh, for it was Hearne's practice to slip his Oxford antiquities into his historical works as appendices.[48]

---

[48] T. Hearne (ed.), *Guilielmi Neubrigensis Historia* (Oxford, 1719) is illustrated by Oxford Castle, Godstow, and Binsey.

St Margaret's Church in 1892 by Henry Taunt. (English Heritage Archive)

The Burghers illustration is of value in showing the church as it was prior to the nineteenth-century restorations. There are two bellcotes rather than the present single one, and wooden shutters on the windows. The nave has one window, so unless it is hidden behind a buttress there was then no window by the pulpit. In 1722 Hearne reported further repairs to the church 'the steeple now done but not yet so as to differ from the Draughts of the old one that I have published.'[49]

Today the church is a small, simple stone building on a two-part plan of nave and chancel, with a porch on the south side. It is built in local limestone rubble, with dressed stone to the windows, buttresses and corners. The south door is Norman, a round arch with chevron (zig-zag) decoration ending in the heads of dog-like beasts. The small columns flanking the door have capitals with a delicate classical ornament, and it must date from the late 1160s, in part reflecting some of the astonishing variety of Romanesque forms to be seen in St Frideswide's Church (Oxford Cathedral) but not exactly paralleled there.[50] How much of the church belongs to this period can only be guessed, but the lack of Norman windows in the north wall perhaps shows that much of it belongs to a later rebuilding. The tall lancet window in the south wall of the chancel indicates that there was a substantial rebuild in the thirteeenth century. This was a 'low side window', a common feature that

[49] R & C Thomas Hearne VII, O.H.S. 48, (1906), 344.
[50] I am grateful to Richard Halsey for his discussion of the Binsey portal. See R. Halsey, 'The 12th-Century Church of St. Frideswide's Priory', Oxoniensia 53 (1988), 115–67.

St Margaret's Church in 1903. (Robert Mealing)

once provoked an endless controversy amongst ecclesiologists, and which can readily be seen to be designed to provide light to the priest's desk—an understandable need at Binsey with its lack of artificial light even though this one has now been blocked in the lower part. The (rebuilt) chancel arch would also be of this period, with its plain chamfered arches and delightful stone knots in the responds on either side, but the chancel roof may be of later date, since from what we can see of its arch-braced collar construction it is more likely to be of the fourteenth century or later. The porch may be of the thirteenth or fourteenth-century, and scratched mass dials can be seen on the right of the (modern) door.

A phase of late medieval reconstruction is evidenced by the 'perpendicular' tracery in four-centred arches in the chancel, and the square-headed windows in the nave. The chancel was perhaps now rebuilt with the addition of buttresses all having characteristic curved tops. The Royal Commission Inventory dates the nave and chancel windows to the fifteenth century, though the nave ones may be older than the chancel.[51] The new east window and south window will have given more light than earlier and smaller windows, as did the two windows in the south and west walls of the nave. The east window was glazed (and some remains of medieval glass have been placed there again), but the windows on the south side were shuttered and may not have been glazed. The shutter hinges can still be seen, and the Burghers engraving shows them in place.

The chancel has a medieval roof, of which the curved arch braces supporting the collar beam can be seen, though the rafters are obscured by the plaster ceiling. This may date from the fourteenth or fifteenth century. The nave roof is rather later, and made to a

---

[51] Royal Commission on Historical Monuments, *An Inventory of the Historical Monuments in the City of Oxford* (1939, 1949), 148 (with plan).

more rustic pattern, with purlins running the length of the roof, supported by curved windbraces, and may date from the sixteenth century or later. The possible nave altar on the south of the chancel arch has been mentioned, and the blocked door opposite in the north wall may have led up to a rood loft or to an external building (on the north wall of the nave is another blocked opening, leadng slightly further west).

Apart from the font, possibly a Norman bowl on a (restored) thirteenth-century base of clustered columns, there are no ancient fittings. Fragments of ancient glass have been brought together in the east window, and include a female figure (perhaps St Margaret), a priest's head, and the possible figure of a pilgrim with an indeterminate number of legs, some of them of the feathered angel variety. Two wall memorials commemorate the Prickett and Tawney families, and there is a board with the royal arms of Queen Anne that perhaps commemorated the application of her 'Bounty' to augment the living in 1746.[52] One of the bells is dated 1652, serving as a pleasing note of defiance in dangerously republican times when such things were disapproved of by Puritans.

Pews, reading desk and pulpit date from the nineteenth-century restorations, and the stone floor, incorporating memorial slabs, has been re-laid in one of the restorations. The church was restored and chancel rebuilt by Christ Church in 1833, again in the 1875 under the Revd T.J. Prout, and in the 1890s with Revd C.E. Adams in 1892 (when Christ Church contributed to the chancel repairs).[53] The Taunt photograph from the late nineteenth century shows the newly restored church with some rather small yew trees in front of it. One later restoration is of some interest. A small silver plaque in the chancel floor commemorates the life of Arthur Bellamy Clifton (1863–1933), whose benefaction paid for a restoration in 1933–34. He was the son of an Oxford physics professor, and must have known Binsey as a child. As a young solicitor he visited Oscar Wilde in Reading Gaol, and later became an art dealer at the Carfax Gallery in London, exhibiting modern artists such as Epstein, Augustus John, etc. Neither his will nor the parish records record the exact nature of his benefaction (he left everything to his wife, who made the arrangements) but he may be responsible for the modern sculpture added to the inside of the pulpit.

Binsey has always attracted visitors, and both poets and artists have celebrated the western views of Oxford from its hills and valleys. J.M.W. Turner, William Turner 'of Oxford', and Peter de Wint have drawn views of Oxford with the western fields in the foreground. Walkers along the riverside have strolled as far as The Perch, or continued to The Trout at Godstow, but a surprising number have found their way along the twisting lane to the church at its end. Some (like Dodgson and the Liddell sisters) have rowed as far as Godstow and perhaps picnicked on the bank. They may lament the loss of the more recent generation of poplars that must have replaced Hopkins' trees, as walkers resent the hard edge of council kerbstones that diminish the character of an unspoilt country lane. In the skies they will see buzzards from Wytham contest with kites from the Chilterns (and perhaps have some effect on the rabbit population). Some may note the signs of badger sets, and recognise the standards planted in the enclosure hedges, others will see the ridge and furrow in the setting sun or beneath a light covering of snow. Beyond this only the low bank of Frideswide's enclosure remains, and in the still moments when the distant traffic is hushed in the imagination one can still think back to recall the little church and place of safety amongst the thorn trees.

---

[52] Papers relating to Queen Anne's Bounty, and Parliamentary Grants, for Augmentation of Maintenance of Poor Clergy, 1703–1815, 97.
[53] *The Oxford University and City Guide* (Slatter and Rose, *c.* 1860), 274; *VCH Oxon* iv, 271; Ch Ch Archives, *Governing Body Minutes 1885–1901*, 153.

BINSEY AND LEWIS CARROLL

EDWARD WAKELING

An amorous Mercian king, a virtuous Saxon woman, an ancient place of healing, and the author of *Alice's Adventures in Wonderland* are all linked by the little hamlet of Binsey, Oxfordshire. The story begins far back in the seventh century.

According to medieval legends, Frideswide, born around AD 675, was the beautiful daughter of a Christian Saxon nobleman who lived in Oxford. Some say she was a princess. King Algar of Mercia sought her as his bride, but she refused to marry him. Not to be thwarted, Algar pursued Frideswide to her home, but she ran away and found refuge in the woods at Bampton on the banks of the Thames. The ancient chronicler, Robert of Cricklade, from whom the history of Frideswide mainly derives, was clearly confused about the facts. Writing in around 1160, he described Frideswide as residing for three years with a swineherd and his wife. He names the wood as Binsey, though this is nowhere near Bampton. Here Frideswide lived a humble life with the country-folk. Soon, her reputation as a miracle worker began to spread; a blind girl had her sight restored, and a fisherman possessed of demons was cured. Gradually, Frideswide gathered a number of supporters (holy sisters) around her, working on the land, and committed to a life of Christian devotion. Robert of Cricklade suggests that Frideswide, over this period of time, moved from Bampton to Binsey. In an attempt to cross the river by boat on her way back to Oxford, she and her companions reached Binsey and decided to remain there for a further period of quiet contemplation and solitude. They built an oratory and other buildings for their religious needs. Binsey, being some way off from the river, was not very convenient for collecting water, so she suggested the construction of a well for the sisters' daily needs. She gave religious significance to the well through her prayers to St Margaret, and, from the holy water, miraculous healing took place for those that drank from the well and prayed there.

Much of the preceding account may have stemmed from Robert of Cricklade's imagination, who, as prior of St Frideswide's monastery, came to write the history of the life of his founder-saint. Nevertheless, there is independent evidence to show that Binsey was a holy place of religious activity at this time with links to Godstow nunnery not far away.

In the meantime, Algar marched with his army to the gates of Oxford, but was struck blind by lightening in a storm. His pursuit of Frideswide was given as the cause of this unlucky event. Legend suggests that he went to St Margaret's well at Binsey, and his blindness was cured. Algar was convinced that his misfortune was caused by his attempt to make the virtuous Frideswide his wife, and that his subsequent cure resulted from her intervention and forgiveness. He repented his selfish and lecherous attitude and left Frideswide in peace to pursue her monastic ambitions. At some later stage, Frideswide returned to Oxford and established a religious house for her followers. On her death, around AD 735, she was made a saint, and a shrine to her memory was created at the beginning of the eleventh century in St Frideswide's Priory. The site later became part of the cathedral college of Christ Church. The shrine was destroyed in the sixteenth century, but fragments survived. In recent times the shrine has been reconstructed and is situated in the cathedral, just below the famous Burne-Jones window that depicts her life. She is now the patron saint of Oxford, commemorated on her feast-day, 19 October, by a memorial service in the cathedral attended by the bishop of Oxford, the dean and canons, the vice-chancellor of the university, the proctors, and the mayor and people of Oxford.

The holy well at Binsey, named after St Margaret, survives in the churchyard. As time passed, the healing-well became known as the Treacle Well, the word 'treacle' being used in its medieval sense of a healing liquid rather than a sweet sticky confection. Over time, the well disappeared among the undergrowth. The living of the parish of Binsey eventually came under the gift of Christ Church, and the vicar was, in Victorian times, appointed by the Dean and Chapter. Thomas Jones Prout (1823–1909), Senior Student at Christ Church, was appointed vicar of Binsey in 1857, a post he held until 1891. One of Prout's first tasks as the new vicar was to locate and restore the well. He was a classical scholar and undoubtedly knew the history of St Frideswide and her connection with Binsey.

Change was afoot at Christ Church in the late 1850s. Up to this time, the management of the college and cathedral was entirely in the hands of the Dean and Chapter—the latter consisting of the canons of the cathedral. The income generated from college fees and its estates dotted around the country was divided by them, with the lion's share going towards their stipends and a small proportion used as the salaries of the academic staff. The differential between the income of clerical and academic staff was greatly in favour of the former, much to the discontent of the latter. In 1865, the senior Students (the equivalent of fellows in other colleges) challenged the absolute power of the Dean and Chapter. Various meetings were held to discuss tactics, and Prout was a leader among the Students in this respect. The outcome brought successful changes to the status and financial position of the Students, so much so that Prout became known as 'The man who slew the canons'. Another key Student who took part in the challenge was Charles Lutwidge Dodgson (1832–1898), better known to us as the author Lewis Carroll.

At the time when Prout had taken over the living of Binsey, Dodgson was befriending the children of the Dean of Christ Church. In 1855, Henry George Liddell (1811–1898), formerly headmaster of Westminster School, was appointed Dean of Christ Church by Lord Palmerston, Prime Minister. This was a royal appointment, and Queen Victoria approved the selection. Liddell was an undergraduate at Christ Church from 1829 until he took his BA in 1833. He gained a first class degree in classics and a first class in mathematics. As a graduate he was appointed joint sub-librarian with Robert Scott (1811–1887) and together they embarked on a monumental scholarly work, the *Greek-English Lexicon*, which was first published in 1843. Liddell took his MA in 1835 and was ordained soon after, as deacon in 1836 and priest in 1838. He became a tutor at Christ Church in 1836, and held this position for the next ten years. He was classical examiner to the university in 1844 and 1845, and chosen as select preacher on two occasions in 1842 and 1847. Eventually, he was appointed Whyte's professor of moral philosophy in 1845, but held the post for only one year before taking over the headship of Westminster School. For a time he was domestic chaplain to Queen Victoria's husband, Albert, Prince Consort, and in this role became known personally to the Royal Family. Liddell married Lorina Hannah Reeve (1826–1910), daughter of James Reeve of Lowestoft, in 1846. When the Liddells came to the Deanery at Christ Church, they had one son, Edward Henry 'Harry' (1847–1911), and three daughters, Lorina Charlotte (1849–1930), Alice Pleasance (1852–1934), and Edith Mary (1854–1876). A second son, James Arthur Charles (1850–1853), contracted scarlet fever during an outbreak of the disease at Westminster School, and died just before his third birthday. Further children were born at Christ Church; Rhoda Caroline Anne (1859–1949), Albert Edward Arthur (1863, died aged 8 weeks), Violet Constance (1864–1927), Frederick Francis (1865–1950), and Lionel Charles (1868–1942).

Charles Lutwidge Dodgson was educated at Richmond School in Yorkshire and then at Rugby. He entered Christ Church in January 1851. He graduated with a third class in classics and a first class in mathematics at the end of 1854. He gained the highest score in mathematics that year, and was asked to remain at Christ Church as a tutor, being made sub-librarian to supplement his income. Dodgson's lecturer in mathematics, Robert Faussett (1827–1908), was about to leave Christ Church to take up a position as an army officer in the Crimean War. This created an important vacancy at Christ Church, and Dodgson realised that he stood a good chance of getting the post. But he was at a disadvantage having only a bachelor's degree—he had yet to take his MA (usually purchased from the University after a given number of terms had elapsed). The Chapter, on the appointment of a new Dean, gave one honorary BA and one honorary MA to members of the college, and Dodgson was made MA of the House (an internal promotion with privileges within Christ Church, but not in the university as a whole). Nevertheless, it cleared the way for Dodgson to be appointed mathematical lecturer by Liddell within months of him becoming Dean. Dodgson noted the new Dean's decision in his diary in August 1855, but he did not take up the lectureship until January 1856.

In the meantime, Dodgson became acquainted with the Dean's children. Liddell spent the first few winters on the island of Madeira for the sake of his health, which had deteriorated in the unhealthy atmosphere surrounding Westminster School, and his wife, but not his children, accompanied him. The children were left at Christ Church in the capable hands of Mary Prickett (1833–1916), their governess. Her father was James Prickett, butler at Trinity College, and it appears that he had relatives at Binsey. There are a number of gravestones in Binsey churchyard that are memorials to the Prickett family. Miss Prickett, or 'Pricks' as the children called her, was not particularly well educated, but certainly able to instil values of good behaviour and society correctness among her young charges—Lorina, Alice, and Edith. Harry was sent to boarding school. Academic accomplishments for girls, apart from basic skills such as reading and writing, were not favoured by the Victorians, although the Dean's children had the advantage of lessons from his university colleagues. John Ruskin, for example, taught Alice the rudiments of art and painting. She was also taught to write and speak French, probably by a university tutor.

Dodgson took pity on the parentless children living at the Deanery. For up to three months they did not see their mother and father. Dodgson made many trips to the Deanery to cheer them up and entertain them. Story-telling was probably the main entertainment, and they would also sing and play the piano for him. He invented games for them and taught them to play croquet. He became a regular visitor to the Deanery, even after the return of the Dean and Mrs. Liddell, often at the invitation of the children (with their parents' permission). Dodgson was an amateur photographer—a relatively new invention in the 1850s—and he took photographs of all the children. He set up his camera in the Deanery Garden and used many opportunities to get portraits of the Liddell sisters. As they grew older and more confident, the entertainment included excursions, walks, and river-trips. On one memorable day, 4 July 1862, the river-trip turned out to be a very special occasion indeed. The trip had been delayed by a day due to bad weather, so the anticipation was heightened and the expectation of an afternoon of singing and story telling without the constraints of the prim governess to curb their enthusiasm added to the excitement. They set off—the three sisters, Dodgson, and a further companion chosen by the children—Revd Robinson Duckworth (1834–1911), renowned for his wonderful singing voice; a crew of five rowing from Folly Bridge to Godstow.

Alice was then aged ten, her sisters, Lorina thirteen, and Edith eight. Dodgson was thirty and Duckworth was twenty-eight, so the crew was youthful, and the occasion was probably lively and frequently punctuated with the singing of popular songs of the day. The rowing was left to the two young men. Alice acted as cox. The journey by river from Oxford to Godstow was long—probably taking two or more hours each way. They had no reason to rush. The main entertainment was a story invented for the occasion by Dodgson—unplanned and purely from his fertile imagination—a story of a little girl named Alice who chases a White Rabbit down a rabbit-hole into Wonderland. The invention of the story included real people, real places, and real events, and much of the fun for the three girls was to identify which parts of the story were based on the truth, often heavily disguised. The whole crew became part of the story, especially in the scene where Alice, having fallen into a pool of her own tears, meets a number of creatures all trying to get dry. Alice was herself, of course, but Lorina was the Lory (a kind of small parrot), Edith was the eaglet, Dodgson was the dodo, and Duckworth was the duck. Other characters may have been instantly recognisable to the children—the rude and rather abrupt marchioness (later to become the duchess) was probably based on their governess, Miss Prickett. The eccentric hatter (who appears in the published version of the story) was probably modelled on Theophilus Carter (d. 1904), furniture and hat salesman with premises in The High at Oxford.

At the end of the day, young Alice asked if Mr. Dodgson would be kind enough to write out the stories he had invented for them. He agreed. But what a task it must have been—an impromptu story told without notes invented for the occasion. We know that Dodgson began immediately to jot down headings and ideas to help him remember the story, and this continued on a railway journey to London he made on the following day. Eventually, bit by bit, he reconstructed as much of the story that he could remember, and began writing it on sheets of paper in his best handwriting, leaving spaces for some illustrations he intended to add. This manuscript was begun on 13 November 1862, more than four months after the boat-trip. It took him three months to write out the story, which he completed in spare moments between his main job of lecturing to the undergraduates at Christ Church. He noted in his diary that the text was complete on 10 February 1863. Then came the task of filling in the illustrations, and to be sure these were done well, he practised first. Christ Church Library has several sheets of preliminary drawings, some containing goblins and elves which were eventually omitted from the story. One of his brothers, Wilfred Longley Dodgson (1838–1914), who graduated at Christ Church in 1860, may have helped with some of the ideas for the drawings. A sketch of the Gryphon has the initials 'W.L.D.' clearly inscribed in the bottom-right corner, although all the pictures added to the final text are in Dodgson's hand.

Various people read the story, probably before the sheets were bound up and the book was not yet finalised. One such family who had the opportunity to try out the story was the MacDonalds. Dodgson met the novelist and poet George MacDonald (1824–1905) sometime around 1860, and they immediately became friends. MacDonald was also a writer of children's stories, so they had that in common. Dodgson visited the MacDonald family on several occasions, getting to know a large family of children, and he let Mrs Louisa MacDonald borrow his manuscript story to read to her children. Their response was very enthusiastic and this positive encouragement, probably with support from George MacDonald, made Dodgson consider publication for his story. In the meantime, he had the final corrected sheets bound up in green leather, and he presented this manuscript, which he entitled 'Alice's Adventures Under Ground' to Alice Liddell as an early Christmas gift on Saturday 26 November 1864, two and a half years after the tale was first told. Even before this event, Dodgson had taken steps to have the book published, but in a greatly expanded version with all references to Oxford and the Liddell children heavily disguised or removed. Initially, he thought that his own illustrations would suffice, and he had even drawn one on wood and had it engraved for the purpose. But advice from friends, particularly Thomas Woolner (1825–1892), a Pre-Raphaelite sculptor, persuaded him to get a professional artist to draw the pictures. With an introduction from another friend, Tom Taylor (1817–1880),

Dodgson called on the famous *Punch* illustrator, John Tenniel (1820–1914), in January 1864 and asked him if he would accept a commission to draw pictures for the story. Tenniel accepted the commission on 5 April 1864, and Dodgson sent him the first section of the story set up in type from the manuscript on 2 May. Tenniel was a very busy man, providing illustrations for the satirical magazine *Punch* every week. By 16 December 1864, Dodgson had only received a dozen illustrations for the book; he had planned to have forty-two pictures. He noted that on Sunday 18 June 1865, he received the last three illustrations, and with all haste the book was published, now under the title *Alice's Adventures in Wonderland*. The pages were printed in Oxford by the Clarendon Press (the University Press) between 20 and 27 June, and sent to London to Macmillan and Company for binding and distribution. Dodgson was very keen that a copy should be specially bound in white vellum and sent to Alice Liddell in time for the third anniversary of the boat-trip on 4 July 1865. As it happened, they met each other at the Royal Academy exhibition that day, so it is possible that Dodgson gave his presentation copy to Alice personally. But at this time Dodgson was unaware of a major problem that was brewing. He had asked Macmillan to send him fifty bound copies so that he could present these to friends. We do not know for certain if he received these, but his diary recorded that on 15 July he went to Macmillan's and 'wrote in 20 or more copies of *Alice* to go as presents to various friends'. One recipient must have been Tenniel because within a few days he wrote back to Dodgson saying that he was 'entirely unsatisfied with the printing'. Some of the illustrations had been printed lightly, and on some pages it was possible to see the outline of the text 'bleeding through' from the verso, especially where there was white space at chapter headings. Tenniel was concerned that his reputation as a major artist was at stake if these books were sold. Dodgson was forced to withdraw the complete edition of 2,000 copies. He even went as far as trying to get back the presentation copies he had already given away, and in one surviving letter to one of the recipients he wrote: 'I write to beg that, if you have received the copy I sent you of *Alice's Adventures in Wonderland*, you will suspend your judgment on it till I can send you a better copy. We are printing it again, as the pictures are so badly done'. Not all these presentation copies came back, and as a result, they are extremely rare and now very valuable. The current value of an 1865 edition of *Alice* is about £1,000,000—but most of the known twenty-three or so books are now in institutional libraries and will never be sold.

The book was re-printed and issued as the first published edition in November 1865, although all copies have 1866 as the date on the title page. This time, Tenniel approved the edition, and Dodgson wrote that it was 'very *far* superior to the old, and in fact a perfect piece of artistic printing'. Part of the story has a strong link with Binsey. It is this:

> 'Once upon a time there were three little sisters', the Dormouse began in a great hurry; 'and their names were Elsie, Lacie, and Tillie; and they lived at the bottom of a well – '
>
> 'What did they live on?' said Alice, who always took a great interest in questions of eating and drinking.
>
> 'They lived on treacle,' said the Dormouse, after thinking a minute or two.
>
> 'They couldn't have done that, you know,' Alice gently remarked; 'they'd have been ill.'
>
> 'So they were,' said the Dormouse; '*very* ill'.
>
> Alice tried to fancy to herself what such an extraordinary way of living would be like, but it puzzled her too much: so she went on: 'But why did they live at the bottom of a well?'
>
> 'Take some more tea,' the March Hare said to Alice, very earnestly.
>
> 'I've had nothing yet,' Alice replied in an offended tone, 'so I ca'n't take more.'
>
> 'You mean you ca'n't take *less*,' said the Hatter: 'it's very easy to take *more* than nothing.'
>
> 'Nobody asked *your* opinion,' said Alice.

'Who's making personal remarks now?' the Hatter asked triumphantly.

Alice did not quite know what to say to this: so she helped herself to some tea and bread-and-butter, and then turned to the Dormouse, and repeated her question. 'Why did they live at the bottom of a well?'

The Dormouse again took a minute or two to think about it, and then said, 'It was a treacle-well.'

'There's no such thing!' Alice was beginning very angrily, but the Hatter and the March Hare went 'Sh! sh!' and the Dormouse sulkily remarked, 'If you ca'n't be civil, you'd better finish the story for yourself.'

'No, please go on!' Alice said very humbly; 'I wo'n't interrupt you again. I dare say there may be *one*.'

'One, indeed!' said the Dormouse indignantly. However, he consented to go on. 'And so these three little sisters – they were learning to draw, you know – '

'What did they draw?' said Alice, quite forgetting her promise.

'Treacle,' said the Dormouse, without considering at all, this time.

'I want a clean cup,' interrupted the Hatter: 'let's all move one place on.'

He moved on as he spoke, and the Dormouse followed him: the March Hare moved into the Dormouse's place, and Alice rather unwillingly took the place of the March Hare. The Hatter was the only one who got any advantage from the change; and Alice was a good deal worse off than before, as the March Hare had just upset the milk-jug into his plate.

Alice did not wish to offend the Dormouse again, so she began very cautiously: 'But I don't understand. Where did they draw the treacle from?'

'You can draw water out of a water-well,' said the Hatter; 'so I should think you could draw treacle out of a treacle-well – eh, stupid?'

'But they were *in* the well,' Alice said to the Dormouse, not choosing to notice this last remark.

'Of course they were,' said the Dormouse: 'well in.'

This scene comes from the Mad Tea-Party chapter in *Alice's Adventures in Wonderland*. The three sisters at the bottom of the treacle-well are easily identified as the Liddell sisters; 'Elsie'—or L. C.—is Lorina Charlotte, 'Lacie' is an anagram of Alice, and 'Tillie' is short for Matilda, the pet-name given to the youngest, Edith. The treacle-well that Alice disputes, but eventually admits may exist ('I dare say there may be *one*') is, of course, St Margaret's Well at Binsey, the word treacle being used by Dodgson in its more usual form rather than in the sense of the medieval healing liquid. There can be no doubt that Dodgson visited the church with the children, possibly on the occasion of the river-trip, leaving their boat moored by the river bank at Binsey and walking the half-mile or so to the church. And possibly on some other occasion, Miss Prickett took them on a visit to see her relatives at Binsey. In either case, the children would understand the significance of the treacle-well, and would have no difficulty identifying its location.

The association with Binsey and Lewis Carroll's masterpiece of children's literature, *Alice's Adventures in Wonderland*, is irrefutable, and is the reason why many people now visit the churchyard at Binsey to see the famous treacle-well. They come, not with any intention of trying the healing liquid, but because they remember a most entertaining episode in an internationally-renowned book that has been in print now for almost one hundred and fifty years.

A wooden door carved by Alice Liddell, from the mission church built by Christ Church at Poplar in the East End of London, destroyed in World War II. The top section depicts St Frideswide upon a punt like vessel of plausible 'Dark Age' type. The door survived, and was sent back to Christ Church whose dean, John Lowe gave it to Arnold Mallinson for St Frideswide's, Osney, in Oxford. See A, Mallinson, *Under the Blue Hood. A hotchpotch 1923-1985* (Oxford 1986), p. 283. (Karl Wallendszus)

GERARD MANLEY HOPKINS AND 'BINSEY POPLARS'

BEATRICE AND PETER GROVES

'Of Oxford… I was very fond. I became a Catholic there. But I have not visited it, except once for three quarters of an hour, since I took my degree'.[1]

Gerard Manley Hopkins, a Catholic priest and a member of the Society of Jesus, wrote these words late in 1878, shortly before he was assigned to the very new Catholic parish of St Aloysius in Oxford. Living in its presbytery on St Giles, Hopkins was able to revisit undergraduate haunts, and to relive the many walks in and around the city which had been so formative of his young poetic mind. From such nostalgia came his poem 'Binsey Poplars', composed in March 1879.[2]

'Binsey Poplars' stands in a central position in Hopkins's poetic output. His unique approach to nature as expressive of the creative Word of God is here deployed to portray a sense of loss, of grief for a romanticized past. It reflects a search for rootedness and security which always eluded the angular young Balliol undergraduate who became the too-often unhappy Jesuit priest. Central to the poem's composition is the use of repetition, through which device he both lays down the verbal roots which allow an organic poetic growth, and creates a new poetic history to replace the wasted past now gone. Binsey Poplars, a remarkable piece in its own right, is therefore also a precursor of the famous and desolate sonnets Hopkins composed in Dublin towards the end of his life, only a few years later.

HOPKINS AND OXFORD

In 1863 Hopkins came up to Balliol College, Oxford, as an exhibitioner. His religious enthusiasm found an outlet in the high church movement of the time, and he was quickly drawn into close contact with the leaders of what was seen as the 'Puseyite' or ritualist party. In particular, he developed a friendship and pastoral relationship with Henry Parry Liddon, Dr Pusey's disciple and lieutenant, and with Edward Pusey himself, then in his mid-sixties and thirty-five years into his tenure as Regius Professor of Hebrew. Hopkins's friends and companions were largely like-minded young men, jumping (with the eagerness still characteristic of undergraduates) at the chance to express a passionate and daring form of Christianity, frequently in reaction to the broad church upbringing many had experienced. Hopkins himself had come from an ordinary Church of England family (his father had been churchwarden of Hampstead parish church) but found student rebellion in Tractarianism and ritualism. He flirted (twice) with membership of a fraternity called the Brotherhood of the Holy Trinity, which gathered frequently for worship in the church of St Thomas the Martyr. This group of university men lived by a common rule of prayer and practice, living out in the collegiate context a sort of 'individual ritualism' which allowed them to share in the more dramatic conflicts being fought in such celebrated London parishes as St

---

[1] *The Collected Works of Gerard Manley Hopkins: Volumes I & II, Correspondence*, ed. R.K.R. Thornton and Catherine Phillips (Oxford: OUP 2013), hereinafter cited as *Correspondence*, p.316.
[2] In April 2013, the Bodleian Library purchased a manuscript of the poem, showing a number of revisions. It joins the four other known manuscript copies, all in the Bodleian's Hopkins collection.

The Binsey Poplars today: second or third generation replacements of the poplars whose felling was lamented by Hopkins; photo taken from Port Meadow' (Julian Munby)

Alban's Holborn, and St George's in the East.[3] These conflicts would eventually result in the imprisonment of clergy for 'ritual practices' immediately before and after the mature Hopkins ministered in Oxford.

Gerard remained an excellent student ('the star of Balliol', as Pusey is said to have called him[4]), and his academic success no doubt helped in persuading his parents to accept his ecclesial rebellions with patience. However, their final consequence – his eventual conversion to Roman Catholicism – was not so lightly endured. 'O Gerard, my darling boy, are you indeed gone from me', were his mother's anguished words in a letter pleading with her son to reconsider being accepted into the Roman Catholic church in October 1866.[5]

The proximity of the countryside, and the opportunities for walking, were some of the first staples of the Oxford life which Hopkins knew. His journals, and Liddon's also, record many walks which the two of them took together, and the route north from Folly Bridge – taking in Port Meadow, Binsey, and Godstow – was among his favourites. An early pair of sonnets, entitled simply 'To Oxford', brings out the simple joy he took in the ancient beauty of his surroundings:

> New dated from the terms that reappear,
> More sweet familiar grows my love to thee,
> And still thou bind'st me to fresh fealty
> With long superfluous ties, for nothing here
> Nor elsewhere can thy sweetness unendear.
> This is my park, my pleasaunce…[6]

---

[3] For discussion of the Brotherhood, see Peter Groves, 'Gerard Among the Puseyites: New light from old archives on Hopkins's undergraduate religion', *The Hopkins Quarterly* XXX 3-4, 2003.
[4] Norman White, *Hopkins: A Literary Biography*, (Oxford 1992), p.99
[5] *Correspondence*, p.120.
[6] All quotes from Hopkins's poetry are from *The Poetical Works of Gerard Manley Hopkins*, ed. Norman H. Mackenzie (Oxford, 1990).

Decision and crisis, however, were not far away. In October 1866 four Oxford undergraduates were received into the Roman Catholic church. Hopkins was one. The scandal in the university was intense. The influence of the Tractarian leaders was bewailed. A series of desperate letters flew between Liddon and the Hopkins, as well as between the new convert's father and the Tractarian leaders. Pusey, recognizing all too well the immovability of the brilliantly headstrong Hopkins, refused to see him despite several pleas: the young man's mind was made up, and the good doctor did not propose to waste time by meeting him simply 'to satisfy relations'.[7] In Birmingham, where the young men were received into Roman Catholicism at the new Oratory, that most famous of converts John Henry Newman had played his hand wisely. Knowing that a return to the heart of Oxford life might shake a conviction formed over the long vacation, he initiated Hopkins and his friends before the new term began. The Bishop of Salisbury wrote to Liddon of the matter: 'the attacking party have always the advantage especially as they are a compact body'.[8]

It is difficult to convey the horror with which the secession of Oxford students in the mid-nineteenth century was greeted, but Hopkins own journey was to take him further. The enormity of reception into the Roman Catholic Church was followed by acceptance into the Society of Jesus, and a period of novitiate and study which was followed by parochial ministry in a number of different settings. St Aloysius Oxford was one of these, and it was in December 1878 that he moved back to the university city he loved. His time at St Aloysius was not easy.

PERSONALITY AND POETRY

Hopkins's whole life displays a certain ill-fitting quality. His personal awkwardness was embraced quite lovingly by his Jesuit superiors after he joined the Society, and his pastoral ministry was dedicated but of varying success. A poem such as 'Felix Randal' gives an intensely moving picture of ministry in life and death, but biographical details and letters record an often awkward young curate, sometimes patronizing in his attitudes to his flock, and this is the priest we encounter in his letters and journals throughout his second sojourn in Oxford, one which lasted only ten months. It was, however, a time of poetic productivity. Hopkins had been writing verse since his youth: the beautiful miniature 'Heaven-haven', imagining the call of a young woman to the religious life, dates from his undergraduate days. But his vocation as a poet was never happily realized: his first major work, 'The Wreck of the Deutschland', was refused publication in the Jesuit journal *The Month* – unsurprisingly given the density and complexity of a poem, the syntax, structure and content of which was then unparalleled in English. However, Hopkins continued to write, and continued to send his work to his friend from student days Robert Bridges, the friend who later – as poet laureate – would publish Hopkins's poems.

The later 1870s saw Hopkins compose several of his best known poems on natural themes. Sonnets of genius such as 'As kingfishers catch fire', 'God's grandeur' and 'The Windhover' all date from 1877, for example. 'Binsey Poplars' can be paired with another poem of the past, 'Duns Scotus's Oxford' to demonstrate the sadness of the poet's response to the city and its surroundings, a sadness exquisitely expressed in these two short poems, and presaging the more serious depression which was to plague his later years.

---
[7] *Correspondence*, p.123.
[8] W.K. Hamilton to H.P. Liddon, 27 October 1866, Liddon Papers, Pusey House, Oxford.

THE SEARCH FOR ROOTEDNESS

Roots were important to Hopkins. His religious life meant a reduced intimacy with his family in adulthood, a deracination compounded by the nomadic impermanence of life as a Jesuit, which stopped him becoming rooted in places. Hopkins had to move where and when his superiors told him, and underwent constant upheavals: 'I am, so far as I know, permanently here, but permanence with us is ginger-bread permanence; cobweb, soapsud, and frost-feather permanence.'[9] (The repetition of 'permanence' here, an attempt to create something settled even while describing transience, has a bitter irony.) The importance of Binsey Poplars is its demonstration of Hopkins determination to create the roots he so badly needed. It is not least from a desire for rootedness that the dwelling, caressing repetitions in his poetry comes. Hopkins believed repetition to be poetry's defining characteristic – 'verse then is speech wholly or partially repeating the same figure of sound' – and he invented his own, more repetitive, names for it: *'oftening, over-and-overing, aftering.'*[10]

> Binsey Poplars
> felled 1879
>
> My aspens dear, whose airy cages quelled,
>   Quelled or quenched in leaves the leaping sun,
>   All felled, felled, are all felled;
>   Of a fresh and following folded rank
>   Not spared, not one
>   That dandled a sandalled
>   Shadow that swam or sank
> On meadow & river & wind-wandering weed-winding bank.
>
>   O if we but knew what we do
>   When we delve or hew —
>   Hack and rack the growing green!
>   Since country is so tender
>   To touch, her being só slender,
>   That, like this sleek and seeing ball
>   But a prick will make no eye at all,
>   Where we, even where we mean
>   To mend her we end her,
>   When we hew or delve:
> After-comers cannot guess the beauty been.
>   Ten or twelve, only ten or twelve
>   Strokes of havoc unselve
>   The sweet especial scene,
>   Rural scene, a rural scene,
>   Sweet especial rural scene.

'Binsey Poplars' is a poem written in response to loss. In a letter of February 27, 1879, Hopkins wrote to his friend Richard Dixon:

> 'You will see that I have again changed my abode, and am returned to my Alma Mater…. That landscape the charm of Oxford, green shouldering grey, which is already abridged and soured and perhaps will soon be put out altogether, the Wytham and Godstow landscape.'[11]

---
[9] *Correspondence*, p.307-8.
[10] *The Journals and Papers of Gerard Manley Hopkins*, ed. Humphry House, completed by Graham Storey (London, 1959), p.289-90.
[11] *Letters II*, 20

First page of Hopkins' *Binsey Poplars* manuscript. Oxford, Bodleian Library, MS. Eng. c. 8235, fol. 1r. Reproduced by permission of The Bodleian Libraries, University of Oxford.

His fears were soon justified, for a letter of March 12 carries a March 13 postscript saying 'I have been up to Godstow this afternoon. I am sorry to say that the aspens that lined the river are everyone felled.'[12] His literary reaction to this discovery is saturated with repetition. Finding the links within his own life being severed, he created poetry which held connections within itself.[13]

Wordsworth believed that repetition was either an expression of 'fondness, exultation and gratitude', or indicated a sense of insufficiency.[14] Both these aspects are important to Hopkins's work. He delights in reusing certain words, such as examples connected with mothering: 'dandalled', 'nestle', 'child', 'brood', or beginning with 'thr': 'throng', 'thrust', 'thrush'. He savours words where he senses sound and meaning meeting, such as in 'thwart'

---

[12] *Correspondence*, p.348.

[13] For a discussion of the poem's relationship with verse composed by Hopkins's father, see Jude V. Nixon, "Fathering Graces at Hampstead: Manley Hopkins' "The Old Trees" and Gerard Manley Hopkins' *"Binsey Poplars"*", *Victorian Poetry* 44.2 (2006) pp.191-211.

[14] Wordsworth's note to 'The Thorn' in William Wordsworth and Samuel Taylor Coleridge, *Lyrical Ballads* [1798/1800], ed. R. L. Brett and A. R. Jones, 2nd edition (London, 1991), p.289.

where the triple consonant cluster, unusual in English, takes the reader by surprise, checking her in a mimetic thwarting. In his early poem 'Nondum' he asks God to let patience: 'lead me child-like by the hand.' The symmetry at the centre of 'ch*ildl*ike' caresses the ear, and in combination with the soft 'ch' and 'ld' sounds, makes the word seem gentle. The persistence of certain words and sounds across Hopkins's poetry feels cherishing, but when words are repeated obsessively in close proximity, it appears rather as a craving verbal permanence created to counteract changes that disturb him.

'Binsey Poplars' enables Hopkins's search for rootedness and stability through his lifelong love for trees. Much of his journal is concerned with accurately recording the trees he has seen: 'ashes not out, only tufted with their fringy blooms.. White poplars most beautiful in small grey crisp spray-like leaf.'[15] Lines drawn from detailed observation of trees can be found in works written throughout his career, from 'aspen's silky skirting' (1862) to 'silk-beech, scrolled ash, packed sycamore, wild/ wychelm, hornbeam fretty' (1888). Close attention to the natural world was very much of Hopkins's time (the nineteenth century abounded in amateur botanists) and of course a fervour for looking at nature first hand was one of the most powerful effects of the influence of John Ruskin, for whom such study of the natural world was the basis of the making of true art.

The word 'We' occurs twelve times in Binsey Poplars. It is found in the first stanza in 'weed' and is incorporated into 'sweet' in the end. 'Quelled' and 'felled' mutate into 'delve', 'twelve' and 'unselve'. Sibilance breathes through the poem from 'aspens' and 'shadow', through 'sleek' and 'slender' to the 'sweet' 'scene' of the end. Aural threads such as these are accentuated by the flowing enjambment of the first stanza, but the final three lines are uncharacteristically static. The evolving sound patterns of the poem comes to an abrupt end as Hopkins dwells on the word in the absence of the referent. The repetition is mournful, caressing, and attempts to create something stable and lasting in the midst of a changing reality.

This poem's root system connects it to his other poems. In one of Hopkins's strolls to Binsey as a student he records having heard the song of a wood-lark. He was to record this occurrence later in 'The Woodlark', a poem even richer in aural iteration than 'Binsey Poplars'. It employs *cynghanedd*, a 'chiming of consonants' in Welsh poetry, where the consonants in the first half of the line are repeated, in order, in the second half: 'the blood-gush blade-gash'.[16] The variation of vowel sounds means that the ear does not get tired, for it is listening for the next mutation. But Hopkins abandoned evolution of sound in the poem's final, monotonously repetitive, lines, which run thus: 'with a sweet joy of a sweet joy,/ Sweet, of a sweet, of a sweet joy/ Of a sweet – a sweet – sweet – joy.' This occurrence of 'sweet' and the unusual, solidly repetitive form the last lines of both 'The Woodlark' (1876) and 'Binsey Poplars' (1879), suggests that the latter's ending is a reworking of the earlier poem.

The clinging iteration in the line: 'all felled, felled, are all felled' ('Binsey Poplars') is also an echo of another poem: Cowper's 'The Poplar Field':[17]

> The Poplars are fell'd, farewell to the shade
> And the whispering sound of the cool colonnade,
> The winds play no longer and sing in the leaves,
> Nor Ouse on his bosom their image receives.

---

[15] *Journals and Papers*, p.134.
[16] *Correspondence*, p.267. For a fuller explanation see L. L. Wyn Griffith 'The Welsh Influence on the Poetry of Gerard Manley Hopkins', *New Verse*, 14 (1935), 28-30, p.28.
[17] *The Poems of William Cowper*, 3 vols, ed. John D. Baird and Charles Ryskans (Oxford, 1995), vol. 2, p.25.

Here the repetitions are elegantly coupled: 'fell'd, farewell', 'cool colonnade', 'Ouse' and 'bosom'. The sound alters subtly, delighting the ear with both similarity and difference. Cowper's argument moves seamlessly from the felled trees to human mortality, and the impression is one of structured stateliness. Conversely in Hopkins's obsessively reiterative line there is an inability to move; he remains rooted to the spot. We find here a pre-echo of the misery of his later work, as we shall suggest below.

'Binsey Poplars', despite its syntactic complexity, is a celebration of the natural world. Hopkins's imagination rejoices in wildness unchecked by human hands, a joy borne out in the poem 'Inversnaid':

> This darksome burn, horseback brown,
> His rollrock highroad roaring down,
> In coop and in comb the fleece of his foam
> Flutes and low to the lake falls home.
> A windpuff-bonnet of fáwn-fróth
> Turns and twindles over the broth
> Of a pool so pitchblack, féll-frówning,
> It rounds and rounds Despair to drowning.
>
> Degged with dew, dappled with dew
> Are the groins of the braes that the brook treads through,
> Wiry heathpacks, flitches of fern,
> And the beadbonny ash that sits over the burn.
>
> What would the world be, once bereft
> Of wet and of wildness? Let them be left,
> O let them be left, wildness and wet;
> Long live the weeds and the wilderness yet.

But at Binsey, the weeds and the wilderness, have not been left. The harsh sound of cutting in the line 'Strokes of havoc unselve' is a powerful mimetic of destruction. The soft 's' sounds glide against the languid 'v', only to be punctuated by the brutal 'k' and hard 'c', which bring them up short. The central 'v' sound of 'havoc' is enveloped by these hard consonants in preparation for the final word 'unselve', whereby the reality of a thing, its unique place in God's creation, is undone by the blow of an axe.

WORD AND CREATION

Hopkins is often called a nature poet. This epithet is a useful reminder of the albatross of secularism which hangs over so much academic study. He was indeed fascinated with the natural world, and has a remarkable ability to make that world sing off the printed page, but Hopkins is inspired by nature not as nature, but as creation, as the pouring forth of the love of God which flashes and sparkles from every single instance of the change and motion which surrounds us as we confront the world. One of his most famous poems, 'As kingfishers catch fire', contrasts the secular view of nature with the Christian view of creation: 'Each mortal thing does one thing and the same:/ …Selves – goes itself; *myself* it speaks and spells,/ Crying *What I do is me, for that I came.*' Rather than this individualistic world, Hopkins sees another: 'Í say more: the just man justices;/ Keeps gráce: thát keeps all his goings graces;/ Acts in God's eye what in God's eye he is –/ Christ.'

For Hopkins, as for Christian orthodoxy, creation and redemption are not to be held apart. We are redeemed because, in the incarnation, death, resurrection and the ascension of the Lord, Christ has become our humanity, Christ has transformed our nature so that when God looks on us in our sin, what he sees is Christ in his love. So 'The world is charged with the grandeur of God', not just because it crackles with the electric spark of divine grace in creation, but because that act of creation charges, entrusts creation with the living out of the greatness of grace. Time has trodden on and on, but humanity does not reck, does not heed the guidance of his creator. Despite all this, God's creative act is never spent, the freshness of his love poured unendingly into all that lives:

> Because the Holy Ghost over the bent
> World broods with warm breast & with ah! bright wings.

Again, repetition is key. The beginning and end of this poem, which deal with God's action in the world, have a structurally satisfying triple form. In the first line the consonants 'g' and 'd' are repeated in order three times: 'the world is char*ged* with the *g*ran*d*eur of Go*d*'. The final line repeats the triple consonant cluster, with 'w' followed by 'br': 'because the Holy Ghost over the bent/ *W*orld *br*oods with *w*arm *br*east and ah! *Br*ight *w*ings', except that the last pair are reversed. In the final line the Holy Spirit, in the form of a dove, brings forgiveness and with it comes a gentle turning of the form. The final reversal breathes freshness into the poem and the possibility of hope.

The evolving and patterned possibilities of iteration are also explored in Hopkins's sonnet 'Spring'.

> Nothing is so beautiful as spring—
> When weeds, in wheels, shoot long and lovely and lush;
> Thrush's eggs look little low heavens, and thrush
> Through the echoing timber does so rinse and wring
> The ear, it strikes like lightnings to hear him sing;
> The glassy peartree leaves and blooms, they brush
> The descending blue; that blue is all in a rush
> With richness; the racing lambs too have fair their fling.
>
> What is all this juice and all this joy?
> A strain of the earth's sweet being in the beginning
> In Eden garden. Have, get, before it cloy,
> Before it cloud, Christ, lord, and sour with sinning,
> Innocent mind and Mayday in girl and boy,
> Most, O maid's child, thy choice and worthy the
> winning.

Celebrating the beauty of the season, the poet asks: 'what is all this juice and all this joy?' The answer is: 'a strain of the earth's sweet being in the beginning/ In Eden garden.' 'Strain' means both: 'offspring, progeny' and 'a race, breed; a variety developed by breeding.'[18] The joys of spring are rooted in Eden (are its progeny), but have evolved away from their original (have been altered by breeding). This argument is supported by the phonemic abundance of 'in', which occurs twenty-three times, in words such as: 'r*in*se', 'wr*in*g', 'fl*in*g', 'lighten*ing*s', '*in*nocent' and 'w*in*ning'. Such profusion alerts us to the importance of the line of greatest concentration: 'being in the beginning/ In Eden garden.' The 'in' of 'Spr*in*g' is also present '*in* the beg*in*ning', and that first creation is reenacted in the innocence and freshness of each spring. But the purity has been tarnished, the spring of youth will 'sour

---

[18] *The Oxford English Dictionary*, s.v. "Strain."

with sinning', and the 'in's of the poem bear resemblance to, but have slid away from, the 'en' of 'Ed*en* gard*en*'.

OXFORD AGAIN

These poems of nature, or, as we maintain 'creation', express Hopkins's distinctive approach to the uniqueness of individual things, an approach which has provoked much discussion as to his philosophical influences. Largely because he said so himself, there is a general view that poems such as 'Binsey Poplars' and the sonnets discussed above reflect the teaching of the great Oxford thinker John Duns Scotus. In fact, there is little evidence that Hopkins really understood Scotus. Rather, as an original poetic thinker himself, he saw ideas in Scotus's writings and shaped them into something new. His insistence on the individual createdness of things chimes just as well with Aquinas as it does with Scotus, for example. However, the poem he wrote not long after his mourning the trees of Binsey bears Scotus's name.

> Towery city and branchy between towers;
> Cuckoo-echoing, bell-swarmèd, lark-charmèd, rook-
> racked, river-rounded;
> The dapple-eared lily below thee; that country and
> town did
> Once encounter in, here coped and poisèd powers;
>
> Thou hast a base and brickish skirt there, sours
> That neighbour-nature thy grey beauty is grounded
> Best in; graceless growth, thou hast confounded
> Rural rural keeping—folk, flocks, and flowers.
>
> Yet ah! this air I gather and I release
> He lived on; these weeds and waters, these walls are what
> He haunted who of all men most sways my spirits to peace;
>
> Of realty the rarest-veinèd unraveller; a not
> Rivalled insight, be rival Italy or Greece;
> Who fired France for Mary without spot

We mentioned earlier the fact that Hopkins's time at St Aloysius was not altogether happy. His disappointment at the loss of the Oxford of his past is undoubtedly a factor. The Roman Catholic parish spread far (out as far as Temple Cowley) and Hopkins regularly celebrated mass in the small chapel of St Ignatius, on St Clements, from which a Catholic school was run. The school continues elsewhere: the chapel building survives, set back next to the Port Mahon public house. (The line 'branchy between towers' surely refers to the experience of looking up when crossing Magdalen Bridge from the east towards the High Street, and seeing the tree branches interspersed among the pinnacles of Magdalen tower and chapel.) As he walked east to the working class communities across the river, and north out towards Port Meadow, he met the growing 'base and brackish skirt' which was the terraced housing of the burgeoning industrial community. In place of this he laments the demise of an Oxford seven centuries earlier which his intellectual hero inhabited. What remains of beauty and joy is the 'rural rural keeping—folk, flocks and flowers'.

This poem is the pair of 'Binsey Poplars' because of its regret at a past forever gone. Seeking his own roots in God's natural world, Hopkins also sought his own intellectual identity in the Catholic past of a city which was to him, for the most part, unequivocally

Protestant. The ideal seems to dominate: nature flourishes in the absence of human destruction; beauty flourishes in the absence of urban growth. Loneliness and loss are left to the poet, repeated in melancholy which indulges a desire to find security and roots in an idealized world now past.

ISOLATION

This loneliness, and the repetitions and search for rootedness to which it gives rise, is a pre-echo of the despair which characterizes Hopkins's later sonnets, poems which enunciate the agonizing isolation and depression he underwent. Rather than construct a new past, with newly set-down roots, Hopkins now simply turns upon his own life and history and sees it as failure without hope. As with 'Binsey Poplars', repetition is central.

> To seem the stranger lies my lot, my life
> Among strangers. Father and mother dear,
> Brothers and sisters are in Christ not near
> And he my peace my parting, sword and strife.
> England, whose honour O all my heart woos, wife
> To my creating thought, would neither hear
> Me, were I pleading, plead nor do I: I wear-
> y of idle a being but by where wars are rife.
> I am in Ireland now; now I am at a third
> Remove. Not but in all removes I can
> Kind love both give and get. Only what word
> Wisest my heart breeds dark heaven's baffling ban
> Bars or hell's spell thwarts. This to hoard unheard,
> Heard unheeded, leaves me a lonely began.

In 'To seem the stranger lies my lot' the juxtaposed repetitions ('I:I', 'now; now' 'unheard,/Heard') lead to constant jolts for the reader. The longer mirror images of corrupted chiasmus – 'were I pleading, plead nor do I' – combine with the verbal iteration to give it sterile abundance. The use of familial terms is telling, as is the reference to being 'at a third remove'. Far from rootedness and security, Hopkins finds unfulfilled exile. He fears his own barrenness and in '*Justus quidem tu es, Domine*' pleads for the growth roots bring:

> Thou art indeed just, Lord, if I contend
> With thee; but, sir, so what I plead is just.
> Why do sinners' ways prosper? and why must
> Disappointment all I endeavour end?
> Wert thou my enemy, O thou my friend,
> How wouldst thou worse, I wonder, than thou dost
> Defeat, thwart me? Oh, the sots and thralls of lust
> Do in spare hours more thrive than I that spend,
>
> Sir, life upon thy cause. See, banks and brakes
> Now leavèd how thick! lacèd they are again
> With fretty chervil, look, and fresh wind shakes
> Them; birds build — but not I build; no, but strain,
> Time's eunuch, and not breed one work that wakes.
> Mine, O thou lord of life, send my roots rain.

As discussed above, 'strain' can be expressive of a wonderful fecundity, as it means both 'offspring' and 'pedigree, lineage, ancestry, descent.' But here an awareness of these meanings, which belong to the plants and birds, and couple with 'breed', only serves to heighten its primary meaning of strenuous failure. Fundamentally, the 'work' that Hopkins longs to 'wake' is his poetry. The world around him with its natural productivity makes Hopkins long to be part of it. He feels that to be rooted, to create is the natural order of the world; and he feels separated from it. The metaphorical roots in his plea for fruitfulness assume that he must become incorporated into the natural world to share in its carefree fecundity: 'mine, O thou lord of life, send my roots rain.'

Hopkins's botanical interest works to give accuracy to his plant metaphors. These roots must be watered to allow him time to grow like the plants and produce like the nest-building birds. In 'My own heart let me have more pity on' he gives the 'root' (comfort) space so that the 'plant' (joy) can grow.

> My own heart let me more have pity on; let
> Me live to my sad self hereafter kind,
> Charitable; not live this tormented mind
> With this tormented mind tormenting yet.
> I cast for comfort I can no more get
> By groping round my comfortless, than blind
> Eyes in their dark can day or thirst can find
> Thirst's all-in-all in all a world of wet.
> Soul, self; come, poor Jackself, I do advise
> You, jaded, let be; call off thoughts awhile
> Elsewhere; leave comfort root-room; let joy size
> At God knows when to God knows what; whose smile
> 's not wrung, see you; unforeseen times rather – as skies
> Betweenpie mountains – lights a lovely mile.

Once more aridity is signaled by extravagantly inept repetition; 'all-in-all in all' mimics his inefficacious effort, while the mutating phonemes of 'leave comfort root-room' indicate growth. Those words give the poem's argument a reassuring authority, for almost all of '*comfort*' can be found in '*root*-roo*m*'. That 'root' can be found inside 'comfort' is not an etymology, a true root, but a fortunate find, like the sound of '*tree*' and 'poe*try*' (in his poem '[Ashboughs]'). Hopkins was fascinated by etymologies and lines such as 'but *we* dream we are rooted in earth' (*The Wreck of the Deutschland*, stanza 11) is punningly aware of the shared root of *homo* (man) and *humus* (earth). 'Roots' were a fashionable concept in etymological studies of the time, defined by the historical linguist Max Müller as: 'whatever, in the words of any language, cannot be reduced to a simpler or more original form, e.g. AR: means *to plough*'.[19] Hopkins, who had read Müller's work, used the roots of linguistic expression to seek his own security and growth in the face of disappointment and despair.

CONCLUSION

The darkest of the Dublin sonnets were not the last poems Hopkins wrote, but date probably from 1885, four years before his death (though 'Thou art indeed just, Lord' is from his final year.) They remain unparalleled in English poetry as a combination of extraordinary poetic art and almost unimaginable loneliness and depression. Attempts to find in them a traditional Christian spirituality of darkness are doomed to failure. However, though

---

[19] Max Müller, *Lectures of the Science of Language,* [1861-4], 2 vols (London, 1994), vol. 1, p.239.

written in isolation from other people, they are not isolated as poems from Hopkins's other work. The importance of 'Binsey Poplars' as a signpost in their direction has not always been noticed.

Gerard Manley Hopkins died in 1889, a largely failed and disappointed priest, an unhappy teacher and an unpublished poet. Contemporary records show him to have been quickly forgotten. (An 1899 memoir recording the events of his conversion does not mention him by name.[20]) His friend Robert Bridges, however, having received, read and edited his poems, brought them to publication in 1918 and thus gave to the world some of the most startlingly original religious poetry ever composed in English. The resurrection which Hopkins had called a 'heart's clarion' was for him literary before it was literal. 'Binsey Poplars' offers us not simply an exquisite threnody for an Oxford scene now past, nor merely the reactionary outpourings of a man unhappy with modernity, but the peculiar insight of poetic expression which characterizes all of Hopkins's work: a poetic world which lives on and off the page with all the fertility and creativity of the natural world it describes. The trees destroyed by cavalier humanity live for ever in the meticulous construction of the poem which grieves at their loss. The irony is not tragic but wonderful.

---

[20] V.S.S. Coles, 'Memories of Liddon addressed in 1899 to J.O. Johnston', Liddon Papers, Pusey House, Oxford.

The Perch and its Predecessors

MARK DAVIES

'First the Church and then the Perch!' According to Paul Marriot's 1978 *Oxford Pubs—Past and Present*, this was once a Binsey saying. The phrase can be taken in two ways. In a historical sense it might reflect the greater antiquity of the original Saxon church at Thornbury, compared to the uncertain history of the pub; or, more likely, the customary Sabbath-day order of things: first pay your respects to the Lord, then pay your pennies to the pub landlord!

Whatever, it would seem certain that a pub in as small a place as Binsey could never have survived on local custom alone. Still on the Sunday theme, the Oxford photographer and writer Henry Taunt (1842–1922) wrote that the Perch was dubbed 'Binsey Cathedral' because the landlord was not averse to serving drinks on a Sunday, in breach of licensing laws. Binsey's unusual extra-parochial status—physically on the Berkshire side of the Thames, but falling within the jurisdiction of the city of Oxford—evidently made it a favourite destination for thirsty Oxonians. It would take an exceptionally zealous Proctor to discover University men this far from the city, after all, and likewise for the civic authorities to visit. Yet it did happen: Elizabeth Burton, landlady of the Perch, was convicted of transgressing Sunday licensing laws in 1856, for instance.

Further evidence of the unorthodox nature of the village appears in a handbill from about 1814, advertising 'Backswords and bull-baiting at Binsey' one Whit-Monday. As well as a 'good dinner' (provided surely by the public house) the other attractions included backswords competitions which

> 'will be played, by two sides, consisting of seven, nine, or eleven on each side, for a hat of one guinea value. The prize will be given to that side which breaks the most heads. At 11 the same day two capital bulls will be brought to the stake, and for the greater entertainment of the company, at three in the afternoon a good fresh badger will be baited.'

Of more local significance than the brutal nature of bygone entertainment is the reference to the staking of a bull, suggesting an activity in the neighbourhood which may have been traditional enough to inspire the naming of the nearby Bulstake Stream. Later in the century, Henry Minn (1870–1961), a man who shared Taunt's love of photography and local tradition, recalled from his own observations that in the 1890s the Perch was 'the usual rendezvous of undergraduates to enter their dogs for rat killing and also pigeon shooting contests'.

It is impossible to say just how long Binsey has been the venue for dubious activities of this kind, but it seems likely that a drinking establishment would have been a pre-requisite for them. Parts of the Perch date from the seventeenth century, and from records held at the Oxfordshire Record Office the earliest identifiable licensee of a Binsey alehouse was Thomas Prickett, in April 1651. The Pricketts are a family with as old an association with the village as any, the earliest evidence for this being in a document at Christ Church's archives citing Robert Pricket as one of several Binsey residents complaining in 1598 that they were prohibited from keeping cattle on Port Meadow, a right which had been applied 'since time out of mind'.

Thomas Prickett's name reoccurs in the licensing lists until 1661, followed by other members of the Prickett family—Alicia, John, and (presumably) another Thomas—until the early eighteenth century. Thomas Hearne (1678–1735), the Oxford diarist and Bodleian

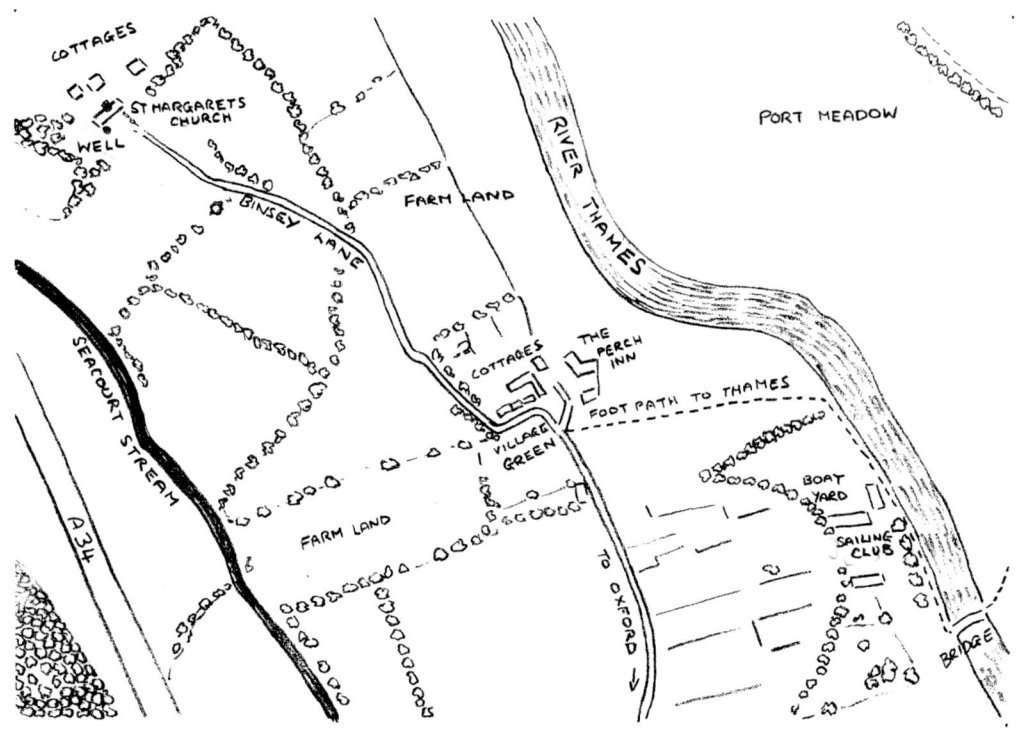

Map of Binsey. (Sue Dewhurst)

librarian, noted two meetings with (again presumably) this second Thomas Prickett (who was born *c.*1648). In 1718 he told Hearne he was a yeoman farmer, and had been sole church warden for thirty-eight years. As farmers the Pricketts continued to be associated with Binsey for many subsequent decades.

MEDLEY

In 1654 comes the first granting of a licence specifically for 'Medley', made to Thomas Feild. By 1659 the licensee was Joan Bonner alias Pitts, a curious combination which Mary Prior's book *Fisher Row* reveals to have been one of the dominant families of sixteenth-century Oxford fishermen (associated also with the important mill at Iffley). The two families were related by marriage, Richard Bonner (alias Pitts) a fisherman of Binsey and St Thomas having married Mary Feild, daughter of Thomas, who was a yeoman and boat owner of Medley manor and presumably also either the Medley publican of the 1650s or his son.

This Pitts/Feild relationship takes an interesting turn in 1662, in which year the licence was issued to Joan England, Bonner having been crossed out. Thenceforth, until 1669 the licensee is named as Joanna or Joanes Ward, the wife, almost certainly, of James Ward (of Islip) who married one Jane England of Binsey on 5 April 1662. The couple were familiar to the Oxford historian Anthony Wood (1632–1695), who kept a journal which often included details of his expenses. He noted his first visit to Binsey in 1661, making payments on this and subsequent visits to a married woman called Jone or Joan, and in 1669 to 'goodwife Ward'—the former Jane England, no doubt.

A place of refreshment at Medley continued until the 1770s. References to pleasure trips to Medley are frequent in Oxford literature, whereas Binsey rates hardly a mention. Medley's superior attractions are summed up in this verse by Mrs Alicia d'Anvers from 1691:

> A place at which they never fail,
> Of Custard, Cyder, Cakes, and Ale,
> Cream, Tarts, and Cheese-Cakes, good Neats Tongues
> And pretty Girls to wait upon's.

It seems evident, therefore, that Medley was the more fashionable and better-known destination, while the forerunners of the nearby Perch were probably unassuming hostelries catering more for a clientele of humble travellers, agricultural labourers, and boatmen, and much less likely to appeal to well-heeled Oxford pleasure-seekers. For there to have been two, sometimes three, pubs consistently so close together in such a small place is indicative presumably of considerable passing trade, either waterborne, horse-drawn, or pedestrian, on the river towpath connecting three important religious buildings of the mediaeval period: the great abbey of Osney to the south, Godstow nunnery to the north, and—much visited in its day, on account of the reputation of the waters of its well—the nearby St Margaret's Church.

It seems likely that the Binsey hostelry would have existed for longer, given that the ford a little to the north of Binsey Green constituted one of the east-west routes into the city, while that at Medley—still indicated in a plan of 1861—seems to have provided more local access to Fidlers Island. Access across the river was obviously well-established in 1731, when Christ Church insisted that the City Council take down the gate and rails at Walton Ford 'to make the passage clear for the tenants of Binsey to pass and repass with their carts and carriages'. It is interesting to note that the ford was still in use—even in the winter—in 1825, as can be discerned from an account in *Jackson's Oxford Journal* of the death of Elizabeth Bale of Godstow, whose drowned body was discovered as a team of horses was crossing Binsey ford, going either to or from Kidlington.

THE FISH

John Prickett was the last male member of that family to hold a victualler's licence in Binsey, in 1711. Or at least, he was the last identifiable member, as the records for 1712 to 1739 are missing. When the records recommence, a new and highly significant name appears in the list of victuallers for the first time. Robert Tawney (1679–1745) probably appears by virtue of his marriage to Margaret Prickett (possibly the daughter, but certainly a relative, of the second Thomas Prickett). He had been an alehouse keeper since at least 1735, according to a manuscript in Christ Church's archives. When Robert died in 1745, the licence was held by his widow until 1761, and then her son Thomas. One of the Tawneys' clients must have been the New College scholar James Woodforde (1740–1803), a man as meticulous as Wood in keeping an account of his expenditure. In the early 1760s he recorded several excursions with friends 'up the water' to 'Binzy for victuals and drink'. They invariably also played 'skettles', the loser usually having to pay for the hire of the boat.

Robert Tawney's brother Richard (1684–1756) was the man who more than any established this family as one of great influence and wealth in eighteenth-century Oxford, trading first as a boatman, then progressing to bargemaster and brewer, and serving as Oxford's Mayor in 1748. When Richard died, he chose to be 'interred with his ancestors at

Binsey' (according to *Jackson's Oxford Journal*). Two of his sons, both three times Mayor of Oxford, were also buried at Binsey: Sir Richard (1721–91) and Edward (1735–1800), whose benefaction paid for the memorial to the Tawneys inside the church.

In 1780 a Binsey victualler called Robert Taylor gained his freedom (i.e. the right to ply a recognised trade in Oxford). This seems certain to be Robert Tawney Taylor (1755–1845), the grandson of Robert Tawney, whose daughter Sarah (*c.*1724–1794) had married John Taylor (?–1764) 'of Hampton Gay' at Binsey in 1754.

The next Binsey victualler to obtain his freedom was John Williams in 1795. He was named as one of five riverside custodians (between Sandford and Binsey) of 'apparatus recommended by the Royal Humane Society for restoring suspended animation' in *Jackson's* of 28 October 1820. This is the first ever mention of a Binsey pub in the newspaper, a full 67 years after its launch! It implies a place with an uneventful history, neither fashionable (as Medley was), nor notorious. Hailing from Cumnor, John Williams had married Robert Tawney Taylor's sister Edith (1762–1840) at Binsey in 1793. His death in 1829 ended the Prickett-Tawney-Taylor-Williams family pub trade going back to at least the 1640s, and perhaps, given the Pricketts' ancient associations with the place, very much longer.

In 1830, an outsider was named as being in occupation of a sizeable Binsey agricultural estate which included the 'well-accustomed' public house identified for the first time by the name of The Fish. His name, from an auction notice printed in *Jackson's* of 14 August 1830, was Richard Gee (*c.*1774–1842). Although not resident, Gee had had considerable business interests in Binsey for several decades, the earliest reference in Christ Church's archives coming in 1811. The pub remained in his possession until his death, when the entire estate was again put up for sale. It is a coincidence that the late Charles Gee acquired Medley Farm in the 1950s. Although some ancient family connection seems likely, it is not now apparent. The 1842 auction is significant in exhibiting the earliest use of the name by which the pub would always subsequently be known, the Perch, being part of an estate which formed 'a very considerable portion of the parish of Binsey'.

THE PERCH

In the census of 1841, the innkeeper is identified as sixty-seven-year-old William Fleetwood, in residence with his wife Mary and three other family members, one being a grandson. At this time he was one of the three individuals in Binsey eligible to vote, the other two being a farmer called James Turner, and, surprisingly, Samuel Beechey, described merely as a labourer – though the church records reveal that he had earlier been a farmer. By 1851, the village's victualler was thirty-nine-year-old Richard Alder, who designated himself also a 'cabinett maker'. At the Binsey baptisms of his five children between 1845 and 1851, Alder called himself a 'publican', and in 1847 at least, he also undertook the role of water bailiff.

By this time, the pub was showing glimmers of the sophistication it would wholeheartedly embrace in more recent times, if the episode described in *Warrior Bard: William Morris* (by Edward and Stephani Godwin) in the spring of 1854 is to be believed. Based on the 'intimate anecdotes and personal reminiscences' of Morris' daughter Mary, it tells of a walk made by Morris and Edward Burne Jones to Wytham. 'Let's stop at the Perch and drink a bottle of red wine—they have fine old Stilton, too, as a rule,' Morris is portrayed as saying. But there's a hint too of why respectable Oxford men might consistently have preferred Medley to Binsey: 'The air inside the dark, low-ceilinged parlour was conscious with hoary ancients, so they carried their bottle and cheese out to a seat in the garden'.

Morris loved the Thames, and took at least two long river trips to inform the writing of his Utopian novel *News From Nowhere*. In his journal, Morris mentioned that he completed

The Perch in 1924. (Oxfordshire County Council - Oxfordshire History Centre)

the journey from Medley Lock to his home at Kelmscott 'in two pair oared boats towed respectively by William Bossom and one of his men'. William Bossom (1838–1919) and his wife Ellen were pioneers of a distinctive Oxford lifestyle: residential boating. Their 'houseboat' in the 1861 census is the first such dwelling ever noted in the city, along with one occupied by Maximilian Davis (1806–1879) and his wife Amelia. The Bossoms were an influential boating dynasty of St Thomas's parish, and with his brother Jack (1828–1915), William ran the firm which even today still trades under the Bossom name.

The next known proprietor of the Perch was Elizabeth Burton (c.1821–1863), she of the 1856 out-of-hours conviction, whose sudden demise was noted in the *Jackson's* of 22 August 1863 some six weeks after she had ceased to run the pub. She had moved to lodge at the Port Mahon in St Clements, where she died suddenly the day after taking a walk to Port Meadow, no doubt revisiting familiar haunts, to try to shake off a persistent headache.

The landlord seems to have changed frequently in the 1860s, with both William Jennings and John Thomas Smith describing themselves as 'publicans' at the baptisms of their children in 1863, and likewise Henry Edmonds (c.1838–?) in 1869. In between came William Venables, named in directories of 1864 and 1867. In 1874 comes the first reference to a name which would be associated with the pub right through to the next century. And of especial interest is the fact that Henry Goatley was described as a boatbuilder as well as a victualler, the first time, as far as can be told, that the two occupations were combined. Indeed, Henry's brother Thomas (c.1851–?) was also a boatbuilder from at least 1874, which is the year he married at Binsey, taking as his wife a local girl Mahalah Howse. Howse is a very significant name in the river context of Oxford; one John Howse, way back in 1583, had been the very first Oxford 'boteman' to take out his freedom, thus establishing the fundamental importance of the occupation to the city, and setting the foundations for families like the Tawneys subsequently to become such powerful establishment figures. Howse (*c*.1534–?) was called in evidence at the 1598 claim that Binsey men had grazing rights on Port Meadow – but on the side of the freemen, who maintained that it was only they who had that privilege.

Other known proprietors of the Perch were William Doe (*c*.1852–?), who added a touch of sophistication by describing himself as a 'vintner' as well as a 'publican' in the census of 1881. Listed in subsequent surviving directories are Edwin Powell Thomas in 1887 and 1895, and Mrs Elizabeth Powell in 1899 and 1903. But by 1911 the Goatleys were back, in the form of George Goatley who, like his father Thomas, had been a boatbuilder at the time of his children's baptisms between 1903 and 1909, but then ran The Perch until at least 1935.

It must therefore have been Goatley who featured in this reminiscence from *On the Chariot Wheel*, the autobiography of J.C. Masterman, whose responsibilities at Christ Church in the 1920s included matters of discipline. He relates how a wealthy Christ Church undergraduate was accused of having assaulted the staff of the Perch when they'd refused to serve him a few minutes after closing time. At the hearing, the landlord produced a battered set of false teeth, his wife a pair of mangled spectacles, and the barman a pile of bloodied clothing, all of which, oddly enough, they claimed to have been brand new at the time of the incident. To avoid public scandal, an out-of-court settlement was agreed. Masterman commented: '£20 turned the woebegone faces of the victims into smiling rejoicing. I seemed to hear the innkeeper murmuring that the undergraduate could return at any time and have the same entertainment for the same price'.

C.S. Lewis made his first visit to Binsey around the same time, cycling there with a friend called Alfred Jenkin. He noted in his diary for 21 November 1922: 'As it was a gloomy and fogged day I suggested that we should seek out 'fountain heads and pathless groves or any melancholy place which would underline the mood of the day'. Jenkin suggested Binsey, and off they went, ending up at the 'sad church by a woodside'. In later years it would seem that the Perch, if not the church, became a favourite destination for Lewis.[1] Another literary giant known to have frequented the Perch (and, sad to say, far too many other pubs in addition!) is Dylan Thomas, who was often to be seen there with his wife and children on Sunday mornings while the Welsh poet was living in South Leigh in the late 1940s.

About the same time, George Scott's autobiography *Time and Place* maintains that 'the Perch became the Saturday night rendez-vous for the most thirsty and insatiable party-seekers in Oxford ... with some of the best "swing" musicians, voices and drinkers in regular attendance, as well as ex-schoolgirls eager to learn quickly about life'. This fame, Scott avers, is on account of two of his more charismatic friends, who took up residence there while still students—'I can't think how they got permission for that' (at a time when students, even ones who had seen recent action in the war, were forbidden to drink in pubs). One of these two friends, Michael Croft, was a former seaman. In the absence of any other evidence, perhaps there is a connection with the Perch ghost alluded to in Marriot's *Oxford Pubs*: a 'phantom sailor' who could often be discerned on a stool at the end of the bar, and was understood to be a petty officer who drowned himself in the Thames after falling into debt.

And as 'Time' is called on this article, it may be well to heed a cautionary tale which is more easily verified despite its far greater antiquity. Was it a forerunner of the Perch which Adam de la Wyke visited on the day of his death in 1299? We shall never know for sure, but

---

[1] The pub is also possibly mentioned by another Inkling, J.R.R. Tolkien, in *The Fellowship of the Rings*. There it is called the Golden Perch; Sam Gamgee praises the establishment's ale and regrets the travellers must bypass it.

it seems as likely as not. Because Adam was a resident of Wyke, just to the south of Binsey, by the Bulstake Stream, and the circumstances of his death, recorded on a Coroner's Roll for 1299, were that his body was found by his wife Alice, he 'having fallen in a ditch when trying to get home one night from the pub', For Adam, poor chap, it would therefore seem to have been a funereal case of 'first The Perch, and then the Church'!

The Perch in 2002. (Mark Davies)

The view of Oxford across the river from Binsey. (Robert Mealing)

Meeting God at Binsey: Holy Ground, then and now

Martin Henig

What did Frideswide think she was doing when she came to her refuge at Binsey, and what do we hope we are we doing when we follow in her footsteps to enter St Margaret's church or linger in the churchyard today?

Perhaps we intend to attend a formal service, either a morning Mass early one cold winter's Sunday, the frost thick upon the ground and a weak sun providing just a glimmer of physical heat, or perhaps Evensong on a warm summer afternoon, when our hearts praise the Lord of the Heavens in which *'he hath set a tabernacle for the sun'* (Psalm 19.4)? Here is a garden, but is it the Garden of Eden or the Garden of Gethsemane? Most likely when we come here to worship God we are alone with our hopes and fears, with our thoughts and with our prayers. There are wild flowers laid lovingly beside the well or floating on its waters. Birds chirp and sing in the trees, as though they too are hymning the Creator-God. It is clear here, in the messages written in the visitors' book, and in the lone, silent pilgrim on her knees, deep in prayer, that we have entered holy ground. Metaphorically, at least, we take off our shoes and fall to our knees.

Here we enter into the world of Frideswide and her contemporaries, amongst whom we might single out St Guthlac at Crowland in the Fens, who fought devils who appeared very visibly to him as well as showing his miraculous powers by healing the sick.[1] In the same region Bede tells us of St Fursey's monastery at *Cnobheresburg,* where St Fursey too is exercised in fighting the demons.[2] A third instance, possibly dated to Frideswide's own time, has a powerfully literary flavour. If Michael Lapidge is right to see the great English epic about confronting dragons, Beowulf, as the product of the same Wessex monastery that produced the *Liber Monstrorum* in the late seventh century, and that monastery was Malmesbury where the great scholar St Aldhelm was Abbot from about 675 until the end of the century, we have a powerful key to the heroic perception of such a solitary life.[3] Although such cenobitic monasticism, whereby the holy man or holy woman confronts not just the loneliness of being outside society but also spiritual temptations, has frequently been considered as the hallmark of Celtic Christianity, as noted previously in this volume, the tradition it represents goes even further back to the Life of St Antony and to the Desert Fathers—indeed to such works as St Jerome's *Vita S. Hilarionis.* Here, it is hybridized with another, local tradition, and British monks and nuns face the familiarly named dragons and devils of their solitude.

Is that so far from our twenty-first century world? It is actually in the mainstream of Christian Life, at least that very large part of Christian life not concerned simply with business, with organizing parishes or charities. In modern terms Binsey, to a more intimate degree than at many larger and more formal retreat-centres, is a place where we can come to fight our own demons and to seek God's help in our lives. As Katie Seal has perceptively remarked of a sojourn in St Columba's Iona in the Hebrides:

> I found parts of it stressful, difficult and dark. And yet, I sense that it is a place of immense healing. For

---

[1] J. Roberts, 'Hagiography and Literature: The case of Guthlac of Crowland', pp.69–86 in M.P. Brown and C.A. Farr, *Mercia: An Anglo-Saxon Kingdom in Europe* (Leicester 2001) citing Felix's *vita sancti Guthlaci*.
[2] Rackham, *Transitus Beati Fursei*
[3] M. Lapidge, 'Beowulf, Aldhelm, the Liber Monstrorum and Wessex', in *Anglo-Latin Literature 600–899* (London and Rio Grande 1996), 271–312.

Sunrise on Iona. (Katie Seal)

> those of us who are prepared to stand in the centre of our God-given humanity. And not just accept it, but try to embrace it. It seems to me that we are all called simply to sit in an often dark place, usually having climbed a hill, and wait...[4]

At Binsey the hill is inevitably metaphorical but the sentiment remains the same, and it could not be put better than Katie has put it here.

In St Frideswide's day a civic focus would have been difficult to sustain, after large parts of the Roman Empire (including Britain) had been badly affected by the near total collapse of the monetary economy in the early fifth century. In other parts of Europe, some of them major areas of mission such as Ireland and parts of Germany, there had never been a monetary economy. Cities and towns had never emerged and thus could not be viable *foci* for ecclesiastical life, which had thus to be centred on the monasteries. Is there a message for our age here too? Will a faith founded on God, focused on quiet, solitary prayer, outlast our self-obsessed trivial concern for constantly increasing and illusive material well-being?

Faith should never be dependent on material wealth and comfort. This is of course most apparent when we recall the flourishing Early Celtic sites of seventh- and eighth-century Britain mentioned above, and also our little church of St Margaret's, Binsey, with no artificial light and no heating to act as barriers between us and nature. There are few tiny

---

[4] Parish magazine, St Paul's, Winchester, November 2010. I am very grateful to Katie for her wise counsel and for sharing with me her insights into the meditative search for God.

St Ishow (St Issui) Church, Partrishow, Breckonshire. A comparative example, also with a sacred well. (Martin Henig)

churches which call so insistently to us. St Issui, Partrishow is another, and for the same reason, its solitude and simplicity. Even when wealth eventually came to some places of high sanctity like Iona in Scotland, Holy Island in Northumbria, or St Albans Hertfordshire, or rather later in the Middle Ages to such great pilgrimage shrines as that of Our Lady at Walsingham in Norfolk or that of the Holy Blood at Hailes Abbey in Gloucestershire, the concept of 'poor' sacred places where the religious could find silence and the pilgrim peace retained immense spiritual value.[5] That Binsey never developed as fully as it might have done is our gain today. It never even had its own regular hermit or anchorite, even though in the twelfth century, prior to founding the nunnery at Godstow just up river, lady Edith Lancelene spent time in retreat at Binsey where 'muche holy lyfe she ledde'.[6] In this she reminds us of St Godric, who at much the same period escaped from Durham to Finchale on a bend in the River Wear where according to Reginald of Durham he lived simply in a little hut with a nearby chapel, and communed with nature and especially with the animals also created by God.[7] Unlike Finchale, no priory was ever built at Binsey; it remains simple and unadorned to this day. The church was only slightly enlarged in the later Middle Ages, and is still basically a Norman two-cell church like its neighbours, St Lawrence, North

---

[5] P. North and J. North, *Sacred space. House of God, Gate of Heaven* (London, 2007) centres on Walsingham.

[6] Quoted by E.A. Jones, 'The Hermits and Anchorites of Oxfordshire', *Oxoniensia* 63 (1998), 51 note 3.

[7] Sir Charles Peers, *Finchale Priory, Durham* (Guidebook, London 1993). I am grateful to Margaret Coombe who is working on a new edition of the Life for discussing this most attractive saint with me. The close connection with animals (see for example the Life of St Cuthbert) is an important feature we should do well to note. Nature is also a major theme in Welsh, and indeed other Insular, praise-poetry and hymnology. Cf. O. Davies, *Celtic Christianity in Early Medieval Wales*, 25–6, 68–9, 73–4 and passim.

Hinksey and formerly (until their rebuilding) those at All Saints, Wytham and St Peter's, Wolvercote.

Most ancient places demand an immediate response. The tourist visits a castle or a country house, and after noting its salient features, buys a guidebook and moves on. It is all too often the case that cathedrals and large churches have become part of the same experience, and the occasional person who has come to pray has almost become an oddity, an embarrassment. The tourist with 'spiritual' interests pays his or her money and expects to be entertained. Even services, especially evensong in such places, can be regarded as merely a performance—as the flashing of cameras at the quaintly surpliced choir reveals. It is not at all impossible to encounter God in such untoward circumstances, but it can be much harder than it should be.

Some cathedrals make a real effort to cater for the prayerful visitor, especially those that do not rattle collecting boxes and contrive to leave the pilgrim in peace. Amongst them is St Alban's Abbey (now the cathedral) the resting place of Roman Britain's most famous martyr and little St Woolo's (i.e. St Gwynllyw's), the cathedral of Monmouthshire, on its hill above Newport. These are both ancient and special sites which powerfully evoke prayer. To them I add the former Benedictine monastery of St Peter's, Gloucester, another personal favourite, where a very conscious decision has been made to maintain the Benedictine tradition of hospitality above the modern pressures of tourism. What gives them the character of sacred space and has made them so important in my personal journey of faith is not just their high archaeological interest, but their *palpable holiness* as houses of prayer. St Margaret's, Binsey has several attractive architectural and archaeological features but in fact does not possess a great deal to detain the casual tourist. Yet people come here to sit, to meditate, to find healing and relief from problems, just as they do in Gloucester cathedral. In the past the well was often the major attraction of the site; it is clear from ribbons and tokens hung on overhanging trees that it is still regarded as a focus for healing. The church still stands as God's House, here without the bustle of sacristans and even priests. There may be no service that day but yet God is palpably here. And the churchyard is more than a place to sit and take a rest at the end of a walk before returning to busy Oxford. One can, in any case, go no further, for the road stops here. What was once a route that led onwards to the west now ends at the church: the earthly goal of the pilgrimage into the Divine Light.

This is not another Walsingham. For me the Walsingham experience is immensely valuable, albeit built around what I believe was the fortuitous discovery in the Middle Ages of a Romano-British temple![8] Sanctified by faith, and by the experiences of fellow pilgrims (as at St James, Compostella in North West Spain, Fatima in Portugal, or any other major centre), Walsingham radiates out on its votaries what has been invested in it, both in past times and now. What it lacks is the *silence* of the desert place, the sort of holiness which nobody can mock as being just slightly tacky. I don't always want to go on pilgrimage to Walsingham, because it is so easy for a particular response to be manufactured at such places. Binsey is different. You may enter the worn gate yourself. There is no-one here to bar your way; it is always open. And yet, and yet He is here. Let us tiptoe with reverence: we are close to that place where we just might find ourselves compelled to take off our shoes, knowing that here we are alone with God, alone with Christ ... on holy ground ... as the trees rustle overhead, the goats bleat in the paddock and the little birds sing. Binsey is one of those places where we are reminded of God who breathed life into all animals, not just of human beings. We are at one with the many saints who lived in quiet places and who

---

[8] J. Bagnall Smith, 'Votive objects and objects of votive significance from Great Walsingham', *Britannia* 30 (1999), 21–56 is suggestive.

offered themselves to God, with St Cuthbert, St Godric and here, especially, St Frideswide in praising the Creator:

> He sendeth the springs into the valleys, which run among the hills.
> They give drink to every beast of the field: the wild asses quench their thirst.
> By them shall the fowls of the heaven have their habitation, which sing among the branches.
>   (Ps.104, 10–12).

St Frideswide, St Margaret, and Blessed Mary, ever Virgin, intercede for us!

Skellig Michael a remote holy island off the west coast of Ireland. (Revd John Lee)